'*Cultures of the Sublime* gives access to hard-to-find texts, suggesting the breadth of the discourse of the sublime in the eighteenth and nineteenth centuries and its relevance to areas far afield of aesthetic philosophy. This book will allow students and scholars a far more comprehensive sense of the meaning of the sublime.' – **Nick Williams**, *Indiana University*

'provides a valuable contextualising role in the study of Romantic literature and the sublime.' – **Steven Vine**, *Swansea University*

This critical anthology examines the place of the sublime in the cultural history of the late eighteenth century and Romantic period. Traditionally, the sublime has been associated with impressive natural phenomena and has been identified as a narrow aesthetic or philosophical category. *Cultures of the Sublime: Selected Readings, 1750–1830*:

* recovers a broader context for engagements with, and writing about, the sublime
* offers a selection of texts from a wide range of ostensibly unrelated areas of knowledge which both generate and investigate sublime effects
* considers writings about mountains, money, crowds, the Gothic, the exotic and the human mind
* contextualises and supports the extracts with detailed editorial commentary.

Also featuring helpful suggestions for further reading, this is an ideal resource for anyone seeking a fresh, up-to-date assessment of the sublime.

Cian Duffy is Reader in English Literature at St Mary's University College.

Peter Howell is Senior Lecturer in English and Programme Director at St Mary's University College.

Cultures of the Sublime

Selected Readings, 1750–1830

Edited by

Cian Duffy and Peter Howell

palgrave
macmillan

First published 2011 by
PALGRAVE MACMILLAN

Palgrave Macmillan in the UK is an imprint of Macmillan Publishers Limited, registered in England, company number 785998, of Houndmills, Basingstoke, Hampshire RG21 6XS.

Palgrave Macmillan in the US is a division of St Martin's Press LLC, 175 Fifth Avenue, New York, NY 10010.

Palgrave Macmillan is the global academic imprint of the above companies and has companies and representatives throughout the world.

Palgrave® and Macmillan® are registered trademarks in the United States, the United Kingdom, Europe and other countries.

ISBN 978–0–230–29965–8   hardback
ISBN 978–0–230–29966–5   paperback

This book is printed on paper suitable for recycling and made from fully managed and sustained forest sources. Logging, pulping and manufacturing processes are expected to conform to the environmental regulations of the country of origin.

A catalogue record for this book is available from the British Library.

A catalog record for this book is available from the Library of Congress.

10 9 8 7 6 5 4 3 2 1
20 19 18 17 16 15 14 13 12 11

Printed and bound in China

Contents

Introduction

For most readers of eighteenth-century and romantic-period writing today, the sublime is effectively synonymous with dramatic natural phenomena, with mountains and oceans, storms and deserts, the so-called natural sublime. The natural sublime, in this context, is investigated primarily in philosophical treatments of aesthetics, and secondarily in creative arts. This anthology recovers a broader context for engagements with, and writing about, the sublime during the 'long eighteenth century', offering a selection of texts from a wide range of ostensibly unrelated areas of knowledge which both generate and investigate sublime effects. On the basis of this selection, we make two claims about the place of the sublime in the cultural history of the romantic period. First: that the 'natural sublime' was only one of a number of different species of sublimity present in British culture of the late eighteenth century and romantic period. Second: that these various popular constructions of the sublime played a more significant role in the cultural history of the romantic period than the substantial body of philosophical speculation about the nature and causes of sublime experience produced during the eighteenth century, what Peter de Bolla has called 'the discourse on the sublime'.[1] A key aim of this anthology, then, is to enable readings of romantic-period engagements with the sublime which are not confined by traditional assumptions about eighteenth-century British and German philosophical aesthetics. The sublime should not be understood, we contend, as an isolated or abstract philosophical concept, but rather as embedded in the cultural practice of the late eighteenth century and romantic period. It was as a ubiquitous trope rather than as a philosophical category that the sublime rose to its eminence in the cultural history of the romantic period.

Eighteenth-century Britain witnessed an explosion of interest in the sublime, with numerous publications purporting to define and explain the phenomenon. The academic study of this 'discourse on the sublime' began, in the twentieth century, with Samuel Holt Monk's seminal *The Sublime* (1935).[2] Monk links the

---

1 Peter De Bolla, *The Discourse of the Sublime: Readings in History, Aesthetics and the Subject* (Oxford: Basil Blackwell, 1989), p. 12.

2 Samuel Holt Monk, *The Sublime* (Ann Arbor: University of Michigan Press, 1935); references are to the second, revised edition (1960). De Bolla defines the 'discourse on the sublime' as the ongoing attempt 'to describe how an experience is sublime and what caused it' (*The Discourse on the Sublime*, p. 12). This analytical discourse is to be distinguished from what De Bolla calls the 'discourse *of* the

growth of interest in the sublime to the publication, in the late seventeenth and early eighteenth centuries, of influential French and English translations of a treatise on the sublime by the classical Greek literary critic Longinus.[3] Longinus is concerned almost exclusively with the production of sublime effect through writing and oratory, the so-called 'rhetorical sublime', and has comparatively little to say about the sublime effect of natural phenomena. But speculation about the natural sublime also burgeoned in the early part of the eighteenth century: witness, for example, Joseph Addison's discussion in his 'pleasures of the imagination' essays, published in his *Spectator* newspaper in June 1712. Arguing in parallel to Monk, Marjorie Hope Nicolson's 1959 study of the discourse on the sublime, *Mountain Gloom and Mountain Glory*, suggests that this early eighteenth-century interest in the *natural* sublime stemmed from the gradual transfer of the emotional responses previously evoked by the idea of God to those aspects of the natural world which seemed to reflect or partake of divine grandeur: initially, the seemingly limitless universe revealed by new astronomical instruments, and eventually any natural phenomenon capable of suggesting the infinite.[4] Both hypotheses are valid: the circulation of Longinus' treatise appears to have supplied eighteenth-century Britain with a vocabulary appropriate for expressing new attitudes to the natural world.

While Monk and Nicolson differ about the origins of the discourse on the sublime, however, they share a core argument about the development of that discourse in eighteenth-century Britain: both read the major British discussions of the sublime – by figures like John Dennis, Edmund Burke and Archibald Alison – as precursors to Immanuel Kant's 'analytic of the sublime' in his *Critique of Judgement* (1790). There are two assumptions at play here: first, that it is possible to produce a complete and objective definition of the sublime, which transcends specific historical or cultural circumstances (an assumption shared by Kant's 'analytic'); second, that Kant's work constitutes this definition. Many academic studies of the discourse on the sublime have granted these assumptions largely unquestioningly; for example Thomas Weiskel's quasi-Freudian *The Romantic Sublime*, Frances Ferguson's *Solitude and the Sublime* and, more recently, Philip Shaw's *The Sublime*, all of which cast Kant's 'analytic of the sublime' as the culmination of eighteenth-century speculation.[5] Discussions of individual romantic-period authors have often similarly taken for granted that

sublime': 'a discourse which produces, from within itself, what is habitually termed the category of the sublime' (p. 12).

3 Nicolas Boileau-Despréaux translated Longinus' *On the Sublime* into French in 1674; William Smith published a widely read English translation in 1739.

4 Marjorie Hope Nicolson, *Mountain Gloom and Mountain Glory* (Ithaca: Cornell University Press, 1959). See also E. L. Tuveson, 'Space, Deity, and the "Natural Sublime"', *MLQ*, 12/1 (March 1951), pp. 20–38.

5 Thomas Weiskel, *The Romantic Sublime: Studies in the Structure and Psychology of Transcendence* (Baltimore: Johns Hopkins University Press, 1976); Frances Ferguson, *Solitude and the Sublime* (New York: Routledge, 1992); Philip Shaw, *The Sublime* (London: Routledge, 2006).

Kant's analytic offers the definitive interpretative paradigm for the experience of the sublime; for example, Leighton's *Shelley and the Sublime*, Knapp's discussion of Coleridge in *Personification and the Sublime*, Ende's readings in *Keats and the Sublime*, and Wlecke's *Wordsworth and the Sublime*, all of which use Kantian theory as the basis of their analyses.[6]

The dominance of the Kantian 'analytic' in scholarly accounts of eighteenth-century British discussions of the sublime was first seriously challenged by Andrew Ashfield and Peter De Bolla's 1996 anthology *The Sublime*, which drew attention to the constructed nature of Monk's and Nicolson's teleological reading and explicitly sought to 'de-couple the British eighteenth-century tradition of the sublime from the Kantian analytic'.[7] The central tenet of Kant's discussion of the sublime is its insistence on the so-called disinterestedness of the individual's experience of the sublime, the supposed freedom of that experience from ethical or other culturally specific concerns. The Kantian 'analytic' is problematic, we contend, precisely because of this refusal to acknowledge the role of cultural and historical factors in constructing the individual's response to sublime effect. The British discussion of the sublime, conversely, is distinguished from the Kantian 'analytic' by what Ashfield and De Bolla describe as its 'refusal to relinquish' the intermixture of cultural elements in the individual's experience of the sublime, by its insistence that the experience of the sublime cannot be divorced from 'other forms of understanding and experiencing the world'.[8] Recent studies of the place of the sublime in the work of individual eighteenth-century and romantic-period figures, such as Furniss's *Edmund Burke's Aesthetic Ideology* and Duffy's *Shelley and the Revolutionary Sublime*, have tended to support this view of the encounter with the sublime as less a matter of disinterested aesthetic judgement than the site of a complex interaction between different discourses.[9] This anthology further documents that view, illustrating both the range of contexts in which an individual might expect to encounter sublime effect during the late eighteenth and early nineteenth centuries, and the extent to which that effect is generated by cultural and historical information specific to both the individual concerned and to the particular phenomenon encountered. Hence the first section of the anthology, on Mountains, which offers a selection of texts engaging with scenery very familiar from romantic-period writing about the sublime – the Alps, and the Italian volcanoes Vesuvius and Etna – reveals not 'disinterested' responses to blank geographical features but

---

6 Angela Leighton, *Shelley and the Sublime* (Cambridge: Cambridge, University Press, 1973); Steven Knapp, *Personification and the Sublime* (Cambridge, MA: Harvard University Press, 1985); Stuart Ende, *Keats and the Sublime* (New Haven: Yale University Press, 1976); Albert Wlecke, *Wordsworth and the Sublime* (Berkeley: University of California Press, 1973).

7 Andrew Ashfield and Peter De Bolla, eds, *The Sublime: A Reader in Eighteenth-Century British Aesthetic Theory* (Cambridge: Cambridge University Press, 1996), p. 3.

8 Ashfield and De Bolla, *The Sublime*, pp. 3–4.

9 Tom Furniss, *Edmund Burke's Aesthetic Ideology* (Cambridge: Cambridge University Press, 1993); Cian Duffy, *Shelley and the Revolutionary Sublime* (Cambridge: Cambridge University Press, 2005).

rather highly 'interested' responses to _landscape,_ to geographical features richly inscribed with a range of cultural associations. Indeed, the authors included in this section often draw attention precisely to the 'interested' nature of their own responses to the natural sublime. A general distinction between landscape and geography had been in circulation since at least 1701, when Joseph Addison described Italy as 'classic ground' in his _Letter from Italy_:

> For here the Muse so oft her harp has strung
> That not a mountain rears its head unsung,
> Renowned in verse each shady thicket grows,
> And every stream in heavenly numbers flows.
>   (12–16)[10]

What Addison registers here is, exactly, the effective impossibility, for an educated traveller, of a 'disinterested' aesthetic response to a landscape which has long possessed a range of specific historical and cultural associations, and this impossibility is repeatedly recognised in cotemporary engagements with the natural sublime. By the beginning of the eighteenth century, Vesuvius and Etna were already well established as 'classic ground' (see Mountains; extracts from Brydone, Eustace, and Swinburne). But what the texts presented in the first section of this anthology also reveal is the process by which, during the late eighteenth century, the Alps – a region largely unknown to European culture until the 1740s – _became_ 'classic ground', a landscape with profound implications for an individual's understanding of matters as diverse as science, religion, politics, individual subjectivity, even the history of civil society.

Subsequent sections of the anthology – dealing with writings about Money, with the Gothic, with descriptions of Crowds, the Mind and the Exotic – similarly reveal the encounter with sublime effect in these various contexts to have been the locus of a complex interaction between different discursive elements. The writings presented in our section on Money, for example, typify this interaction, documenting the beginnings of the modern discipline of economics in the simultaneously horrified and fascinated responses of eighteenth-century and romantic-period thinkers to the enormous national debt contracted by the British government during the eighteenth century in order to finance various foreign wars. Anxiety or enthusiasm was prompted by the seemingly limitless and unstoppable power of interest to accumulate over time, bringing immeasurable wealth or irretrievable ruin inevitably in its wake. Debates consequently took place about the need to incorporate these vast sums in a paper currency that was no longer tied to an equivalent value in precious metal or other commodity.

---

10 Joseph Addison, _A Letter from Italy_ (London: 1703). The rediscovery in the twentieth century of the distinction between landscape and geography can be traced to the work of the American geographer Carl Otwin Sauer, particularly to his 1925 essay 'The Morphology of Landscape', _University of California Publications in Geography 2_ (1925), pp. 19–53.

What the texts presented in the Money section suggest, in other words, is that the formulation of the modern discipline of economics involved, at least in part, what can best be described as a discourse on the sublime: an attempt to characterise and come to terms with financial processes that are both enthralling and terrifying, and resemble *natural* processes in their apparent autonomy, their transformative power, and their entire disregard for individual human circumstances.

A similar discursive overlap characterises many of the writings about psychological processes that we have included in the Mind section of this anthology. Explorations of the encounter between the human mind and the natural sublime make up some of the most familiar moments of canonical romantic-period literature; for example, Wordsworth's account of the Simplon Pass and the ascent of Snowdon, in Books VI and XIII of *The Prelude* (1805), Shelley's 'Mont Blanc' (1816) and Byron's *Manfred* (1817). Over-reliance (sometimes inaccurate) on Kant's description of the encounter with the natural sublime as an ultimately successful attempt by the mind to impose itself upon, and thereby transcend, the initially overwhelming external force of the sublime landscape has meant that many influential scholarly readings of these important passages have been restricted to an attempt to discern the mapping, by the poetic speaker, of subjective, internal space onto objective, external nature.[11] However, as the writings about the mind presented in this anthology reveal, eighteenth-century and romantic-period writing about the human mind – perhaps taking a hint from David Hume's call for a 'mental geography' in his *Enquiry Concerning Human Understanding* (1748) – repeatedly uses images of the natural sublime to figure psychological processes, describing the abysses and summits of psychological experience, the storms of passion, and so on, thereby complicating the relationship between internal and external space, between mind and things.[12] Nor let it be thought that this is simply a matter of the pathetic fallacy. These texts formulate influential cotemporary alternatives to the Kantian model of the relationship between internal and external space, alternatives which refuse definitively to prioritise internal over external, mind over things. They stand at the head of a tradition which carries on into twentieth-century writing about the mind through the likes of Gerard Manley Hopkins's assertion that the 'mind has mountains; cliffs of fall / Frightful, sheer, no-man-fathomed'.[13] In other words, eighteenth-century and romantic-period writing about the human mind shows the nascent discipline of psychology to have been vitally informed, at the moment of its inception, not only by writing about landscape and travel, but by a discourse on the sublime, by a dizzying confrontation with the dark abysses of the unconscious.

A key claim of this anthology, then, is not only that the encounter with sublime effect, during the eighteenth century and romantic period, was a moment of

---

11 See, for example, Samuel Monk's remarks about *The Prelude* VI in *The Sublime*, pp. 3–4; and Angela Leighton's reading of 'Mont Blanc' in *Shelley and the Sublime*, pp. 58–72.

12 David Hume, *An Enquiry Concerning Human Understanding* (Edinburgh, 1748), I, p. xiv.

13 Gerard Manley Hopkins, 'No Worst, There is None' (1918), 9–10.

complex interaction between different discourses, but that writing from a wide range of ostensibly unrelated disciplines was connected by a common engagement with sublime effect. In practical terms, this means that these different writings have, in common, tropes and topoi which were, from the beginning of the eighteenth century, increasingly associated with the sublime. In his treatise *On the Sublime*, Longinus notes five characteristics of speech or writing that is capable of generating sublime effect: grandeur of conception; the provocation of a powerful emotional response; skilful deployment of imagery; elegance of expression; and overall structural coherence. At the beginning of the eighteenth century, British discussions of the rhetorical sublime tended to afford each of these characteristics equal weight, as in John Dennis's influential discussion of the sublime *The Grounds of Criticism in Poetry* (1704), which draws heavily on Longinian paradigms. As the eighteenth century wore on, however, interest shifted away from the rhetorical sublime towards other modes of sublimity. One consequence of this shift was that the extreme emotional response associated with the sublime – both the nature of this response and the manner by which it was elicited – became the primary focus of investigation in philosophical aesthetics.

In his 1712 'pleasures of the imagination' essays, Joseph Addison links the emotional response associated with the sublime to the encounter with grandeur and the uncommon (or 'novel'), broadening the application of Longinus' model of the rhetorical sublime to include a wide range of experiential phenomena, such as landscape, architecture and crowds. By the end of the eighteenth century, the fascination of the uncommon remained a key trope of the sublime, as the texts included in the sections of the anthology dealing with the Exotic and Crowds make clear. A version of this same fascination with the uncommon also informs the repeated valorisation of originality, during the eighteenth century and romantic period, as a mark of genius in the creative arts (see Mind; e.g. extracts from Young, Duff).

Addison's adaptation of the Longinian concept of 'grandeur' had an equally significant legacy in eighteenth-century British writing about the sublime. Longinus suggests that the sublimity of a speech or text depends, in part, upon the grandeur of the artist's conception. Addison extends this suggestion beyond the sphere of the creative arts, arguing that grand or elevated *ideas* are integral to the encounter with all modes of sublimity and play a key role in eliciting the extreme emotional response by which that encounter is characterised. This argument, based partly on Addison's own concept of 'classic ground', is encapsulated in his often-quoted assertion that 'a spacious horizon is an image of liberty', an assertion which links the encounter with the natural sublime to ideas of personal and political freedom, a link echoed by much subsequent writing about the natural sublime, as well as by a number of British commentators on the French Revolution (see Crowds).[14] At the beginning of the eighteenth century, then, Addison's seminal discussion of the tropes of grandeur and the uncommon affirms the essential

---

14 *The Spectator* 412 (June 23) 1712.

'interestedness' of both the individual mind and public opinion in the encounter with the sublime, and it is precisely this same 'interestedness' which has remained unrecognised by conventional descriptions of romantic-period engagements with the sublime steeped in Kantian ideas of aesthetic 'disinterestedness'.

The material included in the Gothic section of the anthology focuses what has undoubtedly become one of the most familiar tropes in academic discussions of the sublime: terror. Longinus considers the role of terror in the emotional response to the sublime, and his remarks are expanded by early eighteenth-century British commentators on his work, including Addison and, in particular, John Dennis, whose *Grounds of Criticism in Poetry* contains an extended discussion of how 'ideas producing terror contribute extremely to the sublime' and are integral to the process by which the rhetorical sublime 'commits a pleasing rape upon the very soul of the reader'.[15] But the most significant eighteenth-century commentator on the relationship between terror and the sublime was Edmund Burke, whose *Philosophical Enquiry into the Origin of Our Ideas of the Sublime and the Beautiful* (1757) has become, after Kant's 'analytic', the most referenced text in academic studies of the place of the sublime in eighteenth-century and romantic-period culture. Burke argues that 'the terrible' is fundamental to the encounter with the sublime: the 'source of the sublime', according to the *Philosophical Enquiry*, is 'whatever is in any sort terrible, or is conversant about terrible objects, or operates in a manner analogous to terror'.[16] Burke's model of the sublime, like most pre-Kantian discussions, is therefore essentially empirical, locating the 'source of the sublime' in the properties of external phenomena, in things, rather than in the individual mind. But mediation is also crucial to the process Burke describes. The 'terrible', the *Philosophical Enquiry* suggests, must be experienced vicariously in order for a sublime effect to be generated: 'when danger or pain press too nearly', Burke writes, 'they are incapable of giving any delight, and are simply terrible; but at certain distances, and with certain modifications, they may be, and they are, delightful'.[17]

'At certain distances', 'with certain modifications': what Burke registers in this account of the process by which experiential phenomena ('pain', 'danger') are 'modified' by being experienced vicariously is precisely the process which the texts presented in this anthology register again and again: the amalgamation of empirical phenomena and cultural value, the inscription of ideas on things to create a shared cultural vocabulary, or *discourse*. Consider, in this respect, Burke's discussion of the rhetorical sublime in the final section of the *Enquiry*, 'Of Words'. Through a series of commentaries on examples of the sublime in literature, Burke draws conclusions about the rhetorical sublime which anticipate certain aspects

---

15 John Dennis, *The Grounds of Criticism in Poetry* (London, 1704), p. 79. This striking formulation, taken from Longinus, was repeated throughout much of early eighteenth-century speculation about the sublime.

16 Edmund Burke, *A Philosophical Enquiry into the Origins of Our Ideas of the Sublime and the Beautiful* (London, 1757) I, vii, p. 58.

17 Burke, *Enquiry*, I, vii, p. 60.

of poststructuralist theories of representation and discourse.[18] The best example is Burke's often-cited examination of the sublime effect generated by Milton's phrase 'a universe of death', in *Paradise Lost* II 620: 'here', Burke suggests, 'are two ideas not presentable but by language [i.e. 'except through language']; and a union of them great and amazing beyond conception'.[19] For Burke, in other words, the rhetorical sublime consists in, and enables, the perception of some 'thing' for which there is no empirical original, something 'beyond conception'. But it is important to understand the basis of Burke's conclusion. This is not necessarily a philosophically idealist assertion of the priority of mind over things: Burke reminds the reader, in the final lines of the *Enquiry*, of the argument maintained throughout the text: that the sublime is a property of 'things in nature'.[20] Rather, in maintaining the priority of 'words before ideas', Burke's account of the rhetorical sublime moves towards poststructuralist theories about the linguistic basis of 'the real', as well as towards Lyotard's and Derrida's descriptions of the sublime as the sign of the unrepresentable.[21] Hence for Burke, as for Addison and many other eighteenth-century British commentators on the sublime, we contend, sublime effect is understood not as the disinterested transcendence, by the individual mind, of empirical phenomena, but rather as the individual's response to the specific cultural values with which certain empirical phenomena have been, or are capable of being, or are in the process of being, inscribed.

This anthology traces the history and documents the range of those inscriptions. One effect of this process is to question the extent of the influence of Burke's ideas about the connection between 'the terrible' and the sublime on his contemporaries. We have already noted that Burke's *Philosophical Enquiry* is, after Kant's 'analytic', the most referenced text in academic discussions of the place of the sublime in eighteenth-century and romantic-period culture. The 'terrible' is certainly a significant trope in a number of the texts presented here, and by no means only in the material we have included in our section on the Gothic. However, what this anthology also reveals is that the 'terrible' is far from being so ubiquitous a component of late eighteenth-century and romantic-period descriptions of the sublime as many academic studies of the subject suggest. Indeed, the trope of 'the terrible' was not generally recognised in the two episodes from Burke's own *Reflections on the Revolution in France* that his contemporaries most frequently referenced as instances of the sublime: the description of the flight of Marie Antoinette from her bedchamber during the assault on Versailles in the early hours of 6 October 1789, and the account of

18 Burke's account of the workings of language in literature also bears comparison with descriptions of 'defamiliarisation' by the Russian formalist critics Viktor Shklovsky and Mikhail Bakhtin.
19 Burke, *Enquiry*, V, vii, p. 338.
20 Burke, *Enquiry*, V, vii, p. 341.
21 See Jean François Lyotard, *The Postmodern Condition*, transl. G. Bennington and B. Massumi (Manchester: Manchester University Press, 1984); Jacques Derrida, *The Truth in Painting*, transl. G. Bennington and I. McLeod (Chicago: University of Chicago Press, 1987).

the forced removal of the French royal family from Versailles to the Tuilleries later that day.[22] The *Philosophical Enquiry* itself also had a number of influential, contemporary detractors. Foremost amongst them was Richard Payne-Knight who, in his *Analytical Inquiry into the Principles of Taste* (1805), quipped of Burke's emphasis on the role of terror in generating sublime effect that if Burke himself

> had walked up St. James's street without his breeches, it would have occasioned great and universal *astonishment*; and if he had, at the same time, carried a loaded blunderbuss in his hands, the astonishment would have been mixed with no small portion of *terror*: but I do not believe that the united effect of these two powerful passions would have produced any sentiment or sensation approaching to sublime.[23]

Payne-Knight's undeniably witty critique actually rather misses the point: Burke's model of the sublime insists, as we have seen, that sublime effects are generated only when the 'terrible' is experienced vicariously, 'at certain distances, and with certain modifications'. But the criticism of Payne-Knight and others, coupled with the relative absence of the trope of the 'terrible' from many of the texts presented in this anthology, suggests that the importance given to Burke's *Enquiry* by academic studies of the place of the sublime in eighteenth-century and romantic-period culture says more about the assumptions informing those studies than it does about Burke's actual influence on his contemporaries, even as mediated through undoubted disciples like the Gothic novelist Ann Radcliffe. That is to say that the importance afforded to Burke in academic histories of the sublime reflects the tendency of those studies, first noted by Ashfield and De Bolla, to read eighteenth-century British discussions of the sublime as a precursor to the Kantian 'analytic'. Indicatively, then, such studies tend to downplay the physiological aspects of Burke's arguments, and his insistence on the empirical basis of the sublime as a property of things – elements which Burke himself felt constituted his distinctive contribution to the British discussion – in favour of those aspects of the *Enquiry* which seem better to anticipate the philosophically idealist approach to the sublime taken by Kant's 'analytic' and its inheritors. What is left out in these attempts to position Burke within an assumed history of aesthetics is, precisely, Burke's characteristic refusal to relinquish the basis of sublime effect in the *dialogue* between words and things. What is added is an inflated sense of the importance of the trope of 'the terrible' in late eighteenth-century and romantic-period engagements with the sublime.

We have pointed to the common ground between Burke's account of the rhetorical sublime and poststructuralist discussions of the relationship between

---

22 Edmund Burke, *Reflections on the Revolution in France*, 10th edition (London, 1791), pp. 105–7.
23 Richard Payne-Knight, *An Analytical Inquiry into the Principles of Taste*, 3rd edition (London, 1806), III, i, 67, pp. 380–1.

representation and the 'real', of the role of discourse in determining our perceptions of the 'real'. The texts presented in this anthology show a number of eighteenth-century and romantic-period writers, across a range of different disciplines, moving towards a similar sense of the discursive basis of the sublime, towards a sense that the sublime object is a kind of text, and that the encounter with the sublime is an act of reading, paralleling Wordsworth's perception of 'the characters of the great apocalypse, / the types and symbols of eternity' in the sublime Alpine landscape encountered during his crossing of the Simplon Pass.[24] Nowhere is this sense of the encounter with the sublime as an act of reading more evident than in the material included in our section on Crowds. Descriptions of the vast populations of London and China, and of the revolutionary crowds in Paris, configure the sublime of 'the crowd' as a dizzying excess of signification. Similar configurations occur in a number of the writings about debt included in our section on Money, and in some descriptions of the Exotic. In these texts, then, we have the beginnings of that genealogy of the sublime which finds its most recent expression in the works of postmodern critics like Lyotard and Slavoj Žižek and their configurations of the sublime as the sign of the inexpressible, the unrepresentable. And these beginnings are materialist, empirical, rooted in everyday relationships between cultural values and things.

As a contribution to the history of the aesthetic, therefore, this anthology has significant implications not only for scholarly interpretations of romantic-period engagements with the sublime, but also for critical understanding of 'the sublime' *per se*. The thriving and diverse romantic-period cultures of the sublime that we recover here question the assumption that it is possible to formulate any objective definition of 'the sublime' as a phenomenon independent from given historically or culturally specific encounters with sublime effect. To put it more precisely, the cultures of the sublime that we recover here suggest that, during the romantic period at least, the encounter with sublime effect was entirely culturally determined, a moment (often consciously anticipated) of complex interaction between different, but increasingly familiar, discourses.

We can best begin to appreciate the significance of this recovery for scholarly interpretations of canonical romantic-period writing about the sublime by returning to that well-known moment in *The Prelude*, to Wordsworth and his 'fellow … mountaineer', Robert Jones, high up on the Simplon Pass in the summer of 1790.[25] Wordsworth's refashioning of this moment from his first visit to the Alps has become, in Alan Liu's words, 'one of a handful of paradigms capable by itself of representing the poet's work'.[26] Fifty years after Samuel Monk first described the same lines as the 'apotheosis' of 'the experience that lay behind the eighteenth-century sublime', the episode also remains the accepted literary

---

24 William Wordsworth, *The Prelude* (1805) vi, 570–1.
25 Wordsworth, *The Prelude* (1805), vi, 339–40.
26 Alan Liu, *Wordsworth: The Sense of History* (Stanford: Stanford University Press, 1989), p. 4.

paradigm of the 'romantic' encounter with the natural sublime, a 'set piece of the sublime', as Thomas Weiskel puts it in *The Romantic Sublime*.[27] Wordsworth's apostrophe to the Imagination – 'that power' which recovers the mental 'prowess' initially 'usurped' by the 'soulless image' of Mont Blanc – is routinely read as a poetic equivalent of the transcendental-idealist paradigms of the sublime outlined in Kant's 'analytic', where the mind recovers from the initially overwhelming impressions of the sublime object by appropriating those impressions to itself.[28] Hence, for example, Monk's claim 'that there is a general similarity between the point of view of the *Critique of Judgement* and *The Prelude*'.[29]

Recent Wordsworth criticism has re-examined *Prelude* VI and offered a number of different interpretative contexts for its address to the imagination. In particular, Alan Liu's seminal re-reading of the passage proposes that the struggle which it records is not so much between self and nature as between self and *history*: the vocabulary of Wordsworth's apostrophe records a specific engagement, Liu suggests, with Napoleon's 1800 crossing of the Alps, and hence the notable absence of the episode from Wordsworth's first account of his Alpine tour in his 1793 *Descriptive Sketches*.[30] However, while Liu's and other recent reassessments undoubtedly reveal the referential richness of Wordsworth's text, they do not – they are not intended to – interrogate the adequacy of the Simplon Pass episode as a paradigm of an idealist and idealising 'romantic sublime', defined, after Kant, as an ultimately transcended conflict between the mind or self, and something *not* self, be that something nature or history.

But let us consider: what exactly is involved in this assumption of a 'general similarity' between Kant's and Wordsworth's 'point of view' on the sublime? First: the suggestion that Wordsworth, in 1805, articulates essentially the same model of the encounter with the sublime that Kant outlined in his 'analytic of the sublime' in 1790. Second: by extension, the assumption that 'the sublime' is a phenomenon which *can* be described objectively, irrespective of historical or cultural difference. Third: by implication, that the interpretation of Wordsworth's text should be governed by the paradigms of Kant's 'analytic', because Kant's philosophical treatise has chronological (and assumed generic) priority over Wordsworth's poem. What is lost, conversely, is any sense of the innumerable historical, cultural and experiential differences between Kant in 1790 and Wordsworth in 1805, between Kant's study in Königsberg and the Alps.

In order to quantify this loss, let us compare Wordsworth's account of the Simplon Pass with our extract from Louis Ramond de Carbonnières's 'Observations on the Glaciers and Glacieres' (see Mountains). On a walking tour of the Alps in the late eighteenth century, Wordsworth and Jones were

---

27 Weiskel, *The Romantic Sublime*, p. 196.
28 Wordsworth, *The Prelude* (1805), vi, 527, 545, 533, 454.
29 Monk, *The Sublime*, p. 4.
30 Liu, *Wordsworth: the Sense of History*, pp. 3–31.

following what was quickly becoming, in James Buzzard's phrase, 'the beaten track' to modern European tourism.[31] Indeed, it is now generally accepted that the pair followed an itinerary laid out in the 1789 edition of William Coxe's *Travels in Swisserland*, one of the most influential of the numerous contemporary Alpine guidebooks.[32] Carbonnières's 'Observations' originally formed part of his 1781 translation of the first edition of Coxe's *Sketches* (1779); English translations of the 'Observations' were included in subsequent editions of Coxe's *Sketches*, and a second translation was published by Helen Maria Williams as an appendix to her *Tour in Switzerland* (1798). Wordsworth had certainly read the original French text of the 'Observations' before 1793, since the notes to his *Descriptive Sketches*, his first verse account of his 1790 tour, acknowledge his debts to 'M. Raymond's interesting observations annexed to his translation of Coxe's Tour in Switzerland'.[33] There is no record of his having read either of the English translations (although it seems likely that he knew both), but his ongoing awareness of the French text is confirmed by a 26 December 1823 letter to Henry Taylor, in which he accuses Byron of having, in the third canto of *Childe Harold's Pilgrimage* (1816), 'taken an expression' from Carbonnières's description of Schaffhausen and 'beaten [it] out unmercifully into two stanzas which a critic in the *Quarterly Review* is foolish enough to praise'.[34]

In the final movement of the 'Observations', Carbonnières examines the effect on the spectator of the 'sublime' glacial landscapes above Chamonix. 'Everything' about this 'immense chaos of mountains', he concludes, 'concurs to make our meditations more profound; to give them ... that sublime character which they acquire, when the soul, taking that flight which makes it contemporary with every age, and co-existent with all beings, hovers over the abyss of time'. As well as echoing Rousseau's account of the Upper Valais in our extract from *Julie*, the vocabulary and imagery of this sentence evidently anticipate Wordsworth's account of the rise of the imagination – out of 'the mind's abyss', in the 1850 text of *The Prelude* (vi 594) – to recover the 'glory' that the 'soul' had previously 'lost' to the 'soulless image' of Mont Blanc, and to reveal that 'our destiny, our nature, and our home / Is with infinitude'.[35] Carbonnières then proceeds to formulate his own apostrophe to the 'Imagination', registering the

---

31 James Buzzard, *The Beaten Track: European Travel, Tourism and the Ways to 'Culture', 1800–1918* (Oxford: Oxford University Press, 1994).

32 See C. N. Coe, 'Did Wordsworth Read Coxe's *Travels in Switzerland* before making the tour of 1790?' *Notes & Queries* 195 (1950), pp. 144–5.

33 William Wordsworth, *Descriptive Sketches: In Verse. Taken During a Pedestrian Tour in the Italian, Grison, Swiss, and Savoyard Alps* (London: 1793), p. 28n.

34 *The Letters of William and Dorothy Wordsworth: III The Later Years (1821–1828)*, ed. Ernest De Selincourt, rev. Alan Hill (Oxford: Oxford University Press, 1978), pt. 1, p. 234. Wordsworth also recommends Carbonnières to Henry Robinson in a letter of 28 November 1828 (*The Later Years*, pt. 1, p. 674).

35 Wordsworth, *The Prelude* (1805), vi, 532, 538–9.

impossibility of ever arriving, via rational enquiry, at any idea of the enormous geological time-scale implied by this landscape:

> In vain would reason strive to count by years. The solidity of these enormous masses, opposed to the accumulation of their ruins, startles and confounds all its calculations. Imagination seizes the reins which Reason drops, and in that long succession of periods, catches a glimpse of the image of eternity. ... Thus, our most extended ideas, and our most elevated and noble sentiments, have their origin in the wanderings of the imagination; but let us forgive its chimeras, for what would there be great in our conceptions, or glorious in our actions, if finite was not, through its illusions, continually changed into infinite, space into immensity, time into eternity, and fading laurels into immortal crowns!

In this passage, we suggest, there is a clear and – from a contextual point of view – immediately relevant antecedent for Wordsworth's apostrophe to the imagination as the agent of the mind's 'prowess' in the encounter with the natural sublime. Just as Wordsworth's account of the natural sublime identifies the 'imagination' as the 'strength' and 'greatness' of a mind whose 'home/ Is with infinitude', so, in Carbonnières's account of the natural sublime, it is the 'imagination' which transforms 'finite into infinite, space into immensity, time into eternity, and fading laurels into immortal crowns', an image surely not lost on the author of *The Prelude*. But Carbonnières's heavily qualified apostrophe to the imagination is neither idealist nor idealising. Rather, with its conviction that the 'wanderings of the imagination' produce 'chimeras' and 'illusions', Carbonnières's apostrophe is closer to David Hume's scepticism about the limitations of rationalism, to Hume's vindication of the imagination as the only faculty of the mind capable of going beyond the limitations of sensation towards the formulation of general hypotheses about the empirical world.[36]

The point, then, is not simply that Carbonnières's 'Observations' may constitute a previously unrecognised influence on Wordsworth's account of the role of the imagination in the encounter with the natural sublime in Book VI of *The Prelude*, although that seems likely. The point is, rather, the extent to which traditional claims of a 'general similarity' between Kant's and Wordsworth's 'point of view' on the natural sublime tend to play down the relationship between Wordsworth's text and the various historical and cultural discourses from which it emerged and to which it responds. The consequence of this elision is to limit both the interpretation of Wordsworth's text and to restrict critical understanding of the diversity of 'the sublime' in romantic-period culture.

In the 'Dedication' to *Don Juan*, written in autumn 1818, Byron remarked that 'Time' had made 'the word *Miltonic* mean *sublime*'.[37] Our intention, in assembling

---

36 See, for example, Hume's discussion of the imagination in his *Treatise of Human Nature* (1740) I, pt. iii.

37 Byron, *Don Juan: Cantos I–II* (1819), 'Dedication', 76–7.

this anthology, has been to counteract the restriction of critical engagements with the 'romantic sublime', during the twentieth century, to the paradigms of the Kantian analytic. We aim to make clear, in this anthology, the extraordinary range of the romantic period's cultural engagement with the sublime. However, we are conscious that we have given only a flavour of the diverse 'cultures of the sublime' which flourished during the eighteenth century and romantic period. Indeed, by offering as representative of these 'cultures' writings about Mountains, Money, the Gothic, Crowds, Mind, and the Exotic, we are aware that we have left many equally vibrant and significant 'cultures of the sublime' to one side. Contemporary writings about religion and religious experience, about the law, about morality, about language and speech, evidence equally the importance of sublime effect as a locus of complex interaction between different discursive elements, as a focal point in the development of these disciplines in their modern form. So, too, while we have chosen to include a section examining the place of sublime effect in writing about the Mind, we are conscious that the sublime also played a central and contentious role in cotemporary writing about the body, gender, and sexuality. Theorists of the sublime like Burke and Kant routinely gender the opposition between the sublime and the beautiful as an opposition between male and female, and, as critics like Barbara Freeman and Anne Mellor have long since pointed out, the 'sublime' played a significant role in eighteenth-century and romantic-period constructions of masculinity and masculine 'authority' of varying sorts.[38] A thorough examination of these other but no-less-important 'cultures of the sublime' would require multiple volumes. We hope that the numerous interactions of writing about religion, law, linguistics, the body, and gender, with those discourses on which we have chosen to focus here, will give a sufficient indication of their interdependency and suggest fruitful avenues for further inquiry.

What we offer in this anthology, then, is a window on the cultural history of the sublime during the late eighteenth century and romantic period, a history encompassing an extensive range of disciplines and discourses. It is to these different cultures of the sublime – to geologists and mountaineers in the Alps, to economists in the City of London, to political theorists in Revolutionary France, to travellers in the Middle and Far East, to explorers of the human mind – that we must return if we are to understand both the place of the sublime in the romantic period and the continued relevance of the sublime to contemporary critical theory and popular culture.

---

38 Barbara Freeman, *The Feminine Sublime: Gender and Excess in Women's Fiction* (Berkeley: University of California Press, 1995); Anne Mellor, *Romanticism and Gender* (London: Routledge, 1993).

1

Mountains

The sublimity of mountainous terrain has long been a commonplace of both popular culture and writing about aesthetics. Such landscapes – in particular the Alps and the Italian volcanoes Vesuvius and Etna – became a major focus of writing about the sublime during the eighteenth century and romantic period. In *Mountain Gloom and Mountain Glory*, Marjorie Hope Nicolson suggests that this intense interest in the so-called natural sublime resulted from the gradual transfer of the affective responses traditionally evoked by the idea of God to those natural phenomena which seemed most to partake of and to reflect the attributes of God: the grandeur of the natural sublime, in other words, became a figure for the grandeur of its supposed creator.[1] Religious ideas certainly played a significant role in responses to the natural sublime during the period covered by this selection, both in the writings of those whose pious responses to the mountain sublime support Nicolson's claim (e.g. Bridges, Glover), and in the work of radical and liberal thinkers (e.g. Rousseau, De Staël) who formulate the corollary hypothesis: that religious ideas *originated* in the reaction of primitive cultures to sublime natural phenomena beyond their comprehension. But what the following extracts also demonstrate is the extraordinary *variety* of connotations that sublime mountain landscapes possessed for these different writers. By the beginning of the eighteenth century, Vesuvius and Etna were already well established on the cultural map of Europe as what Joseph Addison called 'classic ground': a landscape richly imbued with historical and cultural associations.[2] The Alps, too, had their historical associations – with Hannibal, who led his armies over them en route to attack the Roman Empire (see De Carbonnières), and with William Tell, the celebrated Swiss republican. However, following the European 'discovery' of Chamonix-Mont Blanc by William Windham's expedition in 1741, the Alps became the subject of ever more intense scientific and cultural interest, peaking though certainly not concluding with the first ascent and subsequent high-profile ascents of Mont Blanc, the highest mountain in Western Europe, in the 1780s (see De Saussure).[3] To put it in other words, during the eighteenth century the Alps became the locus of a protracted debate between liberal

---

1 Marjorie Hope Nicolson, *Mountain Gloom and Mountain Glory* (Ithaca: Cornell UP, 1959).
2 Joseph Addison, *A Letter from Italy* (1701), p. 12.
3 Windham, W., *An Account of the Glacieres or Ice Alps in Savoy, in Two Letters* (London: 1744).

(republican, scientific) and conservative (religious) world views. The following extracts therefore offer significant and influential contemporary alternatives to Kant's model of the 'disinterestedness' of the aesthetic judgement in the encounter with the natural sublime. Conversely, what these extracts make clear is that, in responding to the mountain sublime – to Alps or volcanoes – these writers were responding to *cultural* rather than to simply *natural* objects.

1.1 Jean Jacques Rousseau, *Julie, or, the New Héloïse: Letters of Two Lovers who Live in a Small Town at the Foot of the Alps* (1761), Part I, Letter XXIII; trans. William Kenrick (London, 1761), pp. 112–19.

The Swiss philosopher and political theorist Jean Jacques Rousseau (1712–1778) contributed significantly to both the development of democratic aspirations in France prior to the Revolution, and to the valorisation of nature and the natural in romantic-period writing. Rousseau's lengthy epistolary novel, Julie, *was enormously popular, and controversial, during the closing decades of the eighteenth century. Telling the story of an illicit romance between the aristocratic Julie and her tutor St Preux,* Julie *emphasises the power of sexual desire to transgress social boundaries, ultimately formulating a vision of love free from class or religious constraints, and relating this vision explicitly to the physical and ethical purity of the sublime Alpine environment. The following extract is taken from* Letter XXIII *of Part One of* Julie, *in which St Preux describes for Julie his journey to the Upper Valais (Wallis), the mountainous region of southwest Switzerland. Rousseau's emphasis on the moral, physical, and intellectual benefits of the encounter with the natural sublime sets the tone for decades of writing about the region, establishing key tropes such as the correlation between physical, aesthetic and moral elevation, and validating the idea that democracy is the 'natural' state of society, linking revolutionary politics directly to the experience of the natural sublime.*

I have employed scarce eight days in surveying a country that would require some years [...] I set out dejected with my own sufferings, but consoled with your joy; which held me suspended in a state of languor that is not disagreeable to true sensibility. Under the conduct of a very honest guide, I crawled up the towering hills, through many a rugged, unfrequented path. Often would I muse, and then, at once, some unexpected object caught my attention. One moment I beheld stupendous rocks hanging ruinous over my head; the next I was enveloped in drizzling cloud, which arose from a vast cascade that dashing thundered against the rocks below my feet; on one side, a perpetual torrent opened to my view a yawning abyss, which my eyes could hardly fathom with safety; sometimes I was lost in the obscurity of a hanging wood, and then was agreeably astonished with the sudden opening of a flowery plain. A surprising mixture of wild and cultivated nature points out the hand of man, where one would imagine man had never penetrated [...]

But it is not labour only that renders this strange country so wonderfully contrasted; for here nature seems to have a singular pleasure in acting contradictory to herself, so different does she appear in the same place in different aspects. Towards the east the flowers of spring – to the south the fruits of autumn – and northwards the ice of winter. She unites all the seasons in the same instant, every climate in the same place, different soils on the same land, and, with a harmony elsewhere unknown, joins the produce of the plains to those of the highest Alps. Add to these, the illusions of vision, the tops of the mountains variously illumined, the harmonious mixture of light and shade, and their different effects in the morning and the evening as I travelled; you may then form some idea of the scenes which engaged my attention, and which seemed to change as I passed, as on an enchanted theatre; for the prospect of mountains being almost perpendicular to the horizon, strikes the eye at the same instant, and more powerfully than that of a plain, where the objects are seen obliquely and half concealed behind each other.

To this pleasing variety of scenes I attributed the serenity of my mind during my first day's journey. I wondered to find that inanimate beings should over-rule our most violent passions, and despised the impotence of philosophy for having less power over the soul than a succession of lifeless objects. But, finding that my tranquillity continued during the night, and even increased with the following day, I began to believe it flowed from some other source, which I had not yet discovered. That day I reached the lower mountains, and, passing over their rugged tops, at last ascended the highest summit I could possibly attain. Having walked a while in the clouds I came to a place of greater serenity, whence one may peacefully observe the thunder and the storm gathering below – Ah! too flattering picture of human wisdom, of which the original never existed, except in those sublime regions whence the emblem is taken.

Here it was that I plainly discovered, in the purity of the air, the true cause of that returning tranquillity of soul, to which I had been so long a stranger. This impression is general, though not universally observed. Upon the tops of mountains, the air being subtle and pure, we respire with greater freedom, our bodies are more active, our minds more serene, our pleasures less ardent, and our passions much more moderate. Our meditations acquire a degree of sublimity from the grandeur of the objects that surround us. It seems as if, being lifted above all human society, we had left every low, terrestrial sentiment behind; and that as we approach the ethereal regions the soul imbibes something of their eternal purity. One is grave without being melancholy, peaceful but not indolent, pensive yet contented: our desires lose their painful violence, and leave only a gentle emotion in our hearts. Thus the passions which in the lower world are man's greatest torment, in happier climates contribute to his felicity. I doubt much whether any violent agitation, or vapours of the mind,[4] could

---

4 *vapours of the mind*: eighteenth-century medicine ('physic') believed that gasses produced by the internal organs could cause a wide range of physical and mental disorders. Rousseau's

hold out against such a situation; and I am surprised that a bath of the reviving and wholesome air of the mountains is not frequently prescribed both by physic and morality [...] Imagine to yourself all these united impressions; the amazing variety, magnitude, and beauty of a thousand stupendous objects; the pleasure of gazing at an entire new scene, strange birds, unknown plants, another nature, and a new world. To these even the subtlety of the air is advantageous; it enlivens the natural colours of objects, renders them more distinct, and brings them as it were nearer to the eye. In short, there is a kind of supernatural beauty in these mountainous prospects which charms the senses of the mind both into a forgetfulness of one's self and of everything in the world.

I could have spent the whole time in contemplating these magnificent landscapes, if I had not found still greater pleasure in the conversation of the inhabitants. In my observations you will find a slight sketch of their manners, their simplicity, their equality of soul, and of that peacefulness of mind which renders them happy by an exemption from pain, rather than by the enjoyment of pleasure.[5] But what I was unable to describe, and which is almost impossible to be conceived, is their disinterested humanity and hospitable zeal to oblige every stranger whom chance or curiosity brings to visit them. This I myself continually experienced – I who was entirely unknown, and who was conducted from place to place only by a common guide. When, in the evening, I arrived in any hamlet at the foot of a mountain, each of the inhabitants was so eager to have me lodge at his house that I was always embarrassed which to accept; and he who obtained the preference seemed so well pleased that, at first, I supposed his joy to arise from a lucrative prospect; but I was amazed, after having used the house like an inn, to find my host not only refuse to accept gratuity, but offended that it was offered. I found it universally the same. So that it was true hospitality, which, from its unusual ardour, I had mistaken for avarice. So perfectly disinterested are these people, that during eight days it was not in my power to leave one patagon[6] among them. In short, how is it possible to spend money in a country where the landlord will not be paid for his provisions, nor the servant for his trouble, and where there are no beggars to be found? Nevertheless, money is by no means abundant in the Upper Valais, and for that very reason the inhabitants are not in want; for the necessaries of life are plentiful, yet nothing is sent out of the country; they are not luxurious at home, nor is the peasant less laborious. If ever they have more money they will grow poor, and of this they are so sensible, that they tread upon mines of gold, which they are determined never to open [...]

What I found particularly agreeable whilst I continued among them was the natural ease and freedom of their behaviour. They went about their business in

---

suggestion was borne out by the development of Alpine sanatoriums during the nineteenth century.

5 Cp. Edmund Burke's theory of the relationship between sublime sensation and 'delight', defined as the emotion experienced upon 'the removal of pain or danger', and contrasted with 'positive pleasure' (*A Philosophical Enquiry into the Origins of the Sublime and the Beautiful* (1757) I iv).

6 *patagon*: old Swiss coin.

the house as if I had not been there; and it was in my power to act as if I were the sole inhabitant. They are entirely unacquainted with the impertinent vanity of *doing the honours of the house*,[7] as if to remind the stranger of his dependence. When I said nothing, they concluded I was satisfied to live in their manner; but the least hint was sufficient to make them comply with mine, without any repugnance or astonishment. The only compliment which they made me, when they heard that I was a Swiss, was, that they looked upon me as a brother, and I ought therefore to think myself at home. After this, they took but little notice of me, not supposing that I could doubt the sincerity of their offers, or refuse to accept them whenever they could be useful. The same simplicity subsists among themselves: when the children are once arrived at maturity, all distinction between them and their parents seems to have ceased; their domestics are seated at the same table with their master; the same liberty reigns in the cottage as in the republic, and each family is an epitome of the State.

1.2 Patrick Brydone, *A Tour through Sicily and Malta. In a Series of Letters to William Beckford, Esq ... The Second Edition, Corrected.*, 2 vols (London, 1774), I, pp. 186–7, 195–200, 202–5, 210–18.

In this extract from his Tour, *Scottish traveller Brydone (1741–1819) describes 'one of the greatest objects of our expedition; the examination of mount Etna' (i, 163). Brydone's account of the volcanic sublime is based around a number of contrasts: the conflict of ice and fire on Etna's summit; the tension between the overwhelming emotional impact of the landscape and the desire to provide reliable scientific witness of it; the conflict between mental and spiritual rewards of the ascent and the physical hardships involved, etc. What Brydone's account also makes clear is the extent to which Etna, like Vesuvius, was already 'classic ground', to use Addison's phrase: a landscape richly imbued with historical and cultural associations which effectively augmented the natural sublimity of the scene. Brydone, in other words, responds, here, as much to a cultural as to a natural phenomenon: his engagement with the volcanic sublime is in no sense a 'disinterested' aesthetic judgement.*

It is indeed a curious consideration that this mountain should reunite every beauty and every horror; and, in short, all the most opposite and dissimilar objects in nature [...] we wander over these beauties [...] considering that hell, with all its terrors, is immediately under our feet; and that but a few yards separate us from lakes of liquid fire [...]

But our astonishment still increases, on casting our eyes on the higher regions of the mountain. There we behold, in perpetual union, the two elements that are at perpetual war; an immense gulf of fire, forever existing in the midst of snows

---

7 *doing the honours of the house*: acting as hosts.

which it has not power to melt; and immense fields of snow and ice forever surrounding this gulf of fire, which they have not power to extinguish.

   [*having emerged from the forests covering Etna's lower slopes, Brydone's description continues*]

The prospect before us was of a very different nature; we beheld an expanse of snow and ice that alarmed us exceedingly, and almost staggered our resolution. In the centre of this, but still at a great distance, we descried the high summit of the mountain, rearing its tremendous head, and vomiting out torrents of smoke. It indeed appeared altogether inaccessible, from the vast extent of the fields of snow and ice that surrounded it [...]

   The ascent for some time was not steep; and as the surface of the snow sunk a little, we had tolerable good footing; but as it soon began to grow steeper, we found our labour greatly increase: however, we determined to persevere, calling to mind in the midst of our labour, that the emperor Adrian and the philosopher Plato[8] had undergone the same; and from the same motive too, to see the rising sun from the top of Etna. After incredible labour and fatigue, but at the same time mixed with a great deal of pleasure, we arrived before dawn at the ruins of an ancient structure, called *Il Torre del Filosofo*, supposed to have been built by the philosopher Empedocles, who took up his habitation here the better to study the nature of mount Etna.[9] By others, it is supposed to be the ruins of a temple of Vulcan[10], whose shop, all the world knows [...] was ever kept in mount Etna [...]

   We now had time to pay our adorations in a silent contemplation of the sublime objects of nature. The sky was clear, and the immense vault of the heavens appeared in awful majesty and splendour. We found ourselves more struck with veneration than below, and at first were at a loss to know the cause; till we observed with astonishment, that the number of stars seemed to be infinitely increased; and the light of each of them appeared brighter than usual. The whiteness of the milky way was like a pure flame that shot across the heavens; and with the naked eye we could observe clusters of stars that were invisible in the regions below. We did not at first attend to the cause, nor recollect that we had now passed through ten or twelve thousand feet of gross vapour, that blunts and confuses every ray, before it reaches the surface of the earth. We were amazed at the distinctness of vision, and exclaimed together, What a glorious situation for

---

8 *Adrian and ... Plato*: the Roman Emperor Hadrian I (76–138 AD) and Greek philosopher Plato (428–347 BC) are both said to have ascended Etna.

9 *Il Torre del Filosofo ... Empedocles*: The philosopher Empedocles was born at Agrigentum, a Greek outpost in Sicily, c. 490 BC; he is supposed to have ascended Etna and constructed an observatory near the summit ('the tower of the philosopher'), although the actual origins of the structure so-called remain unknown (another tradition says it was constructed by Hadrian I). Brydone recounts the legend of Empedocles' death below.

10 *Vulcan*: Roman god of fire (= Greek Hephaestus), often identified as a blacksmith, hence Brydone's reference to his workshop.

an observatory! Had Empedocles had the eyes of Galileo what discoveries must he not have made! We regretted that Jupiter was not visible, as I am persuaded we might have discovered some of his satellites with the naked eye, or at least with a small glass which I had in my pocket [...]

[Brydone continues to describe his party's ascent to 'the highest summit of the mountain, where we arrived in full time, to see the most wonderful and most sublime sight in nature', the sunrise]

But here description must ever fall short; for no imagination has dared to form an idea of so glorious and so magnificent a scene. Neither is there on the surface of this globe, any one point that unites so many awful and sublime objects. – The immense elevation from the surface of the earth, drawn as it were from a single point, without any neighbouring mountain for the senses and imagination to rest upon; and recover from their astonishment in their way down to the world. This point or pinnacle, raised on the brink of a bottomless gulf, as old as the world, often discharging rivers of fire, and throwing out hot burning rocks, with a noise that shakes the whole island. Add to this, the unbounded extent of the prospect, comprehending the greatest diversity and the most beautiful scenery in nature; with the rising sun, advancing in the east, to illuminate the wondrous scene [...]

The senses, unaccustomed to the sublimity of such a scene, are bewildered and confounded; and it is not till after some time, that they are capable of separating and judging of the objects that compose it. – The body of the sun is seen rising from the ocean, immense tracks of both sea and land intervening; the islands of Lipari, Panarea, Alicudi, Stromboli, and Vulcano,[11] with their smoking summits, appear under your feet; and you look down on the whole of Sicily as on a map...The view is absolutely boundless on every side; nor is there any one object, within the circle of vision, to interrupt it; so that the sight is everywhere lost in the immensity [...]

We now had time to examine a fourth region of this wonderful mountain, very different, indeed, from the others, and productive of very different sensations; but which has, undoubtedly, given being to all the rest; I mean the region of fire [...]

Near the centre of the crater is the great mouth of the volcano. That tremendous gulf so celebrated in all ages, looked upon as the terror and scourge both of this and another life; and equally useful to ancient poets, or to modern divines, when the Muse, or when the Spirit inspires. We beheld it with awe and with horror, and were not surprised that it had been considered as the place of the damned. When we reflect on the immensity of its depth, the vast cells and caverns whence so many lavas have issued; the force of its internal fire, to raise those lavas to so vast a height, to support it as it were in the air, and even force it over the very summit of the crater, with all the dreadful accompaniments; the

11 *Lipari* [...] *Vulcano*: the Aeolian Islands, off the north coast of Sicily.

boiling of the matter, the shaking of the mountain, the explosions of flaming rocks, etc. we must allow that the most enthusiastic imagination, in the midst of all its terrors, hardly ever formed an idea of a hell more dreadful [...]

[Brydone's party then begin their descent]

On our arrival at the Torre del Filosofo, we could not help admiring, that the ruins of this structure have remained uncovered for so many ages, so near the top of Etna, when thousands of places at a great distance from it, have been repeatedly buried by its lavas, in a much shorter time. A proof that few eruptions have risen so high in the mountain [...]

Empedocles was a native of Agrigentum, and is supposed to have died 400 years before the Christian era. Perhaps his vanity more than his philosophy led him to this elevated situation; nay, it is said to have carried him still much further: – That he might be looked upon as a god, and that the people might suppose he was taken up to heaven, he is recorded to have thrown himself headlong into the great gulf of mount Etna, never supposing that his death could be discovered by mankind; but the treacherous mountain threw out his slippers, which were of brass, and announced to the world the fate of the philosopher who, by his death, as well as life, wanted only to impose upon mankind, and make them believe that he was greater than they.

However, if there is such a thing as philosophy on earth, this surely ought to be its seat. The prospect is little inferior to that from the summit; and the mind enjoys a degree of serenity here, that even few philosophers, I believe, could ever boast of on that tremendous point. – All Nature lies expanded below your feet, in her gayest and most luxuriant dress, and you still behold united under one point of view, all the seasons of the year, and all the climates of the earth. The meditations are ever elevated in proportion to the grandeur and sublimity of the objects that surround us; and here, where you have all Nature to arouse your admiration, what mind can remain inactive?

It has likewise been observed, and from experience I can say with truth; that on the tops of the highest mountains, where the air is so pure and refined; and where there is not that immense weight of gross vapours pressing upon the body; the mind acts with greater freedom, and all the functions both of body and soul are performed in a superior manner. It would appear, that in proportion as we are raised above the habitations of men, all low and vulgar sentiments are left behind; and that the soul, in approaching the æthereal regions, shakes off its earthly affections, and already acquires something of their celestial purity. – Here, where you stand under a serene sky, and behold, with equal serenity, the tempest and storm forming below your feet: The lightning, darting from cloud to cloud, and the thunder rolling round the mountain, and threatening with destruction the poor wretches below; the mind considers the little storms of the human passions as equally below her notice. – Surely the situation alone, is enough to inspire philosophy, and Empedocles had good reason for choosing it.

But, alas! how vain are all our reasonings! In the very midst of these meditations, my philosophy was at once overset, and in a moment I found myself
relapsed into a poor miserable mortal; was obliged to own, that pain was the
greatest of evils; and would have given the world to have been once more arrived
at those humble habitations, which but the moment before, I had looked down
upon with such contempt [...][12]

1.3 Marc Bourrit, *A Relation of a Journey to the Glaciers in the Dutchy of Savoy*, transl. C. & F. Davy (1775), pp. 90–117.

*The Swiss artist and explorer Marc Théodore Bourrit (1739–1819) made a number
of unsuccessful attempts to climb Mont Blanc during the second half of the eighteenth century. The following extract is taken from his widely read account of his
journeys to Chamonix in 1770–3 (named subscribers included Burke, Beckford and
Walpole), and describes the Mer de Glace, one of the glaciers which descends from
the Vallée Blanche, at the foot of Mont Blanc. Like Rousseau, Bourrit stresses that
the encounter with the sublime Alpine landscape delivers not only aesthetic but
also moral and intellectual rewards, confirming that a gain in altitude equates
not simply with a more sublime view, and hence with greater aesthetic pleasure,
but also with greater scientific insight into the natural processes governing the
landscape. Bourrit also registers, here, the interplay between imagination and
reason in the encounter with the natural sublime: the sublime Alpine landscape
triggers a (potentially hazardous) stimulation of the viewer's imagination, which
must be tempered by a rational understanding of the situation. This interplay is
comparable to the process that Kant describes in his account of the experience
of the sublime in the third* Critique, *but the context for Bourrit's remarks is less
'disinterested' than explicitly aware of the emerging cultural significance of the
landscape.*

We descended into the valley, about three quarters of an hour after sunrise [...]
scarcely had we gained our feet upon the ice, when we found ourselves retarded
by the clefts,[13] that opened quite across the valley. We passed a number of
them with the utmost gaiety and spirit; but others soon appeared, it seemed
impossible to clear; nor could we even look at them without terror. Our guides
accustomed to such objects ventured over boldly, provided with a staff or pole
of seven or eight feet only in length; they sprung with an amazing strength,
agility, and resolution, and encouraged, and instructed us to do the same.
The farther we advanced, we met with openings wider yet, as well as deeper,
and where even our guides were under the necessity of taking every possible
precaution [...]

---

12 Brydone sprained his ankle during the descent.
13 *clefts*: meaning crevasses, deep cracks that occur in glaciers.

We now were soon to see an end of these alarming hazards, and of our excessive labour. Arriving near the fall of rocks upon the ice, we employed ourselves in search of crystals [...] The farther we advanced, the more we saw of objects to admire; yet surrounded by these beauties, we could not but reflect with horror, at the sight of this eternal frozen lake, its yawning clefts, and deep abysses; whilst the mountains which environed us, their venerable antiquity, their several different slopes, and the varied magnificence of their forms, together with those hills of ice, which broken off, had rolled into the valley, struck us with amazement.

In short, we were astonished at the recollection of our being in a place thus severed from the world, so vast, so extraordinary, where there reigned an universal stillness, in the midst even of a thousand dangers.

As we now proceeded forward, the valley was expanded wider, and the ice became more even; but although we had already walked upon it four hours, from our setting off, we had not yet reached the place at which the valley is separated into two branches: we gained this point however at last: what a picture was before us! we were surprised to a degree of transport, and incapable of expressing our admiration, but by frequent acclamations.

We beheld a spacious icy plain entirely level; upon this there rose a mountain all of ice, with steps ascending to the top, which seemed the throne of some divinity. It took the form moreover of a grand cascade, whose figure was beyond conception beautiful, and the sun which shone upon it, gave a sparkling brilliance to the whole: it was as a glass, which sent his rays to a prodigious distance: a polished mirror, upon which the objects were designed with such a perfect mixture of light and shade as ravished our sight; and to complete the beauty of the prospect, this even glassy lake was crowned with mountains differently coloured, and enlivened by a varnish of the clearest ice: these altogether, formed a composition of the most delightful splendid objects, heightened by the deeper colour of a single neighbouring mountain, which graduated from top to bottom: whilst this again was interlaced with streams of snow, whose winding currents cast a lustre from the sun. In short, the whole of this enchanting view was terminated with the rocks of crystal, and by others, all whose several tints were richly and profusely varied [...]

New beauties still continued to delight us, astonished as we were at present, by a number of such objects so magnificent and vast [...]

The valley on our right was ornamented with prodigious Glaciers, that shooting up to an immeasurable height between the mountains, blend their colours with the skies, which they appear to reach. The gradual rise of *one* of them, induced us to conceive it practicable to ascend it; and such is the engrossing nature of these objects, that they seem to efface every other idea. We are no longer our own masters; and it is next to an impossibility to stop the impulse of our inclinations. – It would open still new scenes, or more extensive grandeur. – That, as we *certainly* should gain a view beyond the Needles,[14] such

---

14 *the Needles*: the French name (Aiguilles) for a number of rocky summits.

a point of elevation, (beyond which, no mortal whatever had yet gone) would not only present Mont Blanc to us under a new form, and with new beauties, but that in short, looking towards the south, we should have a picture of all Italy before us as in a Camera Obscura.[15] It was thus the wildness of imagination prompted us to think the project possible, and we were in the full enjoyment of our reverie, when a horrid noise from the very same Glaciers put an end to this delightful dream, and shattered all the scenery at once. Reason dictated immediately, that supposing such a fancied picture as we had represented to ourselves, to be real, and that it *were* possible to ascend the height of the Glacier to enjoy a sight of it, the execution of the plan would require our stay all night upon this frozen valley, which was absolutely impossible, from the want of fuel only [...]

By this time rest was necessary to us; and the only situation where we could be safe, was in the middle of the valley; we might here at least be at a distance from the falling down of ice or rocks. The station of Mr. de Saussure[16] appeared most eligible for the purpose, and we were coming to the very spot: it is a massy block of stone, precisely in the middle of the ice; we seated ourselves upon it, and having taken out our necessary refreshments, poured a sparkling libation to the honour of the Professor, as the first person who had resolution enough to penetrate thus far.

We rested here for two hours, our minds voluptuously employed in the contemplation of so many wonders; every moment was distinguished with some new discovery. A single glance over all these Glaciers together, seemed to throw a light upon their correspondence and extent [...]

1.4 Horace Bénédict de Saussure, *Voyages dans les Alpes* (1779–96).[17]

The famous Swiss naturalist de Saussure (1740–99) travelled extensively in the Alps in the latter part of the eighteenth century, and, with Jacques Balmat, completed a successful ascent of Mont Blanc on 2 August 1787. The first extract is taken from de Saussure's description of a failed attempt at Mont Blanc in 1785, on which occasion his party reached Pierre-Ronde; the second extract comes from his description of the successful attempt in 1787. Both register the tension between the overwhelming affective power of the landscape and the need to provide reliable scientific witness to it, configuring the encounter with the Alpine sublime as at once enlightening, exhausting and potentially overpowering.

15 *a Camera Obscura*: a device used for projecting images, most commonly of landscapes, onto a screen.

16 *the station* [...] *Saussure*: The large rock on the surface of the Mer de Glace, where Horace Bénédict de Saussure, Bourrit's great rival in Alpine exploration, rested during his first expedition to the region, in 1760. The rock is still in situ.

17 Quoted from the translation published in John Pinkerton (ed.), *A Collection of Voyages and Travels*, 17 vols (London 1808–14), iv, pp. 677–711.

I shall not undertake to give a detail of the immense heap of mountains which is discovered from this summit, let it suffice to say that it presents the most ravishing prospect to those who delight in such beauties [...] the beauty of the evening, and the magnificence of the spectacle, which the setting sun presented from my observatory [on the summit], consoled me for this disappointment [of not being able to perform scientific experiments because of equipment failure] [...] the repose and profound silence which reigned in this vast extent, still heightened by the imagination, inspired me with a sort of terror; it appeared to me as if I had outlived the universe, and that I saw its corpse stretched at my feet. Sorrowful as ideas of this nature are, they have a sort of charm which can hardly be resisted. I turned my eyes oftener towards this obscure solitude than towards Mont Blanc, whose shining and phosphorical snows still have the idea of movement and life; but the keenness of the air on this isolated point presently forced me to retire [...]

In the chagrin we felt for not having been able to complete our enterprise, it was some consolation to us to know that we had been higher than any other known observer in Europe had ever been before.

[*the next extract comes from de Saussure's account of his ascent of Mont Blanc in August 1787; it opens with his description of an overnight bivouac near the Dome de Goûter, before the ascent to the summit the following morning. De Saussure's party reached the summit at 11 a.m. and remained there, conducting experiments and making observations, until 3.30 p.m.*]

My guides always occupied with the fear of cold, so closely shut all the openings of the tent, that I suffered much from the heat and impurity of the air, occasioned by the respiration of so many people. I was obliged to get out in the night for the sake of taking breath. The moon shone with the greatest lustre in the middle of the sky of a dark ebony colour, Jupiter seemed to throw out strong rays of light from behind the highest summit to the east of Mont Blanc, and the reverberating light all over this extent of snow was so dazzling, that only the stars of the first and second magnitude were distinguishable [...].

[*on arrival at the summit of Mont Blanc, de Saussure continues*]

My eyes were first fixed on Chamonix, where I knew my wife and her two sisters were, their eyes fixed to a telescope following all our steps with an uneasiness, too great without doubt, but not less distressing to them. I felt a very pleasing and consoling sentiment when I saw the flag which they had promised to hoist at the moment they observed me at the summit, when their apprehensions would be at least suspended.

I could now enjoy without regret the grand spectacle I had under my eyes. A light vapour suspended in the lower regions of the air, concealed from my sight the lowest and most distant objects [...] but I did not much regret this loss.

What I had just seen and what I saw in the clearest manner, is the whole of all the high summits of which I had so long desired to know the organisation. I could hardly believe my eyes, it appeared to me like a dream, when I saw placed under my eyes those majestic summits [...] whose bases even had been for me of such difficult and dangerous access. I seized their relation to each other, their connection, their structure, and a single glance cleared up doubts that years of labour had not been able to dissolve [...]

[...] It is said when you walk on the border of a precipice you should not look at it, and it is true to a certain point; but the following advice is the result of my long experience. Before you engage in a dangerous passage you should begin by contemplating the precipice, until you get quite familiar with it, and it has lost its force on the imagination, and you can look at it with a sort of indifference; meantime you should study the way you should go, and mark as you may your steps: after which the danger is no more thought of, and you only think of following the prescribed way. But if you cannot bear the sight of the precipice, and accustom yourself to it, give up the enterprise, for if the path be narrow, it is impossible to look where to place your feet without looking at the precipice at the same time: and this sight if taken unawares dazzles you, and may prove your destruction; this rule of conduct in danger appears to me applicable to moral as well as natural cases [...]

1.5   Louis Ramond de Carbonnières, 'Observations on the Glacieres and the Glaciers' (1781), translated by Helen Maria Williams and published as an appendix to her *Tour In Switzerland; or, A View of the Present State of the Governments and Manners of those Cantons: with Comparative Sketches of the Present State of Paris*, 2 vols (London, 1798), II, pp. 279–88, 347–52.

French aristocrat and explorer Ramond de Carbonnières (1755–1827) composed his 'Observations' as part of the editorial commentary to his 1781 French translation of William Coxe's Sketches [...] *of Swisserland (1779). English translations were published as an appendix to subsequent editions of Coxe, and Helen Maria Williams published a new translation as an appendix to her* Tour in Switzerland *(1798), from which the present text is taken. The 'Observations' were widely read, with both Wordsworth and Byron, for example, referring to them. De Carbonnières refutes Coxe's curiously dismissive account of the impressive glacial scenery around Chamonix, affirming not just the aesthetic rewards of the sublime landscape but also, like Bourrit before him, emphasising the scientific insight it can provide. Much of the 'Observations' appears indebted to Rousseau's account of the Upper Valais in* Julie, *suggesting that the sublime Alpine environment contributes directly to the moral, intellectual and political enlightenment of the percipient. The 'Observations' conclude with a remarkable apostrophe to the imagination, identifying it rather than the reason as the key agent of scientific progress: it is only the imagination, de Carbonnières suggests, which is capable of going beyond the overwhelming sensory impact of the sublime landscape towards an intuition of the natural processes inform- ing that landscape.*

Twenty ages since, when Rome, for the first time, cast a look towards those unknown regions, whence issued the barbarous nations who were most the objects of her dread, she beheld, with astonishment, a chain of summits, bolder than Caucasus,[18] eternally covered with the snows of winter. The civilised world, for a while, believed that Italy was joined by the Alps to the frozen pole of the North.

Whilst the Romans were contemplating these mountains, Hannibal[19] scaled them. He found, as he had conjectured, that the whole of their surface was not covered with snows, and was led by their savage, but free inhabitants, across their wild pasturages, hidden amidst masses of rocks, and the Romans discovered that they were not invincible.

It is not yet precisely determined over what parts of the mountains the Carthaginians passed; nor can we form any just idea of the state of the Alps at the time of their passage, since we know not to what places we ought to apply the descriptions given by the historians who have transmitted to us the account of this astonishing expedition. All that we can conclude from what they have related, is, that the Alps had at that time reached their period of old age; hills had filled up valleys; regular slopes had become abrupt precipices; vast masses rent from their sides, indicated their decay, and the regions of ice which Hannibal crossed, were no doubt the conquests made by the higher glaciers over the territory beneath. This is all that history records, but in what annals shall we trace the youth of these eldest daughters of the earth? To what remote period shall we revert, to discover the infancy of what for so many centuries has passed the boundaries of old age? If a frail machine, the work of an infant, which moves, which feels, which suffers, which lives, which with all its force and ener- gies hastens to decay; if man counts by years, by what numbers or lapses of time shall those passive insensible masses be computed, which are formed to resist, like the globe of which they are a part, that desolation which changes, without intermission, the beautiful scenery of its external form?

Let us then no longer regret the loss of facts which historians have omitted to mention; what information should we gain from annals of such recent date? What are such points of comparison, at the distance only of a few ages from each other? But there is another history, in which the records of nations occupies but an

---

18 *Caucasus*: mountain range dividing the Black Sea from the Caspian Sea.
19 *Hannibal*: Carthaginian military commander (247–c. 183 BC), who led a number of successful campaigns against the Roman Empire before his final defeat at Zama (202 BC); in 218 BC, Hannibal led his army across the Alps in order to reach Italy, thereby outmanoeuvring the Roman army which had been sent to stop him in Southern France. His achievement was often alluded to during the period, especially in the wake of Napoleon's crossing of the Alps in 1800 en route to victory over the Austrians at the battle of Marengo, in northern Italy.

imperceptible space, the history of nature. The mind of genius, which can read its characters, bounds, at one step, over the limits of our short and dubious page, and leaving at a remote distance both nations, and their earliest convulsions, plunges into antiquity far beyond their ken; discovers its periods, and fixes the epochs of its revolutions. From the shores of the sea he departs; there he collects those facts which are most recent; he marks the yesterday of nature; for nations in his sight are but the beings of the day. He then approaches the hills which rise up from the shores, those which the waters last formed when they finally withdrew from the land.[20] Those are long parallel, and but little elevated lines, the work of the waters in their slow retreat, for when the ocean left them behind, it had lost its primitive fury, tending with less impetuosity towards the hollow which it now fills.

As he advances, the mountains raise their heads, and branch off in different chains, the various directions of which leave traces of the struggles of the waters. Here, broad and deep valleys mark the currents; a raging sea has washed the cliffs and precipices above. Vast banks of shells and vegetable productions, are proofs of the long abode which the water has made, and their petrifaction[21] bears testimony to the number of years which have elapsed since the sea has left them.

In a loftier region, every object assumes a bolder shape; everything indicates more violent convulsions, discovers mightier operations, and leads us back to antiquity still more remote. Every step of elevation adds a century to the age of the mountains, and when the observer arrives at length a thousand fathoms above the real level of the seas, he is at the greatest height where traces of their abode are found, and where the most distant period of their known labours is discoverable.

Nevertheless, he is far from having reached the highest points which bristle over the globe. From the bosom of the mountains which he has just scaled, rises a formidable chain of naked rocks, that seem to have held perpetual dominion over the shoreless seas which rolled around the globe. We should seek in vain for comparisons, and epochs between them, and those masses of mountains, which the sea has formed; the annals of nature here leave a vast chasm; there is nothing common in their respective operations; the spoils of the animal and vegetable kingdom, which the secondary mountains contain, prove that our earth was then the theatre of life; but who has witnessed the birth of the primitive mountains, which conceal nothing but the simplest aggregations of the mineral kingdom? when our planet brought them forth, it was nothing but a dry solitude?

Such is the antiquity of these mountains. Their origin is coeval with the infancy of the globe, and must be left to the same conjectures. If we believe in the hypothesis of that conflagration of the earth which kept it so long in a state

20 *the waters* […] *withdrew*: late eighteenth-century geological debate about the formation of the earth's landscapes was essentially divided into two schools: the Neptunists, who believed that water was the principal agent in the process, and the Plutonists, who believed that volcanological action was responsible (de Carbonnières mentions the Plutonist position below).

21 *petrifaction*: meaning fossilisation.

of liquefaction, we may suppose them to have been formed from the unequal connection of its parts, and the tumefactions[22] arising from its first cooling. If, on the contrary, we suppose that the seas were able to maintain themselves for a series of ages, at more than double the height which has commonly been granted, we may believe that their waters, as yet void of inhabitants, rolled on a purely mineral mud, and formed this enormous mass of simple rocks.

But of what importance to us are these different systems? The existence of the primordial mountains, interests us no farther than the epocha when they proceeded from the bosom of the waters, surrounded with their investiture of secondary mountains, softening their forms, smoothing their asperities, and serving as a basis to vegetation, whilst they inter-chain, and stretch themselves in every direction over the drained continent, dividing into different regions its uniform extent, and destroying that level by which it would be exposed to new deluges, and condemned to eternal sterility. Everything in these primitive chains is regular, everything bears the impression of the first designs of nature. Their gentle, and fruitful declivities offer all the gradations of vegetation without confusion, answering, with exactness, to the different strata of the atmosphere, and passing, from the lavish fertility of the plains, to the scantly indigence of the lofty heights. The vegetable kingdom is terminated by moss; everything beyond is absolute barrenness [...]

Let no one imagine that existence is for a moment painful in the midst of these deserts. A temperature, such as the presence of a cloudless sun, is always an enjoyment, notwithstanding the cold of the atmosphere; an air which is respirable at the highest degree, notwithstanding its rarefaction; waters which have preserved the purity they have acquired, when raised to the clouds, because in falling back on the earth they have not crossed the pestilential vapours which hover over our plains; those waters which, offering to the parched traveller no perfidious beverage, engage him to quench his thirst without apprehension of the fatal effects arising from their coolness; these things are what first strike the senses.[23] The most excessive fatigue vanishes in an instant; strength is renewed; courage and tranquillity take place of uneasiness; in a word, the body and mind undergo a transformation which extends and multiplies all their faculties. However wonderful what I have advanced may appear, I shall not want evidences of its truth, and shall only find those incredulous, who have never ascended above the plain. I call these to witness, who have scaled some of the heights of the globe; is there a single person who did not find himself regenerated; who did not feel with surprise that he had left at the feet of the mountains, his weakness, his infirmities, his cares, his troubles, in a word, the weaker part of his being, and the ulcerated portion of his heart? Who among them but will acknowledge that at no moment of his life, in the age even of his warmest passions, in the midst of circumstances which have given the greatest force to his imagination, he has never felt himself so disposed to that kind of enthusiasm which kindles great ideas!

---

22 *tumefactions*: swellings.
23 The remainder of the extract appears to draw on Rousseau's account of the Upper Valais in *Julie*.

In fine, who, in beholding from that station the immensity of the celestial spheres, and the nothingness of our planet, can think without some feeling of contempt on what we call great, or of pity on what we deem important? Let not this appear wonderful; everything in these regions is of colossal magnitude: the eye lost in the immense chaos of mountains which it surveys, thinks it beholds an universe, and this universe is but a point when it contemplates the azure space in which we wander. Nothing distracts or misleads the mind employed on these sublime objects. The silence of these deserts, where nothing breathes, or moves, beyond the tumult of the habitable world; the view of these profound abysses; of valleys which those immoveable cliffs have beheld alternately desert and cultivated, peopled today, tomorrow desolated, the asylum of so many alternately happy and miserable mortals, the theatre of so many changes; everything concurs to make our meditations more profound; to give them that melancholy hue, that sublime character which they acquire, when the soul, taking that flight which makes it contemporary with every age, and co-existent with all beings, hovers over the abyss of time. In vain would reason strive to count by years. The solidity of these enormous masses, opposed to the accumulation of their ruins, startles and confounds all its calculations. Imagination seizes the reins which Reason drops, and in that long succession of periods, catches a glimpse of the image of eternity, which she hails with religious terror. How has everything vanished, which occupies, enchants, and astonishes us here below, when we compare it with the objects of glory that are set before us! Thus, our most extended ideas, and our most elevated and noble sentiments, have their origin in the wanderings of the imagination; but let us forgive its chimeras,[24] for what would there be great in our conceptions, or glorious in our actions, if finite was not, through its illusions, continually changed into infinite, space into immensity, time into eternity, and fading laurels into immortal crowns!

1.6   Henry Swinburne, *Travels in the Two Sicilies*[25], 2 vols (1790), I, pp. 81–90.

Swinburne (1743–1803) offers a rather disappointed account of Vesuvius – he is one of those travellers for whom the long-expected encounter with the natural sublime fails to deliver its imagined promise, prompting a need to find compensation elsewhere (as in Wordsworth's famous appeal to the imagination in Book VI of The Prelude*). Swinburne, in this extract, turns to a relatively minor volcanic event, which he seeks to paint in rather more expressive colours. Unsurprisingly, then, the extract ends not by*

---

24 *chimera*: a mythical beast, with the head of a lion, body of a goat, and tail of a serpent. Enlightenment thinkers frequently identified the imagination as an agent of superstition.

25 *the Two Sicilies*: meaning the Kingdom of Sicily and the Kingdom of Naples (essentially, the southern part of Italy).

registering the bewildering effects of the sublime landscape (a familiar refrain of other
travellers), but rather by emphasising the dangers of misguided attempts to fit that
landscape to the requirements of a preconceived scientific system.

I ascended the steep cone of cinders in a direct line, up to the ankles at every step
in purple lukewarm ashes. The heat was not very powerful till we came within
a few yards of the summit, and there the smoke breaks out through many cran-
nies [...] It is impossible to give a just idea of the fatigue of this climbing. Before
that day I had mounted some very exalted points of the Alps, and clambered up
the highest peak of the Pyrenees,[26] without feeling such oppressive weariness
and exhaustion of spirits and strength as I experienced on Vesuvius. Perhaps
the mephitic effluvium,[27] which attacked my respiration, may also have had a
debilitating effect upon my nerves and muscles [...]
   I confess I was a good deal disappointed on reaching the summit; for the
descriptions I had read had raised in my imagination an expectation of everything that could be glaring and striking in colours, pompous and tremendous in
a scene of igneous phenomena; but the late eruption had, for a time, laid all the
mountain's fury asleep, and everything was dull and dark. The vent, by which
the lava ran out, is much below the top of the mountain, and on that side the
sulphurous streams are very pungent. I was on the point of returning rather
frustrated of my hopes, when a curling column of smoke and flame rose slowly
out of the gloomy abyss, and brought up with it a thick white cloud, that had
hitherto rendered the crater impervious to my sight. The wind quickly caught
hold of this column, and whirled it around the immense cauldron several times
with inconceivable noise and velocity, till it forced part of the smoke to fly off
horizontally from the mountain, and dashed the remainder back into its original cavern. During this conflict, on the opposite side to that where we stood,
I had a peep very far into the crater. The sides seemed all lava and scoria,[28] with
very little variety in the tints, closed at the bottom by an impenetrable screen
of smoke. I have seen old ruined coal pits, that afford a tolerable idea of this
volcanic kettle. As soon as the smoke was driven away, the roaring below grew
loud, and frequent explosions were heard with a hollow sound; and at every
throe; which cause a very considerable commotion in the thin arch on which we
stood, a shower of red-hot stones was shot up; but, not rising many feet above
the mountain, they did not come within the sweep of the wind, and so fell back
perpendicularly into the rumbling gulf [...]
   I shall not presume to investigate minutely the origin, composition, or
operations of the mountain [...] Many writers of dissertations on ignivomous[29]
mountains have been led into a labyrinth of mistakes, false propositions, and

------

26 *the highest* [...] *Pyrenees*: Aneto (3404 m).
27 *mephitic effluvium*: poisonous gasses.
28 *scoria*: lumps of solidified material, ejected from the volcano.
29 *ignivomous*: 'vomiting fire' (*OED*).

false consequences, by trusting solely to the relations of others, and not being at pains of examining the phenomena with their own eyes. Whoever has not had the advantage of inspecting an active volcano, should not presume to write upon that subject, as he must unavoidably fall into error, in spite of all the learning, combinations, and sagacity, the wit of man is susceptible of. Indeed, some authors, who have had Vesuvius before their eyes for forty years, have likewise fallen into strange indefensible opinions concerning its component parts, original formation, and modes of operating. Attachment to system misleads us all, and frequently causes us to see things, not as they are, but as we wish to find them [...] Without prejudices of this kind, could other authors have seen nothing in Monte Somma, and the hills of Naples, but primitive substances, unaltered since the Deluge, when, in reality, every stone bespeaks a fiery origin?

1.7 Madame de Staël, *Corinna, or Italy* (1807), Book XIII, chapter 1; trans. D. Lawlor, 5 vols (London, 1807), III, pp. 207–10.

Because of its lengthy topographical descriptions, Germaine de Staël's story of the doomed romance between the Scottish peer, Lord Nelvil, and the Italian improvisatrice, Corinna, was often used as a guidebook by travellers in Italy – and, indeed, was for many years catalogued as travel literature in the Bibliothèque du Roi, in Paris. This extract describes Nelvil and Corinna's visit to the sublime volcanic landscape of Vesuvius. De Staël presents the volcanic sublime allegorically, using the lava as a figure for the inevitable onslaught of mortality. But she also registers contemporary speculation that this kind of landscape provided the original for human ideas of hell, reprising the French Enlightenment claim that human notions of gods and demons sprang from an anthropomorphic response to sublime natural phenomena. The extract concludes with Nelvil internalising the horror of the landscape, affirming that psychological terrors outstrip anything nature can offer.

The ground which they traversed, before they arrived hither [at the lava flow], gave way beneath their feet, and seemed to repulse them from an abode hostile to all that breathes, where nature no longer appears under the control of man, where she escapes his domination by death. The fire of the torrent is of a dark colour; nevertheless, when it burns the vines or the trees, they produce a clear and brilliant flame; but the lava itself is sombre, as the infernal lake is represented to be; it slowly flows along, sable by day, and red by night. We hear, as we approach it, a little sparkling noise, which terrifies us the more from its being light and trifling, from cunning seeming to unite with strength; thus the tiger steals with slow and measured steps upon his prey. The lava creeps along without hastening or losing a moment; when its passage is opposed by a wall, or an edifice of any kind, it stops, and accumulating its black and bituminous waves, swallows up, in its burning torrent, the obstacle that resisted it. Its progress is not so rapid, that men may not escape it; but, like Time, it reaches the imprudent and the aged, who, seeing it approach, heavily and silently, imagine themselves secure. Its light is so ardent, that, for the first time, the earth is reflected in the sky, producing the appearance of a continual lightning: the sky in turn is reflected in the sea, and nature is inflamed with this triple image of fire.

The wind is heard and seen in the whirlwinds of fire from the gulf whence proceeds the lava. We feel terrified at what passes in the bowels of the earth, which secret storm causes to tremble beneath our feet. The rocks, which surround the surface of the lava, are covered with sulphur and bitumen, whose colours have something infernal in them: a livid green, a yellowish brown, and a gloomy red, form a kind of dissonance in our eyes, and torment the sight in the same manner that the ear would be wounded by the shrill cries of witches, when, by night, they call to the moon to descend upon the earth.

All that surrounds the volcano recalls the idea of hell, and the descriptions of the poets are, doubtless, borrowed from this spot. It is here that we can form an idea of a malevolent power opposing the designs of Providence. In contemplating such an abode, we ask ourselves, whether bounty[30] alone presides over the phenomena of the creation, or whether some hidden principle forces nature, like man, to acts of ferocity. 'Corinna', cried Lord Nelvil, 'is it from these infernal regions that pain proceeds? Does the angel of death take his flight from this summit? Did I not see thy celestial look, I should here lose all recollection of the works of the Deity that adorn the world, and, nevertheless, this infernal aspect, all fearful as it is, to me is less terrible than the remorse that preys upon my heart. Every peril may be braved: but how can he, who is no more, exonerate us from those crimes which we have been guilty of towards him? Never! Never! Ah, Corinna, that is a word of iron – a word of fire. The torments which the imagination has invented, the wheel that turns incessantly, the water that flies the lips of him who approaches it, and the stone that rolls down again in proportion as it is raised to a certain height,[31] give but a feeble image of that dreadful thought – *irreparable*!

1.8 George Wilson Bridges, *Alpine Sketches, Comprised in a Short Tour through Parts of Holland, Flanders, France, Savoy, Switzerland, and Germany, during the Summer of 1814, by a Member of the University of Oxford* (London, 1814), pp. 103–20.

The following extract is taken from Bridges's account of his visit to Chamonix. It exemplifies the popular view of the natural sublime as evidence of the power and grandeur of God, reading the glacial landscape around Chamonix in essentially catastrophist terms, as evidence of a world that had been destroyed by flood. Alongside the moral

---

30 *bounty*: 'goodness'.
31 *the wheel* [...] *the stone*: recalling, from Greek myth, the tortures of Ixion, Tantalus and Sisyphus.

admonishment to be taken from the landscape, however, Bridges also recognises, in terms borrowed directly from Rousseau, the physical and intellectually enlivening effects of the Alpine sublime.

What a contrast between the luxuriant verdure which carpeted the valley, and the enormous masses of ice in the midst, mixing themselves with the richest productions of the earth! One of these accumulations, *the Glacier de Boissons*, looked like the ruins of a vast town, with its towers, its pyramids, its obelisks, some fallen, others falling. [...] We were at the foot of the highest mountains of Europe! [...] It is in this valley that the astonished beholder views three summits charged with an eternal snow. [...] These three summits, which in fact form the stupendous mass of Mont Blanc, are encompassed by a chain of pyramidal rocks, where you may conceive to see realized the fable of the giants [...] But this Mont Blanc, whose head was buried in the clouds, fixed all our attention: the other mountains which gird it appear to exist but for its protection and glory. This theatre of death, these colossal mountains, which we regard as a deformity of the globe,[32] present an admirable picture of the well preserved order of nature, and in the bosom of these barren rocks [...] we may perceive the regularity and all-wise providence of God [...] these frightful and sterile regions [are] the eternal reservoirs of our rivers which distribute luxury and comfort to every part of Europe [...]

> [*Bridges then describes an ascent of Montenvers and the resulting view of the Mer de Glace*]

A new universe opened beneath our view; nature seemed to rise out of chaos [...] Before us was an immense extent of solid ice, many hundred feet deep; like a sea, whose waves running mountains high, were suddenly congealed. Life and movement had fled this terrible desert: a vast silence reigned around, all was dead, and we seemed to be in the very tomb of nature. We perceived pyramids of ice, so bright, so high, so majestic, that the astonished imagination could scarcely measure them [...] I had but one idea; that of the Great Creator of these enormous masses. The Gauls,[33] struck by the religious grandeur of their dark forests, conceived them to be the residence of their gods. More astonished by the awful sublimity of these mountains, I thought I there beheld the hand of the Divinity: everything announced the harmony and magnificence of his works[34] [...] Those who have never been on these heights of the globe, can have no idea of the change which there takes place in the human frame. Fatigue the most extreme vanishes at once. It seems as if we had left below in the valleys, all

---

32 *a deformity of the globe*: Thomas Burnet's (1635–1715) *Sacred Theory of the Earth* (1681) was one of a number of works which identified mountainous landscapes as evidence that an originally Edenic world had been destroyed by Flood.

33 *Gauls*: Ancient Roman name for the inhabitants of central Europe.

34 The remainder of the extract is indebted to Rousseau's seminal account of the Upper Valais in *Julie*.

the cares, the follies, the sorrows, and the passions of humanity; there is more animation in the body; more serenity in the soul. The ideas take a character of the sublime, proportionate to the objects which strike the eye; a voluptuous tranquility seizes us; and it appears as if the soul, in approaching to the ethereal regions, partakes of their unalterable purity [...] Among the Alps alone, are found men, rustic without being ferocious, civilized without being corrupted. Our peasants in England are not to be compared with them: there, living among their equals, they are contented, possess an elevated mind, are generous, and welcome strangers as brothers.

1.9 Sir Humphry Davy, 'Mont Blanc' (5 January 1814), from *The Collected Works of Sir Humphry Davy*, ed. John Davy, 9 vols (London, 1839–40), I, pp. 170–1.

Davy (1778–1829), the famous English chemist, composed this poem at Chamonix during his 1812–14 grand tour of Europe. As one might expect from a scientist of Davy's calibre, the poem takes a comparatively sober view of the sublime landscape, affirming how the glacial waters transmit vital minerals to distant regions, an affirmation repeated in Percy Shelley's 1816 poem 'Mont Blanc', although he is unlikely to have known Davy's poem. Davy then uses this natural process to figure the position of the intellectual in the social world, a figuration comparable to de Saussure's comparison of Alpinism and ethical fortitude.

'Mont Blanc'

      With joy I view thee, bathed in purple light,
      Whilst all around is dark; with joy I see
      Thee rising from thy sea of pitchy clouds
      Into the middle heaven, –
5   As if a temple to the Eternal, raised
      By all the earth, framed of the pillar'd rock,
      And canopied with everlasting snow! –
      That lovely river,[35] rolling at my feet
      Its bright green waves,[36] and winding 'midst the rocks,
10   Brown in their winter's foliage, gain'd from thee
      Its flood of waters; through a devious course,
      Though it has laved the fertile plains, and wash'd
      The cities' walls, and mingled with the streams
      Of lowland origin, yet still preserves

35 *that lovely river*: The Arve, which flows from the snout of the Mer de Glace through the valley of Chamonix.
36 *green waves*: 'green' because of the heavy mineral content of the waters.

15   Its native character of mountain strength, –
            Its colour, and its motion. Such are those
            Amongst the generations of mankind
            To whom the stream of thought descends from heaven,
            With all the force of reason and the power
20   Of sacred genius. Through the world they pass
            Still uncorrupted, and on what they take
            From social life bestow a character
            Of dignity. Greater they become,
            But never lose their native purity.

1.10 John Chetwode Eustace, *A Classical Tour through Italy, Anno MDCCCII; the Fourth Edition, Revised and Enlarged. Illustrated with a Map of Italy, Plans of Churches, an Index, etc.* 4 vols (Livorno, 1817), III, pp. 29–40.

Eustace's Classical Tour *was one of the most influential Italian guidebooks of the early nineteenth century. His description of Vesuvius is predominantly sober and scientific in tone, avoiding the florid style of many contemporary reactions to the volcanic sublime. Like Brydone's account of Etna, Eustace's description of Vesuvius reflects the extent to which the landscape was 'classic ground', a landscape heavily overwritten with cultural associations rather than the scene of the 'disinterested' aesthetic judgement promoted by Kant's analytic of the sublime. In addition to registering Vesuvius's many classical associations, Eustace, like many other liberal writers, draws attention to the likelihood that religious ideas may have originated in the reaction of primitive man to such bewildering landscapes.*

Vesuvius rises in a gentle swell from the shore; the first part or base of the mountain is covered with towns on all sides [...] These are all large towns, and with the villages and villas that encircle them, and extend over the second region of the mountain, may be said, without exaggeration, to cover the lower parts of it with fertility, beauty, and population. The upper tract is a scene of perfect devastation, furrowed on all sides with rivers of lava extended in wide black lines over the surface. This region may be said to terminate at the *Atrio dei Cavalli*[37] so called, because the traveller is obliged to dismount and leave his horse there till his return, as the summit of the mountain must be ascended on foot. This part has the shape of a truncated cone; it is formed almost entirely of ashes, and is extremely difficult of ascent, as it yields under the pressure of the foot, so that one step out of three may be considered as lost. The guides however afford every assistance, and by means of a leathern strap thrown over their shoulders ease the traveller not a little in his exertions. It is advisable to proceed slowly and rest at

---

37 *Atrio dei Cavalli*: 'chamber of the horses'.

intervals, as the fatigue otherwise is sufficient to try even strong and youthful constitutions.

When we reached the summit we found ourselves on a narrow ledge of burnt earth or cinders, with the crater of the volcano open beneath us. This orifice in its present form, for it varies at almost every eruption, is about a mile and a half in circumference, and may be about three hundred and fifty feet in depth; its eastern border is considerably higher than the western. Its sides are formed of ashes and cinders, with some rocks and masses of lave, intermingled; they shelve in a steep declivity, enclosing at the bottom a flat space of about three quarters of a mile in circumference. We descended some way, but observing that the least motion or noise brought great quantities of ashes and stones rolling together down the sides, and being called back by our guides, who assured us that we could not in safety go lower or even remain in our station, we reascended. We were near enough to the bottom however to observe, that it seemed to be a sort of crust of brown burnt earth, and that a little on one side there were three orifices like funnels, from whence ascended a vapour so thin as to be scarcely perceptible. Such was the state of the crater in the year 1802. We reached the summit a little before seven, and as we had ascended under the shade of the mountain we had yet felt no inconvenience from the heat; while on the top we were refreshed by a strong wind blowing from the east, and sat down on the highest point of the cone to contemplate the prospect.

Vesuvius is about three thousand six hundred feet in height, and of course does not rank among the greater mountains; but its situation is so advantageous, that the scene which it unfolds to the eye probably surpasses that displayed from any other eminence [...] I own I do not admire views taken from very elevated points; they indeed give a very good geographical idea of a country; but they destroy all illusions of rural beauty, reduce hills and vales to the same level, and confound all the graceful swells and hollows of undulated surface, into general flatness and uniformity.

The most interesting object seen from the summit of Vesuvius is the mountain itself, torn to pieces by a series of convulsions, and strewed with its own ruins. Vesuvius may be said to have two summits; the cone which I have described, and separated from it by a deep valley, a ridge called *Monte Somma* from a town that stands on its side [...] The valley or deep dell that winds between these eminences is a desolate hollow, formed entirely of calcined stones, cinders, and ashes, and it resembles a vast subterraneous forge, the rocky roof of which has given way, and admitted light from above. Hence it is conjectured that it is part of the interior of the mountain, as the ridge that borders it, or the *Monte Somma*, is the remnant of the exterior, or original surface so much celebrated for its beauty and fertility, previous to the eruption of the year 79 of the Christian era [...]

It is not my intention to describe the phenomena of Vesuvius, or to relate the details of its eruptions, which have been very numerous since the first recorded in history in the reign of Titus, so well described by Pliny the younger in the two well known epistles to Tacitus the historian. I shall only observe that although this eruption be the first of which we have an account, yet Vesuvius had all the features of a volcano from time immemorial. Strabo[38] speaks of it as being hollowed out into caverns, and having the appearances of being preyed upon by internal fires; and Florus[39] relates a stratagem employed by a Roman officer, who, he says, conducted a body of men through the cavities and subterraneous passages of that mountain. These vestiges however neither disfigured its form nor checked its fertility; and it is represented as a scene of beauty and abundance, covered with villas and enlivened by population, when the eruption burst forth with more suddenness and more fury then any similar catastrophe on record. The darkness, the flames, the agitation, the uproar, that accompanied this explosion, and extended its devastation and its terror so widely, might naturally excite among many of the degenerate and epicurean Romans that frequented the *Campanian* coasts, the opinion that the period of universal destruction was arrived, and that the atoms which formed the world were about to dissolve their fortuitous combination, and plunge the universe once more into chaos.

The last eruption took place in 1794; the ashes, cinders, and even water, thrown from the mountain did considerable damage to the towns of *Somma*, *Oltaino*, and all the circumjacent region; but the principal mischief was, as usual, occasioned by the lava, rivers of which, as I have already related, poured down the southern side of the mountain. These and several other torrents of similar matter, but of earlier date, are seen from the summit, and may be traced from their source through the whole of their progress, which generally terminates at the sea. They are narrow at first, but expand as they advance, and appear like so many tracks of rich black mould just turned up by the plough. When their destructive effects are considered, one is surprised to see villas placed in their windings, vineyards waving over their borders, and towns rising in the very middle of their channels. Ravaged and tortured as the vicinity of Vesuvius has been for so many ages, it must appear singular, that is has not been abandoned by its inhabitants and consigned to the *genius of fire and desolation* as his own peculiar territory. But such is the richness of the soil, and so slight the damages occasioned by the volcano, when compared to the produce of the lands fertilized by its ashes; so delightful is the situation, and of its numerous inhabitants so small the number that suffer by its agitations, that the evil when divested of its terrific appearances seems an ordinary calamity, not exceeding in mischief the accidents of fire and inundation so common in northern countries. The alarm is indeed great on the approach of an eruption, because it is usually preceded by earthquakes; but when once the fermenting matter finds vent, the general danger is considered as over, and the progress of the phenomena becomes an object of mere curiosity to all, excepting to the cultivators of the lands which the lava actually rolls over, or seems likely to ravage in its progress.

---

38 *Strabo*: first-century AD Greek author, who compiled a 17-volume *Geography* of the known world.
39 *Florus*: A Roman historian, whose *Epitome de T. Livio Bellorum* describes the early history of the city.

We descended the cone or upper part of the mountain with great ease and rapidity, as the ashes yielding to the tread prevented slipping, and enabled us to hasten our pace without danger. From the *Atrio dei Cavalli* we proceeded towards a bed of lava ejected in the last eruption, and found its appearance very different from that which we had observed from the summit. Thence it resembled long stripes of new plough land; here it was like the surface of a dark muddy stream convulsed by a hurricane, and frozen in a state of agitation; presenting rough broken masses rolling over each other, with a huge fragment resting here and there above the rest, like a wave distorted by the tempest and congealed in its fall. The exterior parts of this torrent of fire are cold, but the sand produced by the friction and the crumbling of the interior parts, although it is now eight years since the eruption, is still too hot to hold in the hand, as is indeed the earth itself under, or in immediate contact with these once glowing masses. We continued our descent, and again reached *Portici*[40] about eleven o'clock.

1.11   Samuel Glover, *A Description of the Valley of Chamouni* (1819), pp. 25–30.

Little is known about the life of Samuel Glover, but this extract from his Description *suggests that he held strong religious views, and was deeply concerned by the burgeoning scientific and philosophical speculation about the sublime Alpine landscape which seemed calculated to undermine the prevalent, popular view of such landscapes as evidence of God's power, by advancing geological arguments against the Biblical account of creation, and by suggesting that religious ideas originated in anthropomorphic reactions to the natural sublime (e.g. De Stäel). Glover begins by offering a panoramic view over the valley of Chamonix from the summit of Le Brévent, and then moves on to imagine a Dante-eqsue hell amongst the Alps. Glover's particularly vitriolic response to atheists suggests that his* Description *might have been motivated, at least in part, by the public controversy surrounding Percy Shelley's inscriptions in the register of various inns at Chamonix during his 1816 visit to the area, in which he signed himself 'Democrat, Atheist, and Philanthropist'. For a detailed account of this controversy, see Gavin de Beer, 'An Atheist in the Alps',* Keats-Shelley Memorial Bulletin *(1958) 1–15.*

To the right of The Sea of Ice,[41] and stretching down the sides of The Mont Blanc into the valley of Chamouni, appear the Glaciers of les Pelerins, – of du Bossons, – of Tacona, – of l'Agria, – of des Ouches, – and of Bionassy: – the eye

---

40 A town at the foot of Vesuvius.
41 *Sea of Ice*: the Mer de Glace, one of the glaciers which flows from the Vallée Blanche into the valley of Chamonix.

follows them alternately, then, gradually rising, continues its course, and, at length, loses itself in the clouds.

Yes! – there, towering in sullen majesty, – fronting The Brévent, – in all its grandeur, – in all its horrors, – mantled with eternal snow and ice, the region of cold and silence, stands the almost inaccessible Mont Blanc,[42] – the gigantic monarch of the vale; – such is its magnitude, that at its presence the circumjacent mountains seem to shrink before him, and 'hide their diminished heads'; the path leading to its summit is carefully pointed out by the guides, but the mind is too much enrapt in meditation on this colossal mountain, – this mighty mass, to spare the least attention; – this alone amply repays your toil and danger, and insensible, indeed, must that heart be, which overflows not with adoration before the wondrous works of The Creator [...]

The descent is now extremely slippery and difficult, but the assistance of the guides diminishes the fatigue, and on the following day you are sufficiently recovered to explore the mysteries of

The Sea of Ice

Mysteries indeed! – such as plunge the reflecting mind in the deepest meditation, and furnish unbounded scope to the imagination: the road conducting thither, contributes greatly to enable you to enjoy in its fullest extent the wonders which await you.

I have already said, that the ascent to the summit of The Brévent is abrupt, – barren, – almost destitute of trees or verdure; – as you rise, the view expands, and terminates, as described, in an extensive scene on one side, and on the other the snow-clad monarch of the vale; – but the path conducting to the Montenvers, which overlooks the Sea of Ice, is gentle, free from rock, and abounding with plants, which invite the research of the botanist; as you advance, the sombre hue increases; dark and gloomy pines rise thick together, and, at length, conceal surrounding objects 'from mortal ken', as if to attune the soul to reflection, 'ere a sight, original in nature, burst on the astonished eye.

On a sudden you emerge from darkness, and at your feet, motionless at The Fiat[43] of Nature's God, appear the once turbulent, once foaming waves of The Sea of Ice.

All is calm around, forming an impressive contrast to the once dreadful uproar of the elements, combating for supremacy; – here, the waves, swelling into mountains, retain their rounded forms; – there, exhausted by their weight, they sink to an even surface; – now, rising into pyramids; – then, gaining their utmost height, frowning and already curved, they are suddenly arrested by That Power, before whom rocks melt, and mountains tremble to their foundations.

---

42 *almost inaccessible*: because Mont Blanc had already been summitted a number of times.
43 *Fiat*: Latin for 'command'.

That the Sea of Ice, seven miles in length and one to three miles in breadth, was once a portion of the valley, smiling in gay luxuriance, the contours of the mountains testify; nor is it presumption to hazard an opinion as to the cause of this wonderful phenomenon.

The surrounding rocks and mountains were buried in snow, on which a sudden heat was permitted to exert its influence, and reducing it to water, it rushed with indescribable impetuosity, submerging a branch of the Valley of Chamouni, and threatening to engulf the whole in indiscriminate ruin; – nature sighed at the havoc; – her plaint was heard; – a voice cried, 'Thus Far Shalt Thou Go, And No Farther'; – a violent wind met the watery element in its devastating career; – its waves recoiled upon themselves, and a sudden frost transfixed them immoveable in their multifarious forms; – still they frown and bend, threatening to bury in their yawning gulfs the mortal, who treads this once liquid element, and dares to explore its mysteries.

Atheist! stand here; – here, amid this chaos of mountains, – these shapeless and gigantic rocks; – fancy thyself spectator of 'this war of elements'; – darest thou, unappaled, listen to the dreadful uproar, or fearlessly behold the mighty conflict? thinkest thou the phantom, to whose creation thou arrogantly attribut-est the wondrous universe; thinkest thou, presumptuous man, that *chance* could save thee from destruction? – impossible!!! – in prostrate adoration thou wouldst abjure thy impious precepts, implore celestial aid, and own the presence of that God, who sits above in the heavens enthroned in majesty supreme, – whom *chance* approaches not, – whose will is fate [...]

[*after a discussion of the cave at the foot of the Mer de Glace from which the river Arve emerges, Glover moves on to imagine an Alpine hell*]

It is a generally received opinion, that the fate allotted to the wicked is eternal purgatory in flames of liquid sulphur; but as fire is the consumer of all things, I cannot digest the idea, that the spirits, which are precipitated therein, can possibly survive the plunge, and lest they escape the just punishment due to their crimes, I have determined, in despite of the imprecations of Pluto, the howlings of Cerberus, and the furious gestures of Old Charon, for loss of fees, to debar all future access to flaming Tartarus,[44] and consign the evil spirits to the regions of eternal ice and snow; – for instance, the wicked of various denomina-tions I confine beneath the Glaciers, which occupy the lower valleys of the Alps; the thunder, proceeding from the bursting of these Glaciers, and attributable to the heat of the Meridian sun,[45] are the ravings of these spirits; and as it is a well-known fact that the Glaciers rise and fall, advance, and then recede, it is

---

44 *Pluto* [...] *Tartarus*: in classical Greek myth, Pluto was the god of hell (Tartarus); the gates of hell were guarded by Cerberus, a three headed dog; Charon was responsible for ferrying the spirits of the dead across the river Styx, into the underworld.
45 *Meridian Sun*: midday sun.

occasioned by an universal struggle of these impious spirits to escape from their cold and dreary prisons; but their efforts serve to increase their torments, by condensing more closely the ice-mountains, which envelop them.

In those masses of snow, the remains of the Avalanches, which encumber the verdant meadows, and defy the summers' heat, are incarcerated those scourges of the human race – those depopulators of nations, who, like the thundering Avalanches, resistless in their course, swept all before them in their fury, marking their progress with destruction. Where now is the pride and pomp of war – the plumed helmet – the blood-stained sword – the crimsoned spear – the gaudy banner, reeking with human gore? – No more the marshalled legions, the licensed murderers swarm around them and obey their nod: – beneath their snowy prisons' shade, screened from the mid-day sun, the shepherds and their flocks repose in safety; and instead of glowing at the war-denouncing trumpets' sound, the infuriate spirits of these mighty conquerors are roused to frenzy by the music of the pastoral pipes, breathing the airs of happiness and peace.

Yon towering glaciers, which proudly advance into the valleys, aping a stately march, entomb the spirits of those sovereigns, who, forgetful of their first, great duty, the happiness of their subjects, abandon them themselves to every vice disgraceful to humanity: the smaller glaciers, which precede and follow them, contain the spirits of Court parasites, – of evil Counsellors, – of Ministers, who, blind to their country's good, and deaf to the peoples' cries, were solely intent on the means of furthering their interest and advancing their ambition; – but their punishment is in the highest degree humiliating; the smaller glaciers, impregnated with a portion of these grovelling spirits, instead of solid ice, are soft and porous; – in spring, to preserve the corn from sudden frosts, the Mountaineers[46] strew their fields with the substance of these glaciers; this disgraceful proceeding takes place in the vicinity of the towering Glaciers, the receptacles of the spirits of kings, and makes them tremble for their fate.

Within those icicles which adorn the spiring rocks, or fringe the precipices' edge, are shrouded the worst of spirits; – of mortals, who prostituted their brilliant talents to the nefarious purpose of subverting religion and disproving the existence of God. To the *Atheists* I assign those icicles, clear as crystal, where, suspended high in air, these presumptuous spirits are unceasingly exposed to the storms and tempests which sweep around their icy prisons, and doomed eternally to behold those magnificent works of nature they ever affected to despise: how ardently do they now desire to atone for their impiety, by abjuring before the universe their blasphemous precepts; but, conscious their torments will endure, though 'nature sink in years',[47] despair possesses them; they rave in frantic agony, and with imprecations, such as burst from the agonised bosom of Satan when first he saw the sun, they curse the glorious orb, whose morning rays, chasing the shades of night, illume the scenes they hate [...]

---

46 *Mountaineers*: meaning the local population.
47 Quoting Joseph Addison, *Cato* (1713), V, i, 27.

1.12   William Hazlitt, *Notes of a Journey through France and Italy* (1826), pp. 195, 199–200, 206.

This extract is taken from Hazlitt's account of his visit to the monastery of the Grande Chartreuse, in the mountains above Grenoble, and his subsequent crossing of the Alps into Italy. Unlike Wordsworth's somewhat disappointed account of the crossing of the Alps in Book VI of The Prelude *(1805), which Hazlitt of course could not have known, this extract registers a sublime landscape which exceeds Hazlitt's expectations. He notes the sobering effects of the Alpine sublime upon an 'egotist' but also acknowledges, through the example of Napoleon, who had led his armies across the Alps en route to defeat the Austrians at the Battle of Marengo (1800), the possibility of human mastery of that landscape. In the final paragraph of the extract, Hazlitt then perceives a similar dynamic in his own encounter with the Alpine sublime. This dynamic – the sobering effects of the landscape upon the ego, but the potential for human triumph – is in many respects comparable to Kant's formulation of the relationship between the mind and the world in the encounter with the natural sublime, but Hazlitt's remarks are explicitly 'interested' in, rather than concerned to transcend, the cultural and historical connotations of the landscape.*

It was a scene dazzling, enchanting, and that stamped the long-cherished dreams of the imagination upon the senses [...]

Let no-one imagine that crossing the Alps is the work of a moment, or done by a single heroic effort – that they are a huge but detached chain of hills, or like the dotted line we find in the map. They are a sea or an entire kingdom of mountains. It took us three days to traverse them in this, which is the most practicable direction, and travelling at a good round pace. We passed on as far as eye could see, and still we appeared to have made little way. Still we were in the shadow of the same enormous mass of rock and snow, by the side of the same creeping stream. Lofty mountains reared themselves in front of us – horrid abysses were scooped out under our feet. Sometimes the road wound along the side of a steep hill, overlooking some village spire or hamlet, and as we ascended it, it only gave us a view of remoter scenes, 'where Alps o'er Alps arise',[48] tossing about their billowy tops, and tumbling their unwieldy shapes in all directions – a world of wonders! – Anyone, who is much of an egoist, ought not to travel through these districts; his vanity will not find its account in them; it will be chilled, mortified, shrunk up: but they are a noble treat to those who feel themselves raised in their own thoughts and in the scale of being by the immensity of other things, and who can aggrandise and piece out their personal insignificance by the grandeur and eternal forms of nature! It gives one a vast idea of Buonaparte[49] to think of

---

48 *'where Alps [...] arise'*: misquoting Pope, *Essay on Criticism* 225: 'Hills peep o'er Hills, and Alps on Alps arise!'.

49 *Buonaparte*: Napoleon Bonaparte.

him in these situations. He alone (the Rob Roy[50] of the scene) seemed a match for the elements, and able to master 'this fortress built by nature for herself'. Neither impeded nor turned aside by immoveable barriers, he smote the mountains with his iron glaive,[51] and made them malleable; cut roads through them; transported armies over their ridgy steeps; and the rocks 'nodded to him, and did him courtesies!'[52] [...]

The height, the magnitude, the immovableness of the objects, the wild contrast, the deep tones, the dance and play of the landscape from the change of our direction and the interposition of other striking objects, the continued recurrence of the same huge masses, like giants following us with unseen strides, stunned the sense like a blow, and yet gave the imagination strength to contend with a force that mocked it.

1.13 John Auldjo, *Sketches of Vesuvius* (1832) pp. 1–24.

Auljdo, a Scottish traveller who made a successful ascent of Mont Blanc in August 1827, deploys a number of conventional tropes in this description of Vesuvius, recalling early accounts of the volcanic sublime by Brydone and Eustace. Foremost amongst these are a comparison between the Alpine and the volcanic sublime (between glaciers and lava flows), and a recognition of the tension between an almost indescribable landscape and the wish to describe that landscape soberly and scientifically. Unlike some other travellers (e.g. Swinburne), who suggest that the actual encounter with the natural sublime fails to live up to expectations, Auldjo here affirms that nothing can compare with the 'original'.

Among the enchanting features of the far-famed scenery around the Bay of Naples, the favoured region of poets, none is more attractive than Vesuvius, 'the burning mountain', which has allured the curious and learned, in all ages and from all countries [...] The lower parts of the mountain are studded with towns, villages, and palaces, that rise among vineyards and gardens, the property of men who forget their danger while seeking to derive wealth from the fertility of its soil, though there has not been a period of a hundred years, in which some part of the lands around the base of Vesuvius has not been ruined by earthquakes, destroyed by currents of lava, or covered with ashes. But what is there with which man will not familiarise himself? The eruption over, the inhabitants will return to build their houses on the same spot where terrible experience ought to have made them dread the risk of being buried by some future eruption.

---

50 *Rob Roy*: Robert Roy MacGregor (1671–1734) was a famous outlaw in the Highlands of Scotland; sometimes known as the Scottish Robin Hood, 'Rob Roy' was the subject of Walter Scott's eponymous 1817 novel.

51 *glaive*: sword, or lance.

52 Adapting *A Midsummer Night's Dream* III, i, 174.

[*Auldjo then describes the various possible routes up Vesuvius, and recommends ascent 'in the direction of Fosso Grande'*]

This course lengthens the time required for the ascent by about half an hour, but the path is less difficult and steep, and is, in every respect, better than the other [via the Piano delle Ginestre], except a few yards of the latter part of it, which must be performed on foot. It has the great advantage of a constant change in scenery and, at the same time, it exhibits a section of the mountain that lays its structure open to the view, which cannot fail to afford both pleasure and instruction even to unscientific admirers of Nature [...]

On the summit a scene is presented, which almost baffles description. The field of lava in the interior of the crater, enclosed within a lofty and irregular bank, might be likened to a lake, whose agitated waves had been suddenly petrified; and, in many respects, it resembles the *mer de glace*,[53] or level glaciers of Switzerland; although in its origins and materials so very different. It is intersected by numberless crevices, some deep and wide, others long and shallow. Here one sees masses curled and twisted like cables, there large slabs piled up in various angles against each other, in one part a wide table or platform, in another, a narrow stream, the ripples of which, in pushing each other forward, have maintained their wavy form for a great distance. In the sea of ice, the white, dazzling surface is relieved only by beautiful tints and various shades of blue and green; in its simulacra[54] of stone, the bright yellow and red of the compounds of sulphur and the metals interspersed with the pure white of the muriate of soda, afford a pleasing contrast to the brown and melancholy hue of the lava [...]

The view from the highest peak, is perhaps one of the most beautiful in the world; the height of the mountain being not so great that the features of the fairy land over which the eye roves, are either lost or too much diminished [...]

Having thus proceeded from the bottom to the top, and again, from the summit to the base of this celebrated mountain, and having described, in the order in which they present themselves, the most striking parts of its western or more frequented side, it remains for me to hope that my sketches, however faint and imperfect they may be, will, nevertheless, serve as a general outline of Vesuvius to strangers, and induce those who have the opportunity, to fill them up, by personal inspection, to the variety, magnitude, and sublimity of their original.

---

53 *mer de glace*: one of the glaciers flowing from the Mont Blanc massif into the valley of Chamonix.
54 *simulacra*: an image, or representation of something.

2

Money

The modern discipline of political economy developed, during the period 1750–1830, out of a sustained enquiry into a range of issues surrounding value, commerce, credit and the sublime spectacle of Britain's ever-increasing national debt. It was not until the 1820s that political economy could be said to have become a discipline in its own right, distinct from other fields of enquiry. Hence the extracts included in this section come from the most diverse range of textual genres, including political pamphlets, newspaper articles, parliamentary debates, autobiographical memoirs, and even a self-help manual on investing in stock. This miscellaneous set of documents charts the progress of thinking about money, finance and commerce as responses to phenomena such as the increasing complexity of commercial and monetary systems, the alarming growth of government borrowing, and the material achievements brought about by economic growth. Since these phenomena were often construed by contemporary observers as sublime, the following extracts, taken as a whole, would suggest that the formulation of the modern discipline of political economy involved, at least in part, what can best be described as a discourse on the sublime.

The centrality of a discourse on the sublime to the development of political economy is most apparent in three areas of economic enquiry. The first has to do with interest, and in particular with the manner in which compound interest accrues on debt: the sum owed increases in a geometrical progression, so that a small principal can with time grow to a large amount, and is projected in the imagination as tending towards infinity.[1] Where this is applied to public finances, the nation is figured as increasingly exhausted, labouring against an ultimately irresistible force; where it concerns individuals, the debt is described as a small secret vice, which by degrees, but finally with haste, brings the indebted to destruction. Of course there is also a positive version of compound interest. Where one is *in* credit, a small sum can grow to an extent that sometimes defies belief. Richard Price, in particular, argues that the state should use a sinking fund earning compound interest in order to offset its debt. He illustrates this with the example, which became famous during the ensuing 50 years, of a

---

1 Although the charging of compound interest was considered usurious and therefore illegal in Britain until 1854, compound interest was effectively accrued by the practice, by governments and individuals, of taking out new loans to cover the interest and principal on old loans.

penny put out at compound interest in AD 1 which would now be worth a literally unimaginable sum.

The second area in which the development of political economy involves a
discourse of the sublime is the power of capital accumulation to bring about
social change and progress. For writers like David Hume, Adam Smith and
J. R. McCulloch, the glittering prizes of wealth, when viewed from afar, excite
the imaginations of the enterprising and incentivise innovation. Capital is often
described as being 'omnipotent', possessing a magical quality to overcome adver-
sity. Examples of this potency can be seen in our extracts from the description of
George III's coronation, and the competing claims, in Burke's *Letters on a Regicide
Peace* and Lord Grey's speech to Parliament, on the ability of the British or
French peoples to regenerate themselves from the apparent exhaustions caused
by war during the 1790s. Paper credit has an important function in such work:
the ability of banks to issue paper money, and of individuals to sign securities,
is a kind of alchemy in which belief in the future – that is to say, being able to
imagine future growth enabling later payment – gives the signifier a signified of
infinitely greater value. Once again, however, there is also a negative side to this
species of the sublime: some writers look with horror upon the chasm between
what a piece of paper is said to be worth on the one hand, and, on the other
hand, its actual referent in the real world. In an analysis that looks forward to a
Marxist critique of capital, Piercy Ravenstone figures this capital as an insidious
machine spreading its malign influence to all human activity.

The third area in which economic enquiry intersects with a discourse on the
sublime concerns the field of study itself, which was in the process of being
constituted during the period 1750–1830. As David Hume announces in his essay
'Of Commerce' (1754), this field will be complex, often abstruse, and in need of
expanded horizons on the part of its practitioners. As study makes the objects of
political economy clearer during the ensuing century, so the depth and breadth
of the discipline expands, so that by 1820 McCulloch was able to describe it as
the most powerful of sciences, capable of changing the world to a hitherto unim-
agined degree. Yet again, however, there is a negative, counter-version of this, in
which economists are seen by the likes of Mortimer and Ravenstone as initiates
in a secret, dark art which is there to obscure simple truths by mystifying the
populace. As with debates on debt and interest, and those on capital accumulation, then, opposing views of political economy as a discipline share an enquiry
into the sublime, differing only as to their interpretation of this sublimity as an
ultimately diminishing or aggrandising impetus.

2.1   Anon., *The Necessity of Lowering Interest and Continuing Taxes, Demonstrated* (London, 1750), pp. 7, 9–12, 15–16.

*The following is an extract from an anonymous pamphlet, published in 1750, in
response to a plea, in* The Remembrancer *of 30 December 1749, for a reduction*

of taxes. Since the peace of 1748, Pelham's ministry had been able to renegoti-
ate the terms of most of the national debt down to 3 or 3.5 per cent, and had
reinstituted a sinking fund intended eventually to pay off the principal of the debt
(its interest being paid directly from taxation). The extract expresses widespread
anxieties about the terrifying spectacle of the national debt at this time; that it
was too big, and that it would inevitably grow in size. Unless drastic measures
were taken, a chain of consequences could be imagined: if it were allowed to
grow at all, it would just keep on growing, leading to the complete exhaustion of
British resources and handing absolute power to France. The pamphlet utilises a
number of tropes taken from the discourse of the sublime to describe the country,
such as exhaustion, loss of control, remorselessly expanding burdens, fear at the
threat from France, and impending despair. These images were to become common
features of the debate on the national debt up until 1815. But out of the negative
comes a positive: the terror and awe at the size of the debt lead ultimately to a
greater perceptiveness of the situation, and act as a call to self-mastery (where the
self is the body politic), in this case through the implementation of measures to
reduce the debt.

The present national Debt is near eighty millions; the Produce of the Sinking Fund not nine hundred thousand pounds; and supposing the intended Reduction of Interest should take Place, will not for the next eight Years to come be more than twelve.[2] [...]

FRANCE is at present as much encumbered with Debts as we are, and that Nation which first eases itself of its Burthen will be enabled to give the Law to the other, and to the rest of *Europe.* Sorry I am to say, that, by the Regulation of the *French* Revenue, such a Proportion is set apart for the payment of their Debts, that, in the space of fifteen Years, they will have discharged thirty Millions Sterling.[3] Unless we can therefore in some measure keep pace with them in the Reduction of our Debt, we shall be necessitated to accept the Law from them; and be no longer able to oppose their Attempts for universal Monarchy. This shows how impolitic it would be to lessen the Sinking Fund by an Abatement of Taxes, or to apply any part of it to the current Service of the Year in Ease of the Land. – Fallacious Ease! which would render our Destruction inevitable. – Upon the first disturbance in *Europe* the Taxes must be replaced and mortgaged, and the Land for ever after burdened with four shillings in the Pound[4], without a possibility of Reduction. [...]

---

2 The national debt in 1748, at the end of the War of the Austrian Succession, was £76 million; by the start of the Seven Years' War in 1756, it had been sunk by only £2 million, although with lower rates of interest. At the conclusion of that war, it had risen to £133 million (see J. Brewer, *The Sinews of Power* [London: Unwin, 1989]).

3 In 1749 Louis XV's minister, Machault, attempted (ultimately unsuccessfully) to institute the *vingtième*, a tax of one-twentieth of incomes without exception.

4 *the Land burthened with four shillings in the* pound: A land tax equivalent to 20 per cent of rentable value.

But now let us see what will be the Consequence of a contrary Method. Suppose the Land-tax continued at three Shillings, and that the whole Sinking Fund (not lessened by an Abatement of Taxes, but increased by a Prevention of Frauds in the collecting them) regularly applied to the Discharge of the Debt. In eight Years ten Millions may be made off, and, at that Time, the further Reduction of Interest taking place, and the Salt Duty being then disengaged, there will be a sinking Fund of two Millions; we many then afford to take off Taxes to the amount of five hundred thousand Pounds a Year, and to apply five hundred thousand Pounds more to the Current Service in the Ease of the Land; and yet have a Sinking Fund of a Million to operate upon the Debt. These would be circumstances that would give real Relief to Land and to Trade. We should then be in a condition to figure it in *Europe*; and, by being in that Condition, should be less likely to be attacked, than if we were in the Distress we are at present [...]

Let us now consider what is the true Interest of our Trade. If such Taxes were immediately to be taken off which appear most burthensome, it would certainly be of some present Advantage; but if, in Consequence of that, the Debt was to remain undiminished, who does not see that upon the first Bustle in *Europe*, which demands our Interposition, the same Taxes must be renewed, nay, additional ones must be imposed; and all of them to be mortgaged at an exorbitant Interest to *Jews* and stock-jobbers: so that we might see a Debt of an hundred Millions without a Sinking Fund to discharge it.[5] After which, the Merchant would trade, and the landed Man would plough, not for themselves, but for their usurious Creditors; Persons perhaps who got their wealth by plundering in Office; and thus it would go on, till irretrievable Poverty hurried them into Despair.

2.2 David Hume, 'Of Commerce', in *Political Discourses* (Edinburgh, 1752) pp. 1–4, 13–17.

The Scottish philosopher David Hume (1711–66) was best known in his own time for his History of England *(1754–62), and for his short* Essays *(1741–77) on the subjects of religion, ethics, aesthetics and politics. The passages below are extracts from the essay 'Of Commerce', which introduces the nine-essay cycle on the field that is now known as economics, that is to say, topics such as the rise of commerce, the national debt, paper money and specie, taxation, and interest rates. These essays occupy a vital place in the history of economic thought and were a decisive influence on Hume's colleague Adam Smith, whose work* The Wealth of Nations *is often considered the founding text of the modern discipline of political economy.*

There are two main concerns in 'Of Commerce'. First, a general introduction on the philosophical propriety of the 'vulgar' topics of 'commerce, luxury, money,

---

5 *a Debt of an Hundred Millions*: this became the case in 1760.

interest, &C' is given, in which Hume argues, with typical circumspection, that abstract reasoning and general principles are possible in the field of economics because certain patterns of human behaviour are discernible to the observer. However, this requires an expansion of the field of vision 'beyond [what is currently seen as] the truth', as compared with the 'shallow' thinkers who customarily write on the topic of money; thus the science of money, which Hume enunciates here as being possible, desirable, but not yet in existence, generates sublime effect in the way that its imagined complexity irresistibly pushes out the boundaries of knowledge before its potential can later be realised. Second, Hume describes how the commercial spirit of a nation multiplies in all directions, once one part of a population first gets a feel for the economic and cultural advantages that result. In a commercial nation, individuals are led on ceaselessly to attain those advantages that have come into view but are yet to be achieved, in a virtuous cycle of improvement and expansion. This description of 'progress' – which has come to form an important part of modern thought about economic development – mobilises the dynamic of the sublime in that, whether material improvement be real, ideal or even chimerical, individuals' imaginations have so been expanded by it that they will exert themselves to achieve it, even though the aims to which they aspire will be constantly shifting and hence forever out of reach.

The greatest part of mankind may be divided into two classes; that of *shallow* thinkers, who fall short of the truth, and that of *abstruse* thinkers, who go beyond it. The latter class are by far the most uncommon: and I may add, by far the most useful and valuable. They suggest hints, at least, and start difficulties, which they want, perhaps, skill to pursue; but which produce very fine discoveries, when handled by men who have a more just way of thinking. At worst, what they say is uncommon; and if it should cost some pains to comprehend it, one has, however, the pleasure of hearing something that is new. An author is little to be valued, who tells us nothing but what we can learn from every coffee-house conversation.

All people of *shallow* thought are apt to decry even those of *solid* understand-ing, as *abstruse* thinkers and metaphysicians, and refiners; and never will allow anything to be just which is beyond their own weak conceptions [...] General reasonings seem intricate, merely because they are general; nor is it easy for the bulk of mankind to distinguish, in a number of particulars, that circumstance in which they all agree, or to extract it, pure and unmixed, from the other superflu-ous circumstances. Every judgment or conclusion, with them, is particular. They cannot enlarge their view to those universal propositions, which comprehend under them an infinite number of individuals, and include a whole science in a single theorem. Their eye is confounded with such an extensive prospect; and the conclusions, derived from it, even though clearly expressed, seem intricate and obscure [...]

I thought this introduction necessary before the following discourses on *commerce, luxury, money, interest,* &C. where, perhaps, there will appear some

principles which are uncommon, and which may seem to be too refined and
subtle for such vulgar subjects. If false, let them be rejected: But no one ought to
entertain a prejudice against them, merely because they are out of the common
road.

The greatness of a state and the happiness of its subjects, how independent
they may be supposed in some respects, are commonly allowed to be inseparable
with regard to commerce; and, as private men receive greater security, in the
possession of their trade and riches, from the power of the public, so the public
becomes powerful in proportion to the opulence and extensive commerce of
private men [...]

If we consult history, we shall find, that, in most nations, foreign trade has
preceded any refinement in home manufactures, and given birth to domestic
luxury. The temptation is stronger to make use of foreign commodities, which
are ready for use, and which are entirely new to us, than to make improvements on any domestic commodity, which always advance by slow degrees,
and never affect us by their novelty. The profit is also very great, in export-
ing, what is superfluous at home, and what bears no price, to foreign nations,
whose soil or climate is not favourable to that commodity. Thus men become
acquainted with the *pleasures* of luxury and the *profits* of commerce; and their
delicacy and *industry*, being once awakened, carry them on to farther improvements, in every branch of domestic as well as foreign trade. And this perhaps
is the chief advantage which arises from a commerce with strangers.[6] It rouses
men from their lethargic indolence; and presenting the gayer and more opulent
part of the nation with objects of luxury, which they never before dreamed of,
raises in them a desire of a more splendid way of life than what their ancestors enjoyed. And, at the same time, the few merchants, who possess the secret
of this importation and exportation, make exorbitant[7] profits; and becoming
rivals in wealth to the ancient nobility, tempt other adventurers to become
their rivals in commerce. Imitation soon diffuses all those arts; while domestic
manufactures emulate the foreign in their improvements, and work up every
home commodity to the utmost perfection of which it is susceptible. Their own
steel and iron, in such laborious hands, become equal to the gold and rubies
of the *Indies*.

2.3 'On the Coronation of George III', from *The London Chronicle* (4–6 December 1760), p. 559.

*This short article concerns the preparations for the coronation of George III, which was
to take place in September 1761. However, the immediate current affairs context was*

---

6 *strangers*: foreigners.

7 *exorbitant*: in subsequent editions Hume replaced 'exorbitant' with 'great', no doubt worried by the
   earlier wording's implication of exploitation.

*the approval by the House of Commons of a new loan of £12m to pay for the continu-
ance of the successful campaigns against France in North America, the West Indies
and India. The author opposes the concepts of the martial to the commercial spirits,
as had Hume in his essay 'Of Commerce', but notes with surprise that a nation at war
could still fulfil both its desire for luxury and its capacity to wage a costly war that
required increased taxation and frugality in non-military government spending. As with
Hume, sought-after luxuries are largely imaginary, and once purchased do not bring the
expected satisfaction; as the author puts it, 'such is the difference between hope and
possession [...] that the show will cease as soon as it appears'. But this does not dimin-
ish their psychological power to enthuse and motivate individuals; aspiration forms
itself a sublime object that constantly appears at the edge of vision, only to be replaced
by a greater object once achieved. In fact, what comes out of this piece most strongly
is a sublime sense of astonishment at the British economy's ability to transcend long-
held beliefs about what was possible, by servicing a debt contracted in order to finance
military campaigns, at the same time as it funded a marked increase in industry and
consumption. This continual exceeding of all that was before thought possible can, of
course, be seen to run in parallel to the dynamics of the sublime. Thomas Mortimer
also expresses such astonishment, as does Adam Smith in* The Wealth of Nations,
*although with greater scepticism about the economy's ability to pull off this trick in
the future.*

> *Illam omnis tectis agrisque effusa juventus
> Turbaque miratur matrum & prospectat euntem,
> Attonitis inhians animis, ut regius ostro
> Velet honos levis umeros, ut fibula crinem
> Auro internecta –*
>
> VIRG.[8]

That a time of war is a time of parsimony, is a maxim which Patriots and
Senators have had often in their mouths, and which I do not remember ever to
have been denied.

I know not whether by the acute enquiries of the present age, this opinion has
been discovered to be groundless, and is therefore thrown aside among obsolete
follies; or whether it has happened on this, as on other occasions, that conviction is on one side, and practice on the other; but so it is, that the War, whatever
it has taken from our Wealth, has added nothing to our Frugality. Every place of
splendid pleasure is filled with assemblies, every Sale of expensive Superfluities
is crowded with buyers; and War has no other effect, than that of enabling us
to show that we can be at once Military and Luxurious, and pay Soldiers and
Fiddlers at the same time.

8 Virgil, *Aeneid*, vii, 812–16: 'All the youth, streaming from house and field, and thronging matrons
marvel, and gaze at her as she goes; agape with wonder how the glory of royal purple drapes her
smooth shoulders, how the clasp entwines her hair.'

Among other changes which time has effected; a new species of Profusion has been produced. We are now, with an emulation never known before, out-bidding one another for a sight of the Coronation; the annual rent of palaces is offered for a single room for a single day.

I am far from desiring to repress Curiosity, to which we owe so great a part of our intellectual pleasures; nor am I hardy enough to oppose the general practice of mankind, so much as to think all pomp and magnificence useless or ridiculous. But all passions have their limits, which they cannot exceed without putting our happiness in danger; and although a fine show be a fine thing, yet, like other fine things, it may be purchased too dear. All pleasures are valuable in proportion to their greatness and duration: that the pleasure of a show is not of any long continuance, all know, who are now striving for places; for if a show was long, it would not be rare. This is not the worst, the pleasure while it lasts will be less than is expected. No human performance can rise up to human ideas. Grandeur is less grand, and finery less fine, than it is painted by the fancy. And such is the difference between hope and possession, that, to a great part of the spectators, the show will cease as soon as it appears.

Let me not yet deceive my readers to their disadvantage, or represent the little pleasures of life as less than they are. Those who come to see, come likewise to be seen, and will, for many hours before the procession, enjoy the eyes of innu-merable gazers. Nor will this be the last or the longest gratification; those who have seen the coronation will have whole years of triumph over those who saw it not. They will have an opportunity of amusing their humble friends and rustic acquaintances with narratives often heard with envy, and often with wonder; and when they hear the youth of the next generation boasting the splendour of any future procession, they will talk with contemptuous superiority of the coronation of George the Third.

2.4   Thomas Mortimer, *Every Man His Own Broker; or, A Guide to Exchange-Alley* (London, 1761), ii–v, vii–xi, xiv–xvi, 1–4, 12–14, 15–16, 27–32, 54–60, 72–82.

Every Man his Own Broker is on the face of it a layman's guide to buying and selling stock, particularly Bank of England stock, and was highly influential as a handbook for 40 years, being published in 14 editions between 1761 and 1798. However, it contains within it an argument about the virtues of the national debt for both the private investor and the country as a whole, and an attempt to bypass stockbrokers in trading this stock, whose dubious practices are revealed in the second part of these extracts. Mortimer argues that the national debt, and trade in it through Bank of England stock, is part of a virtuous cycle by which mili-tary supplies are financed in order to enlarge markets for British trade, forming a pattern of low-interest annuities trading at a high price during peacetime, and high-interest annuities trading at a low price during times of war and other crises.

The review of Every Man his own Broker in the Gentleman's Magazine stated, 'This traffic manifestly depends altogether upon the fluctuation of the price of stock, and thus it becomes the interest of those who carry it on to produce this fluctuation.'[9] The idea of public credit as a self-perpetuating augmentation in national wealth and prestige was challenged by the likes of David Hume, Adam Smith and Richard Price, but each position conceptualises the national debt as sublime, with those opposed relating it to the negative sublime of objective expansion and self-diminution, while the likes of Mortimer relate it to a positive sublime of infinite expansion.

The danger for Mortimer lies in the practices of the stock-jobbers, who traded stock, more or less illegally, on the black market. The Bank of England and other stock trading houses had a day, usually at the end of each month and known as the rescountres when stocks were officially traded, dividends paid and accounts reconciled. During each month, jobbers would offer contracts to trade stock at a certain price to investors ('contracts for time', or buying and selling 'for rescountres'), gambling on favourable movements of prices at the end of the month. In practice, no stock would be traded, the account being settled based on the difference between the original price and the price at the end of the month. Mortimer gives a number of examples of how honest tradesmen might be tempted by the spectacle of huge profits to trade in this way, and in effect shows how the positive effects of the ever-increasing profits of stock-trading can be turned into huge losses for the unwary. These descriptions are couched in language reminiscent of the Gothic and orientalist sublime; Mortimer lifts the veil on the mystifications of the stock-jobbers, painting them as magicians practising a (false) alchemy. If this book opens up to greater numbers the opportunity of achieving long-term profits in a win-win negotiation between individual and state, it also lifts the lid on the secrets of 'Change Alley, and illustrates the temptations of spectacular but ultimately unattainable profit.

Sum Solus,[10] I remember, was the motto of a very singular man, after whom the good people of England ran in crowds some few years ago, according to their usual curiosity, and taste for novelty. His excellence consisted in broiling a beefsteak upon his tongue, and eating an infernal soup, composed of various combustibles, without burning his mouth. After this account of him, the sagacious reader will be apt to think, no man has a better title than this, to the motto at the head of the page. Certain it is, however, that my pretensions to it go much further than his, as I have never heard that he favoured the public with a treatise upon his excellent art – no, to me alone it was reserved to teach astonished

---

9 *The Gentleman's Magazine* 32 (1762), pp. 17–20.

10 *Sum solus*: 'I am unique' (Latin); the reference to this artiste is obscure, but it is appropriate that Mortimer should introduce his work with an example of apparently miraculous spectacle, as he consistently uses the language of the magical and the exotic to describe the practices of the London financiers.

Britons, the amazing art of thrusting their hands into the fire[11] without burning their fingers; or, in other words, of learning grown people to walk through the fiery furnace of J _____'s[12] Coffee-house unhurt; a task extremely difficult for a Christian author to perform, and equally hard for a Christian people to attain. Shadrach, Meschach, and Abednego,[13] have indeed granted policies of insurance to all their descendents, and therefore it is rare to see a Jew so much as singe his beard in this mansion of Belzebub; while poor Christians very often consume bills, bonds, and jewels, in a few days, betwixt the hours of one, and three, when its heat is most intense. Arduous as the task is, however, I hope to acquit myself with honour, and to the no small profit, and entertainment of my readers [...]

Among all the various productions of the press, it is amazing that this important subject has never been touched, except in a few satirical pieces on the fatal year 1720;[14] which, though they severely lash the diabolical iniquity of that period, yet have left no solid instructions to the public, how to avoid being the dupes of such sort of schemes, which, though carried on in a less conspicuous manner, are yet in practice to this day. The legislature, indeed, since that time, have taken every prudent measure to put a stop to the infamous practice of Stock-Jobbing[15] but notwithstanding all the wise precautions hitherto taken, only the most palpable and glaring frauds have been entirely suppressed. The Bubbles are indeed burst, and the Race Horses of Exchange-Alley long since dead, but Bulls, and Bears, still subsist in their vigour, and full strength. [...] Yet, as there is every day some new scene of iniquity contriving behind the curtain, it is impossible for me to insure success; which is scarce ever certain, till those troublesome companions, that generally attend the innocent, *viz.*, Honour, honesty and a good conscience, are entirely discarded [...]

---

11 'A phrase well known to the gentlemen of "Change Alley"' (Mortimer's Note). Financier slang for making a risky investment.

12 Jonathan's coffee house, founded by Jonathan Miles in 1680 on Exchange Alley in the City of London. It was frequented by traders, and in 1761 it was the meeting place of a newly formed club to trade stocks, which later became the Stock Exchange.

13 *Shadrach, Meschach, and Abednego*: three Jews who refused to worship Nebuchadnezzar's golden idol, survived their punishment of being thrown into the royal furnace, and were finally appointed to governmental posts in Babylon (Daniel 3:1–30). Mortimer plays on the common stereotype of Jewish financiers as using some kind of dark art to protect themselves, and perhaps insinuating themselves into the state establishment.

14 *1720*: the year of the 'South Sea Bubble', in which fraudulent trading and governmental collusion caused first a great inflation in the price of the South Sea Company, and then a crash, with many unwary investors losing large sums. Mortimer's enthusiasm for Bank of England stocks is partly born out of the widespread paranoia about such crashes happening again.

15 'Vid. an act of Parliament, entitled, An Act for the better preventing the infamous practice of Stock-Jobbing, made in the year 1734' (Mortimer's note). Stock-jobbers were literally the brokers buying and selling stocks, but the term had acquired a pejorative meaning by this time, implying those involved in the practice of making futures contracts to trade in stock of the Bank of England, and the East India and South Sea Companies.

Tremble, O ye Gallic[16] hosts! and thou Monarchy falsely styled, *le bien aimé*,[17] nor ever entertain the idle hope of prevailing against this my native land, for learn to your astonishment, and utter confusion, that her paper credit is arrived at such a height, that her *gentleman brokers* alone (men who live partly on the circulation, but more on the abuse of paper money) can afford to pay twenty-eight thousand, eight hundred livres of your money *per annum*, barely for the use of a room; and two or three valets to receive letters and messages from clients, or more properly (in the language of Drury-Lane, which is synonymous to that of 'Change-Alley) from their culls. Think not, O Rome! that with all the artful sophistry thou canst invent a more absurd proposition than this, that some *Devils* are blacker than others; a proposition, however, which these *gentlemen brokers* have openly maintained, by their separation from their poor brethren. [...]

Surely the breast of every Englishman must glow with rapture and admiration, when he considers, that while the unhappy subjects of other powers engaged in the present war[18] are quite exhausted, and thousands of them totally ruined, by the demands made on them by their arbitrary monarchs, he is voluntarily contributing towards defraying the public expenses of his country, in a manner that is so far from being a burden to him, that on the contrary, he is serving himself at the same time, by lending money on parliamentary security; and on conditions, that though they are not quite so profitable as some others, are yet insured by the credit of the nation, which exceeds all other security whatever [...]

[*Account of Jonathan's Coffee-House*]

As a prose writer, and only a bare narrator of facts, I cannot properly call in the assistance of the fairy train, nor yet conjure up aerial spirits to convey my readers through the jarring elements to the place, where, for my own convenience, I would have them transported; I shall therefore only simply entreat them to awaken the powers of their imaginations, and by their strength, suppose themselves conveyed to the famous college of jobbers, not inferior to any college of Jesuits; where I must leave them to recollect, and call up the idea of Bartholomew Fair, or some country wake, that they may have a just resemblance of that horrid din of confused voices; and that motley appearance of various characters which present themselves to their view, at their entrance into the college – while I for a moment pause – to consider in what language and form, I shall explain the subjects of their wild uproar.

Shall I throw it into dialogue? No, 'tis impracticable; for it consists of such a medley of news, quarrels, prices of different funds, calling of names, adjusting of accounts, &c. &c. continually circulating in an intermixed chaos of confusion,

---

16 *Gallic*: French
17 *le bien aimé*: 'the well beloved' (French), i.e. the inaccurately styled French King Louis XV. The costly Seven Years' War was of course being fought at this time between France and Britain.
18 *present war*: the Seven Years' War (1756–63).

that it will not admit of digesting into that pure decent method of expressing a familiar conversation.

Shall I invoke the comic muse; and in her lively vein of humour expose the deformity of the sons of iniquity? No, the characters are too low, the subject too mean, and the plots too dirty, unless I was writing for a strolling company; and piece to be presented at a booth on a common, in the wilds of Kent.

Since then no borrowed style will suit it, nor no characters aptly represent it, let me give the explanation in their own language. [...]

The grand scene opens a little after twelve at noon, (at which time the transfer of books of most of the offices are shut for the day) and generally the actors hold forth in the following manner, and almost all at once: 'Tickets – Tickets – South-Sea Stock for the opening – Navy-Bills – Bank Stock for the rescounters – Long Annuities – (*here the waiter calls*) Chance – Chance – Chance *Mr. Chance is not here, Sir, he is over at his Office* – Here tickets for August – Omnium gatherum for September – Scrip for the third payment – 3 per Cent. consolidated, gentlemen – Here Mr. Full (*whispers a friend, but is overheard*) they are all BULLS by G[o]d, but I'll be d[amne]d if they have any of my stock, I'll go to Bath, and not come near them till the rescounters – Here Bank Circulation, who buys Bank Circulation – Tickets for the drawing, gentlemen – Well, what have you to do in Tickets for the drawing Mr. Mulberry. – I am a seller of five hundred, Sir – and I am a buyer, Sir, but pray at what price? – Why, as you are a friend, Mr. Point-royal, I shall give you the turn, you shall have them at 14. The turn, Mr. Mulberry, why, do you think I do not know what I am about? they are sellers at 13 – Well then, you shall have them at 13 – I will take them at 12, and no otherwise – Well, you shall have them, put 'em down (for the drawing mind) but, d[amn]n it, where did you get that paste Wig? Why, you son of a b[itc]h, it is as good as your mop. [...] Enter Kit Cot – and Mr. Verjuice, with each a book in his hand – Here every Man his own broker, I am a seller for time – to them Mr. Skin'it, formerly a butcher, Mr. Onion, Sam. Dangerless, Joe Dirty-face, the baker, and Tom Steel the common-concil-man, who all at once demand, what is it? Any new subscription, Mr. Verjuice? I buy, I buy, – no, no, Gentlemen, it is not so good a thing, it is a dammed impudent libel, against all the members of this sacred college; and I would give all Spring-Gardens to see the author punished for his insolence; here he gives directions to buy and sell Stock; and lays open the whole of our transactions; and all forsooth because he has lost money amongst us [...] Tom Steel now interposes – 'Gentlemen you are highly in the wrong to take such notice of this paltry performance, or its author; trust me, the best thing you can do is let him alone, the thing will die of itself ... leave him to me, pass quietly by him in the streets, and do not stare at him as if you saw a monster, for that only marks rage, and a confession of guilt: – I have a safer and more quiet way, it is but arming our knights, and baronets in our cause, and this moth will soon be crushed.'[19]

---

19 The suggestion appears to be that the old aristocracy should be involved in stock trading so as to enlist their support for the activities of the stock-jobbing.

2.5 Richard Price, 'Of Public Credit, and the National Debt', in *Observations on Reversionary Payments; on Schemes for Providing Annuities for Widows, and for Persons in Old Age; On The Method of Calculating the Values of Assurances on Lives; and on The National Debt* (London, 1771), pp. 135–65.

Richard Price (1729–91) was a dissenting minister who is now best known for preaching, in November 1789, a sermon 'Discourse on the Love of Our Country', in support of the French Revolution, to which Edmund Burke was directly responding in Reflections on the Revolution in France *(1790). However, prior to this he had been a celebrated and original thinker in a number of different areas, and had published widely on philosophical and scientific topics. Price's interest in the mathematics of probability led him to undertake a series of actuarial studies on the subject of annuities and life insurance.*

At this time, a number of cooperative societies were being set up to provide financial services such as pensions and insurance to their members. Most of the volume from which the following passages are extracted is devoted to pointing out and correcting the mathematical and actuarial errors these societies had made, and which would inevitably lead to their bankruptcy. In his introduction, Price describes the silent power of compound interest and time. At times this is malevolent:

It cannot be said with precision, how long these societies may continue their payments to annuitants, after beginning them. A continued increase, and a great proportion of young members, may support them for a longer time than I can foresee. But the longer they are supported by such means, the more mischief they must occasion. – So, a tradesman, who sells cheaper than he buys, may be kept up many years by increasing business and credit; but he will be all the while *accumulating distress*; and the longer he goes on, the more extensive the ruin will produce at last.

But it can also be turned to advantage; just as the geometric increase in debt can silently ruin one's finances, so too can the geometric increase in funds make one rich. Hence when he turns to the subject of the national debt, two versions of sublime effect emerge: a negative sublime, which overwhelms and diminishes, and a positive, which suggests infinite expansion. As Price comments, 'the smallest fund of this kind [...] is omnipotent'. Price's footnote on compound interest, although mathematically inaccurate, became a much cited and debated example of what has since been called (possibly first by Benjamin Franklin, Price's mentor) the 'eighth wonder of the world'.

There is no part of this work, in which the public is so much concerned as the [following] chapter. It will here be proved, that had the sums raised for the public since the REVOLUTION, been much greater than they have been, the increase of the public debts to their present state might have been prevented in the easiest manner, and at a trifling expense. A method, likewise, of reducing within due bounds these debts, heavy as they now are, will be proposed. – All competent judges will, I believe, see that this method, being founded on the most perfect improvement that can be made of money, is the most expeditious and effectual that the natures of things admits of. Nor, in my opinion, if the nation is not too near the *limit* of its resources, can there be any *good* reason, against carrying it into execution. – It is well known, to what prodigious sums, money, improved for some time at *compound interest*, will increase.[20] A state, if there is no misapplication of money, must necessarily make this improvement of any savings, which can be applied to the payment of its debts. It need never, therefore, be under any difficulties; for, with the *smallest* savings, it may, in as little time as its interest can require, pay off the *largest* debts [...]

The practice of raising the necessary supplies for every public service, by borrowing money on interest, to be continued 'till the principal is discharged, must be in the highest degree detrimental to a kingdom, unless a plan is settled, for putting its debts into a regular and certain course of payment. When this is not done, a kingdom, by such a practice, obliges itself to return for every sum it borrows infinitely greater sums; and, for the sake of a present advantage, subjects itself to a burden which must always be growing, 'till it becomes insupportable.

This seems now to be the very state of this nation. At the REVOLUTION, an aera in other respects truly glorious, the practice I have mentioned begun. Ever since, the public debt has been increasing fast, and every new war has added much more to it, than was taken from it, during the preceding period of peace. In the year 1700, it was 16 millions. In 1715, it was 55 millions. A peace, which continued 'till 1740, sunk it to 47 millions; and next peace sunk it no lower than 72 millions. In the *last* war, it rose to 148 millions; and, at a few millions less than this sum it now stands, and probably will stand, 'till another war raises it perhaps to 200 millions. – One cannot reflect on this without terror. – No resources can be sufficient to support a kingdom long in such a course. 'Tis obvious, that the consequence of accumulating debts so rapidly; and of mortgaging posterity,[21] and funding for eternity, in order to pay for interest on them; must in the end prove destructive. Rather than go on in this way, it is absolutely necessary, that no money should be borrowed, except on annuities, which are to terminate

---

20 'A *penny*, put out to 5 *per cent*, compound interest at our Saviour's birth, would, by this time, have increased to more money than would be contained in 150 millions of globes, each equal to the earth in magnitude, and all solid gold' (Price's Note). Price's estimate is inaccurate by a factor of three.

21 *mortgaging posterity*: a phrase that Edmund Burke appears to have picked up on in *Reflections on the Revolution in France*, in which the argument is made that the new French government, by incurring debt on forcibly seized lands in order to issue *assignats*, had mortgaged (and then squandered) its inheritance, leaving nothing to posterity. To complicate the issue further, Burke, who had been Price's antagonist in the *Reflections*, then argued in favour of such a mortgage in *Letters on a Regicide Peace*.

within a given period. Were this practised, there would be a LIMIT beyond which the national debts could not increase; and time would do that *necessarily* for the public, which, if trusted to the economy of the conductors of its affairs, might possibly never be done. [...]

These advantages would be, indeed, unspeakably great. [...] I am, however, far from intending to recommend this plan as the best a state can pursue. There is another method of gaining the same end, which is, on many accounts, preferable to it. I mean, by providing an annual saving, to be applied invariably, together with the interest of all the sums redeemed by it, to the purpose of discharging the public debts: Or, in other words, by the establishment of a permanent SINKING FUND.

It is well known, that this plan has been also adopted by our government; but though capable of producing the *greatest* effects in the *easiest* and *surest* manner, it has never been carried into execution. It will abundantly appear from what follows that this observation is just. [...]

The advantages of putting the public debts into such a course of payment, as I have described, are scarcely to be imagined. It would give a vigour to public credit, which would enable a state always to borrow money easily, and on the best terms. And the encouragement to lenders might be always improved, without any inconvenience, by making every loan irredeemable, during the first 20 or 30 years; for, there could seldom be any occasion, for beginning to discharge any *one* loan sooner.

It might easily be shown, that the faithful application, from the beginning of the year 1700, of only 200,000 *l.* annually, would long before this time, notwithstanding the reductions of interest, and every waste that has been made of the public money, have caused above half the public funds to revert to the public, and paid off above 80 millions of its debts. The nation might therefore, some years ago, have been eased of the greatest part of the taxes with which it is loaded. The most important relief might have been given to its trade and manufactures; and it might now have been in much better circumstances, than at the beginning of the last war; its credit firm; respected by foreign nations; dreaded by its enemies; and ready to punish any insult that could be offered to it. The near view, likewise, of such a period, during the course of the last war, would have given higher spirits to the nation, and encouraged it to bear the expense occasioned by the war with more cheerfulness, and to continue it with vigour for two or three years longer; the consequence of which would, probably, have been, gaining a full indemnification from our enemies, and weakening them to such a degree, as would have given us effectual security against them for many years to come. – A new account might also now have been begun; and another fund, not much more considerable, applied in the same way, would, in 60 or 70 years more, have paid, not only all that would have been now unpaid, but also, probably, a great proportion of such further debts as must be contracted within this time. And thus, without any expense that could be sensibly felt, its debts, as soon as they began to grow heavy, might have been constantly reduced to a *half*, or a *third*; and not only all *danger*, but all considerable *inconvenience* from them prevented [...]

Certain it is, therefore, that if our affairs are to be retrieved, it must be by a *fund* increasing itself in the manner I have explained. The smallest *fund* of this kind is, indeed *omnipotent* if it is allowed time to operate, but we are, I fear, got so near to the limits of the resources of the nation, that it cannot be allowed much time: And, in order to make amends for this, it is necessary that it should be *large*.

2.6   Adam Smith, *Inquiry into the Nature and Causes of the Wealth of Nations*, 2 vols (London, 1776), I, pp. 414–21; II, pp. 550–2, 561–5.

Although he is now best known as the founder of modern economics, Smith wrote and lectured on an extraordinary range of topics, including moral philosophy, aesthetics, epistemology, rhetoric, and Law. In fact, Inquiry into [...] the Wealth of Nations *grew out of a series of lectures on Law (or 'Jurisprudence') first given at the University of Glasgow in 1762–3. Smith's concept of 'inquiry' can be seen as a development of an early essay on Astronomy, in which he argues that the will to knowledge comes out of the aesthetic experiences, associated with the sublime, of 'surprise', 'wonder' and 'admiration' at the complexity of the universe.[22] The observer perceives with awe the apparent incomprehensibility of things, but is led on to attempt an explanation to impose order on the universe. If this is the case with astronomy, it must be even more so with society and its relationship to money, which suggest patterns as complex as, but more variable than, the movements of the celestial bodies. The depiction of the political economist as the chaser of sublime objects can be seen as a development of the 'abstruse' thought that Hume argues is necessary to the proper study of economics.*

The two extracts reproduced here exemplify two other ways in which the aesthetics of the sublime interact with his economic thought, although both are significantly bounded by the problems of national debt and taxation. In the first, the virtuous cycle of accumulation of stock, conversion to capital and reinvestment is Smith's subject. He has already stated that accumulation breeds accumulation: 'A great stock, though with small profits, generally increases faster than a small stock with great profits. Money, says the proverb, makes money. When you have got a little, it is often easy to get more. The great difficulty is to get that little' (I.ix.11). Self-improvement is the grand ruling passion of mankind, and the commonest realisation

---

22 See 'The History of Astronomy' in *Lectures on Philosophical Subjects*, ed. W. P. D Wightman (Oxford: Oxford University Press, 1980), pp. 33–47; see also 'General Introduction' in *The Wealth of Nations* pp. 1–5.

of this is the desire to accumulate wealth. While it is true that some spend prodigally without any return, the good sense of the majority more than compensates; this assertion, Smith goes on to argue, is proven by history, but ability to see the evidence depends on the position of the viewer; from close in, where only a short time span can be seen, economies often look like they are contracting, but from further back, where a span of centuries can be seen, constant accumulation and improvement is obvious. A further problem is government expense and taxation, which according to Smith always hinder improvement; but just as the 'unknown principle of animal life' makes a sick body recover despite the ministrations of doctors, so the desire of humans to improve themselves results, despite state incompetence, in inevitable but 'silent' improvement. Smith finally takes this sublime accumulation resulting from a transcendent human characteristic one stage further, by speculating as to the level of accumulation that might have been achieved were it not for political distortions. The subjunctive mood at the end of the first extract describes tentatively a utopian alternative to the contemporary situation of increasing governmental expense and taxation, which is to be aspired to but is nonetheless 'perhaps not very easy to imagine.'

The second extract comes from near the end of The Wealth of Nations, *the later chapters of which are increasingly coloured by the anticipated costs of Britain's new colonial war in America. Smith portrays the terrifying increase in the national debt as sublime, as did many writing on the topic at the time. While it buys time for governments, debt carries on increasing unstoppably, necessitating renewed taxation after renewed taxation, working directly against the accumulation described in the first extract, and leading inexorably, at some point in the near future, to financial catastrophe and national bankruptcy. But Smith also paints the major cause of national debt, war, as a kind of spectacle, put on more or less cynically by governments for the apparent benefit of the public, in order to justify increased taxation; Smith comments that 'remote from the scene of the action', people 'enjoy, at their ease, the amusement of reading in the news-papers the exploits of their own fleets and armies', and entertain 'a thousand visionary hopes of conquest'. Just as the issuing of more and more paper credit produces imaginary money, so the dross of war is sublimated into heroic spectacle by the effect of distance, in a process similar to that described by Burke in* A Philosophical Inquiry. *Governments attempt a number of feints (like currency devaluation) to deflect attention from the fact that they are bankrupt, but still they persist on keeping on colonies as a 'showy equipage' that they cannot in reality afford. Credit's ability to finance fantasy is cyclical and destructive; governments need new wars to justify taxation to fund former expense. The glittering objects of colonial ambition do nothing in reality to pay for their acquisition, leading, in the cycle of the negative sublime, to perpetual indebtedness and perpetual war. However, in a final expression of the aesthetics of the sublime, Smith predicts that terror at the approaching national humiliation will lead the nation to a realisation of the 'mediocrity of its circumstances', the chastened self-belittlement requiring in turn a resolve to proceed with more rational policy.*

[*From 'Of the Accumulation of Capital' (Bk. II, chap. 3, extracts.)*]

It can seldom happen [...] that the circumstances of a great nation can be much affected either by the prodigality or misconduct of individuals: the profusion or imprudence of some being always more than compensated by the frugality and good conduct of others.

With regard to profusion, the principle, which prompts to expense, is the passion for present enjoyment; which, though sometimes violent and very difficult to be restrained, is in general only momentary and occasional. But the principle which prompts to save, is the desire for bettering our condition, a desire which, though generally calm and dispassionate, comes with us from the womb, and never leaves us till we go into the grave. In the whole interval which separates those two moments, there is scarce perhaps a single instant in which any man is so perfectly and completely satisfied with his situation, as to be without any wish of alteration or improvement of any kind. An augmentation of fortune is the means by which the greater part of men propose and wish to better their condition. It is the means the most vulgar and obvious; and the most likely way of augmenting their fortune, is to save and accumulate some part of what they acquire, either regularly or annually, or upon some extraordinary occasions. Though the principle of expense, therefore, prevails in almost all men upon some occasions, and in some men upon almost all occasions, yet in the greater part of men, taking their whole course of life at an average, the principle of frugality seems not only to predominate, but to predominate very greatly. [...]

The uniform, constant, and uninterrupted effort of every man to better his condition, the principle from which public and national, as well as private opulence is originally derived, is frequently powerful enough to maintain the natural progress of things towards improvement, in spite both of the extravagance of government, and of the greatest errors of administration. Like the unknown principle of animal life,[23] it frequently restores health and vigour to the constitution, in spite, not only of the disease, but of the absurd prescriptions of the doctors.

[*Smith surveys economic growth in England from Anglo Saxon times to the present*]

In each of these periods, however, there was not only much public and private profusion, many expensive and unnecessary wars, great perversion of the annual produce from maintaining productive to maintain productive hands; but sometimes, in the confusion of civil discord, such absolute waste and destruction of stock, as might be supposed, not only to retard, as it certainly did, the natural accumulation of riches, but to have left the country, at the end of the period,

---

23 *the unknown principle of animal life*: that which gives life to inanimate matter, a frequent object of enquiry in eighteenth-century natural philosophy.

poorer than at the beginning. Thus, in the happiest and most fortunate period of them all, that which has passed since the restoration, how many disorders and misfortunes have occurred, which, could they have been foreseen, not only the impoverishment, but the total ruin of the country would have been expected from them? The fire and the plague of London,[24] the two Dutch wars,[25] the disorders of the revolution,[26] the war in Ireland,[27] the four expensive French wars of 1688, 1701, 1742, and 1756,[28] together with the two rebellions of 1715 and 1745.[29] In the course of the four French wars, the nation has contracted more than a hundred and forty five millions of debt, over and above all the other extraordinary annual expense which they occasioned, so that the whole cannot be computed at less than two hundred millions. So great a share of the annual produce of the land and labour of the country, has, since the revolution, been employed upon different occasions, in maintaining an extraordinary number of unproductive hands. But had not those wars given this particular direction to so large a capital, the greater part of it would naturally have been employed in maintaining productive hands, whose labour would have replaced, with a profit, the whole value of their consumption. The value of the annual produce of the land and labour of the country, would have been considerably increased by it every year, and every year's increase would have augmented still more that of the next year. More houses would have been built, more lands would have been improved, and those which had been improved before would have been better cultivated, more manufactures would have been established, and those which had been established before would have been more extended; and to what height the real wealth and revenue of the country might, by this time, have been raised, it is not perhaps very easy to imagine.

But though the profusion of government must, undoubtedly, have retarded the natural progress of England towards wealth and improvement, it has not been able to stop it. The annual produce of its land and labour is, undoubtedly, much greater at present than it was either at the restoration or at the revolution. The capital, therefore, annually employed in cultivating this land, and in maintaining this labour, must likewise be much greater. In the midst of all the exactions of government, this capital has been silently and gradually accumulated by the private frugality and good conduct of individuals, by their universal, continual and uninterrupted

---

24 *fire and plague of London*: the Great Plague of London (1665–6) and the Great Fire of London (1666).

25 *the two Dutch Wars*: the Second and Third Anglo-Dutch Wars (1665–7 and 1672–4).

26 *the disorders of the revolution*: the 'Glorious Revolution' of 1688, in which James II was overthrown in favour of Stadtholder Wilhelm of Orange (who became William III).

27 *the war in Ireland*: William III's campaign in Ireland (1689–71) to put down Jacobite resistance to his reign.

28 *French wars 1756*: The War of the Grand Alliance (or 'Nine Years' War') 1688–97; War of the Spanish Succession (1701–14); the campaigns known collectively as the 'War of the Austrian Succession' (1740–8); the Seven Years' War (1756–63).

29 *two rebellions of 1715 and 1745*: Jacobite uprisings against the Hanoverian succession in 1715 and 1745.

effort to better their own condition. It is this effort, protected by law, and allowed
by liberty to exert itself in the manner that is most advantageous, which has maintained the progress of England towards opulence and improvement in almost all
former times, and which, it is to be hoped, will do so in all future times.

[*from 'Of Public Debts' (Book V, III, Chapter iii)*]

In great empires, the people who live in the capital, and in the provinces remote
from the scene of action, feel, many of them, scarce any inconveniency from
the war; but enjoy, at their ease, the amusement of reading in the news-papers
the exploits of their own fleets and armies. To them this amusement compensates the small difference between the taxes which they pay on account of the
war, and those which they had been accustomed to pay in time of peace. They
are commonly dissatisfied with the return of peace, which puts an end to their
amusement, and to a thousand visionary hopes of conquest, and national glory,
from a longer continuance of the war.[30] [...]

[*Smith outlines the history of the rise of the national debt to fund war from 1688
onwards*]

The practice of funding[31] has gradually enfeebled every state which has adopted
it. The Italian republics seem to have begun it. Genoa and Venice, the only two
remaining which can pretend to an independent existence, have been enfeebled
by it. Spain seems to have learned the practice from the Italian republics, and (its
taxes being probably less judicious than theirs) it has, in proportion to its natural
strength, been still enfeebled. The debts of Spain are of very old standing. It was
deeply in debt before the end of the sixteenth century, about a hundred years
before England owed a shilling. France, notwithstanding all its natural resources,
languishes under an oppressive load of the same kind. The republic of the United
Provinces[32] is as much enfeebled by its debts as either Genoa or Venice. Is it
likely that in Great Britain alone a practice, which has brought either weakness
or desolation into every other country, should prove altogether innocent? [...]

When national debts have once been accumulated to a certain degree, there
is scarce, I believe, a single instance of their having been fairly and completely
paid. The liberation of the public revenue, if it has ever been brought about at
all, has always been brought about by a bankruptcy; sometimes by an avowed
one, but always by a real one, though frequently by a pretended payment.

The raising of the denomination of the coin has been the most usual expedient
by which a real public bankruptcy has been disguised under the appearance of

---

30 Elsewhere Smith treats the effect of distance as promoting disinterested judgements; see *The Theory
   of Moral Sentiments*, III, i, 3.
31 *funding*: perpetual funding; see note above.
32 *republic of the United Provinces*: Holland

a pretended payment [...] When it becomes necessary for a state to declare itself bankrupt, in the same manner as when it becomes necessary for an individual to do so, a fair, open, and avowed bankruptcy is always the measure which is both least dishonourable to the debtor and least hurtful to the creditor. The honour of a state is surely very poorly provided for when, in order to cover the disgrace of a real bankruptcy, it has recourse to a juggling trick of this kind, so easily seen through, and at the same time so extremely pernicious.

[*Smith proceeds to discuss options for Britain to increase revenues or decrease expenses, and the cost of the colonial wars of 1740–8 and 1756–63*]

In those two wars the colonies cost Great Britain much more than double the sum which the national debt amounted to before the commencement of the first of them. Had it not been for those wars that debt might, and probably would by this time, have been completely paid; and had it not been for the colonies, the former of those wars might not, and the latter certainly would not have been undertaken. It was because the colonies were supposed to be provinces of the British empire that this expense was laid out upon them. But countries which contribute neither revenue nor military force towards the support of the empire cannot be considered as provinces.[33] They may perhaps be considered as appendages, as a sort of splendid and showy equipage of the empire. But if the empire can no longer support the expense of keeping up this equipage, it ought certainly to lay it down; and if it cannot raise its revenue in proportion to its expense, it ought, at least, to accommodate its expense to its revenue. If the colonies, notwithstanding their refusal to submit to British taxes, are still to be considered as provinces of the British empire, their defence in some future war may cost Great Britain as great an expense as it ever has done in any former war. The rulers of Great Britain have, for more than a century past, amused the people with the imagination that they possessed a great empire on the west side of the Atlantic. This empire, however, has hitherto existed in imagination only. It has hitherto been, not an empire, but the project of an empire; not a gold mine, but the project of a gold mine; a project which has cost, which continues to cost, and which, if pursued in the same way as it has been hitherto, is likely to cost, immense expense, without being likely to bring any profit; for the effects of the monopoly of the colony trade, it has been shown, are, to the great body of the people, mere loss instead of profit. It is surely now time that our rulers should either realize this golden dream, in which they have been indulging themselves, perhaps, as well as the people, or that they should awake from it themselves, and endeavour to awaken the people. If the project cannot be completed, it ought to be given up. If any of the provinces of the British empire cannot be made to contribute

---

33 *But countries [...] as provinces*: the American War had been occasioned by the colonies' refusal to pay taxes to the colonial administration.

towards the support of the whole empire, it is surely time that Great Britain should free herself from the expense of defending those provinces in time of war, and of supporting any part of their civil or military establishments in time of peace, and endeavour to accommodate her future views and designs to the real mediocrity of her circumstances.

2.7   'Debate in the House of Commons on Suing for Peace with France, 26 January 1795', from *The Morning Chronicle* (27 January 1795).

Following the execution of Louis XVI by the French Republic in January 1793, a number of powers joined the 'First Coalition' against France. In response, France declared war on Britain on 1 February 1793, and had by the end of 1795 gained the upper hand on land by, in particular, annexing Holland as the puppet 'Batavian Republic' (which hindered an important British trade route with the Continent), and occupying the Rhineland. After Prussia and Spain had sued for peace, there were increasing calls in Britain to negotiate, in view of military failure, the enormous cost of the war, and the adverse economic consequences of the increased national debt and hindrances to trade. In February 1794, Pitt's ministry successfully asked the House of Commons to approve a budget requiring a new loan, through the Bank of England, of £11m. However on 15 January 1795, the Bank of England effectively refused more credit to the government, and a kind of stand-off between the Bank's Directors and Pitt's Ministry ensued; with the promise of new taxes, Pitt secured loans of £6 million to support Austria and £18 million to pay for British forces.[34] A by-now familiar debate ensued about the ability of the fiscal system and the British economy to service the national debt, the new loans being, as had become usual during the eighteenth century, far greater than anyone had imagined possible. In this debate on the economic effects of war, images of national exhaustion were employed, and the prediction was made of the country being precipitated into an abyss from which it could not recover. Charles Grey argues, in the extract printed here, that the French, on the other hand, like the American rebels in the 1770s, were a people animated by the love of liberty, and would hence be able to issue ever more paper currency against their assets, in an alchemic process by which bank notes can signify an excess wholly unrelated to their referent. It is largely to arguments like that contained in Grey's speech that Burke's Third Letter on a Regicide Peace *is addressed, which claims that the British economy will constantly confound observers and transcend all that it had achieved in the past. As is customary in parliamentary records, proceedings are presented in reported speech, hence the slightly clumsy gram-matical constructions.*

---

34 For a near-contemporary account of public borrowing during the French Revolutionary War, see
   J. J. Grellier, *History of the National Debt* (London, 1810), pp. 375–420.

Mr. Grey's speech[35]

After two years war, marked with a mixture of brilliant successes and melancholy disasters, both of which had contributed to drain this Country of its blood and of its treasure, we were not one point nearer to the object for which it was said to have been undertaken, than at the moment of its commencement. A melancholy reflection this; still more so when the lives of perhaps 50,000 of our countrymen had been sacrificed, and when we had so enormously increased our debt; a debt which had contributed so much, and which will contribute much more, to damp the ardor, cramp the genius, and check the industry of all ranks and descriptions of people in this country; melancholy indeed because, if the war were to subside to-day we shall have added to our national debt perhaps *seventy millions of money*. The Right Honourable Gentleman[36] seemed not to assent to this. He believed it was not an exaggerated account, but in order to avoid disputes upon the sum, he would state it at fifty millions; that he knew was below the mark, but he was content to take it so. Surely then it became the House to deliberate again and again before they added to a burden already so enormous; it became them to pause before they would proceed one step further, where the issue was in itself so hazardous, and the loss so large and certain. [...]

The next point which had been insisted upon by the Minister as a reason why we should expect success in the present War, was the want of resources on the part of the French; that Right Honourable Gentleman had stated, that the French were so exhausted, that he could prove from calculation, they could not continue the War much longer. He had heard, he said, much said upon this sort of reasoning by calculation of the strength of States. He had heard it from the commencement of the present War to this moment, and yet the French had been successful in proportion as we had depreciated their power. (Here he read part of the King's speech of last year). This was the language in the year 1794, and such was the language now. – But the History of the World proved the fallacy of this mode of argument. We were told of the progressive and rapid decay of the resources of the French. Precisely in the same stile the House of Commons was addressed in 1777, when the American War was hardly begun, and upon that occasion a speech was made by a person (the late Lord Chatham[37]), whose authority was such as the Right Honourable Gentleman would certainly pay some attention to. That great Statesman had then asked,

---

35 *Mr. Grey*: later Lord Howick and then 2nd Earl Grey (1764–1845), Prime Minister 1830–4; in 1795 he was a leader of the radical Whigs in Parliament and founder of the democratic but decidedly aristocratic 'Society of the Friends of the People'.

36 *The Right Honourable Gentleman*: William Pitt the Younger (1759–1806), the Prime Minister and key proponent of war with France.

37 *the late Lord Chatham*: William Pitt the Elder (father of Pitt the younger, to whom this speech is largely addressed), who had been Prime Minister during the successful Seven Years' War of 1756–63, but had since gone into opposition.

'where is the man who has the forehead to say he can prove it? I should like to see his face – I should like to look at it.' – Now we all know that the Americans had issued a great quantity of paper money, and they were said on that account to want resources, and it was insisted that therefore they must fall. It was then also stated by way of proof of that assertion, that the debts of the Americans would amount to sixty six millions sterling, and that the whole value of their estates did not amount to thirty three millions. Such were the arguments then, and such they were now; this was the misfortune of having the affairs of this Nation in the hands and under the direction of men who were unable to distinguish between the fallacy of such calculations and the energy of a people struggling for what appeared to them to be their Freedom, and of our being governed by men who thought that their knowledge upon such topics was superior to what was collected from the history of nations. But, if we compared that statement of American resources with those of France, we should find that, even upon that calculation, there was a prodigious advantage in favour of France. The most exaggerated account that had been given of the probable debt of France amounted only to four hundred and twenty millions (about one hundred million beyond the truth), and the value of their landed estate was admitted to be above six hundred million sterling. [...] But this, in truth, great and mighty as the advantage was in the favour of the French, was not the real way to estimate the resources of a people who, in a state of revolution, were contending, as they thought, for their liberties and their lives. They were not to be measured by the common efforts of a people. No, while there was iron in the ground, or grass on the surface of the earth, there was no end to their resources. Besides, if we looked at the population of France, we should find them to amount to one sixth of the population of the whole of Europe; add to this, the distracted and impoverished state of the Allies, and then he believed, that no man in his senses would think of success in another campaign against them; for it was clear, however desirable the thing might be, it was impossible to conquer them. With regard to our own resources, he believed them to be, as the RH Gentleman stated them to be, very great; equal, certainly, to every thing to which they ought to be applied; but not equal to the conquest of France; or of the carrying on War of aggravation, for so he must again state this War to be, as it was avowedly for the destruction of the government of France. He would say again, that whatever we might think of ourselves, we had not, nor could we in the nature of things, have, in the prosecution of this War, the energy and the spirit of the French, for they must fight while there was a man or a shilling left.

[*Grey goes on to consider the poor and hopeless state of the Allies*]

The only question for him to consider now, and that he confessed was the most difficult, was, the general question, How we were to submit to the disgrace of a negotiation? [...] He was asked, should we trust to the mercy of the French government? Certainly not, we were a great power, and had great resources; but that was an additional reason why we should put our affairs in train for negociation. If we did so now, we had the advantage of that power and those resources; but should we exhaust them both, and be at last compelled to negotiate, we should then indeed be at the mercy of the French.

2.8 Edmund Burke, *A Third Letter to a Member of the Present Parliament on the Proposals for Peace with the Regicide Directory of France* (London, 1797), pp. 1–2, 88–92, 94–8, 134, 138–41, 156–8.

The following is extracted from the last of four public letters – although published posthumously as the 'third' – written by Burke concerning the possibility of a peace with France. Due to the collapse of the 'First Coalition' (principally, Britain, Spain, Prussia and Austria) and the previously unimaginable level of public borrowing required to fund British forces and to subsidise the Austrian military failure, such a possibility was widely entertained by a broad spectrum of political opinion, if only to buy some time for state finances to recover. Lord Malmesbury had been dispatched to Paris to see on what terms peace might be sought, and it is these diplomatic overtures that were the immediate concern of Burke in his Letters*. The* Third Letter *is largely about Britain's financial ability to continue the war against France, in view of the ever-increasing level of borrowing that the war required; just before Burke had started writing, in December 1796, the government had negotiated a new loan through the Bank of England of £18 million. Notwithstanding this, the Bank's Directors several times gave stern public warnings to the government about borrowing levels, including a statement on 11 February that further loans 'would prove fatal'.*[38]*

Burke is clearly having none of this. He contrasts first the numbing inertia that has led to Malmesbury's diplomatic exchanges, with the energy of the nation that is consistently able to exceed what was expected of it. In particular, this is the case in the swift and complete subscription to the loan of £18 million raised late in 1795. Burke emphasises that there was no coercion in this loan, but that it was a fair and transparent bargain between 'monied men' and the state. Further, profits made by the financiers are ploughed back into the economy by way of taxation and personal spending, so that the interest paid by the state to its creditors comes back to help the payment of further interest, in a virtuous cycle similar to that envisaged – although as a fraudulent, vicious circle – by Price. This is in sharp contradiction to what Burke says in his* Reflections on the Revolution in France, *where he is critical of the revolutionary French government's practice of issuing paper money ('assignats') based on capital borrowed from financiers against expropriated Church lands. Historical events appear to have backed Burke into this new position, which has more in common with Mortimer than with Hume and Smith. It is also an economically*

---

38 Cited in J. J. Grellier, *History of the National Debt* (London, 1810), p. 402.

similar position to that expressed by Charles Grey of the French in his speech to
the House of Commons. Moreover, in discussing these economic problems, and to
add weight to his claim that Britain is capable of servicing ever-increasing debt in
the cause of national security, Burke mobilises a number of aesthetic categories he
had defined much earlier in his Philosophical Inquiry into [...] the Sublime and
the Beautiful *(1757). By the end of the century, then, it was possible for observers*
from a number of points on the political spectrum to conceptualise state debt not
simply as an ever-increasing object that justly inspired terror in all who beheld it,
but a practice that liberated capital and promised greater and greater economic and
cultural growth.

Dear Sir

I thank you for the bundle of State-papers, which I received yesterday. I have
travelled through the Negotiation; and a sad, founderous[39] road it is. There
is a sort of a standing jest against my countrymen,[40] that one of them on his
journey having found a piece of pleasant road, he proposed to his companion
to go over it again. This proposal, with regard to the worthy traveller's final
destination, was certainly a blunder. It was no blunder as to his immediate
satisfaction; for the way was pleasant. In the irksome journey of the Regicide
negotiations, it is otherwise: Our 'paths are not paths of pleasantness, nor
our ways the ways to peace.' All our mistakes (if such they are) like those
of our Hibernian traveller, are mistakes of repetition; they will be full as far
from bringing us to our place of rest, as his well considered project was from
forwarding him to his inn. Yet I see we persevere. Fatigued with our former
course; too listless to explore a new one; kept in action by inertness; moving
only because we have been in motion; with a sort of plodding perseverance,
we resolve to measure back again the very same joyless, hopeless, and inglori-
ous track. Backward and forward; oscillation not progression; much going in a
scanty space; the travels of a postillion, miles enough to circle the globe in one
short stage; we have been, and are yet to be jolted and rattled over the loose,
misplaced stones, and the treacherous hollows of this rough, ill kept, broken
up, treacherous French causeway! [...]
    I am thoroughly satisfied that if we degrade ourselves, it is the degradation
which will subject us to the yoke of necessity,[41] and, not that it is necessity
which has brought on our degradation. In this same chaos, where light and
darkness are struggling together, the open subscription[42] of last year, with all

---

39 *founderous*: likely to cause a traveller to founder, because full of ruts and holes.
40 *my countrymen*: the Irish.
41 *necessity*: the necessity of treating for peace, because of military failure and economic exhaustion.
42 *open subscription*: in December 1795, Pitt's ministry had published a loan to the general public of
    £18m at the high interest rate of five and five-eighths per cent, which was, to the surprise of many
    observers, quickly subscribed in full.

its circumstances, must have given us no little glimmering hope; not (as I have heard, it was vainly discoursed) that the loan could prove a crutch to a lame negotiation abroad; and that the whiff and wind of it must at once have disposed the enemies of all tranquillity[43] to a desire for peace. Judging on the face of facts, if on them it had any effect at all, it had the direct contrary effect; for very soon after the loan became public at Paris, the negotiation ended, and our Ambassador was ignominiously expelled. My view of this was different: I like the loan, not from the influence which it might have on the enemy, but on account of the temper which it indicated in our own people. This alone is a consideration of any importance; because all calculation, formed upon a supposed relation of the habitudes of others to our own, under the present circumstances, is weak and fallacious. The adversary must be judged, not by what we are, but by what we must know he actually is; unless we choose to shut our eyes and our ears to the uniform tenor of all his discourses, and to his uniform course in all his actions. We may be deluded; but we cannot pretend we have been disappointed. The old rule of, *Ne te quaesiveris extra*,[44] is a precept as available in any policy as it is in morals. Let us leave off speculating upon the disposition of the enemy. Let us descend into our own bosoms; let us ask ourselves what are our duties, and what our means of discharging them. In what heart are you at home? How far may an English Minister confide in the affections, in the confidence, in the force of an English people? What does he find us when he puts us to the proof of what English interest and English honour demand? It is, as furnishing an answer to these questions that I consider the circumstances of the loan. The effect on the enemy is not in what he may speculate on our resources, but in what he shall feel from our arms.

The circumstances of the loan have proved beyond a doubt three capital points, which, if they are properly used, may be advantageous to the future liberty and happiness of mankind. In the first place, the loan demonstrates, in regard to instrumental resources, the competency of this kingdom to the assertion of the common cause, and to the maintenance and superintendence of that, which it is its duty, and its glory to hold, and to watch over – the balance of power throughout the Christian World. Secondly, it brings to light what, under the most discouraging appearances, I always reckoned on; that with its ancient physical force, not only unimpaired, but augmented, its ancient spirit is still alive in the British nation. It proves, that for their application there is a spirit equal to the resources, for its energy above them. It proves that there exists, though not always visible, a spirit which never fails to come forth whenever it is invoked; a spirit which will give no equivocal response, but such as will hearten the timidity, and fix the resolution of hesitating prudence; a spirit which will be ready to perform all the tasks that shall be imposed upon it by public honour. Thirdly, the loan displays an abundant confidence in his Majesty's Government,

---

43 *enemies of all tranquillity*: France and her allies, thus figuring France as the aggressors in the war.
44 *ne te quaesiveris extra*: 'do not look outside yourself' (Latin).

as administered by his present servants, in the prosecution of a war which the people consider, not as a war made on the suggestion of Ministers, and to answer the purposes of the ambition or pride of statesmen, but as a war of their own, and in defence of that very property which they expend for its support; a war for that order of things, from which every thing valuable that they possess is derived, and in which order alone it can possibly be maintained. [...]

After all, it is a great mistake to imagine, as too commonly, almost indeed generally, it is imagined, that the public borrower and the private lender, are two adverse parties with different and contending interests: and that what is given to the one, is wholly taken from the other. Constituted as our system of finance and taxation is, the interests of the contracting parties cannot be well separated, whatever they may reciprocally intend. He who is the hard lender of to-day, to-morrow is the generous contributor to his own payment. [...]

[Burke then considers the claim that higher taxation has led to economic stagna-
tion, and that the country will not be able support the even higher taxation necessitated by increased state borrowing. Through a quantitative analysis he attempts
to show that neither the labouring nor the higher classes have suffered as a result
of the economic exigencies of the war; and that trade in imported, mostly luxury,
commodities is up. He ends with a description of the theatres as symbols of the
strength of the nation.]

If then the real state of this nation is such as I have described, and I am only apprehensive, that you may think, I have taken too much pains to exclude all doubt on this question; if no class is lessened in its numbers, or in its stock, or in its conveniencies, or even its luxuries; if they build as many habitations, and as elegant and as commodious as ever, and furnish them with every chargeable decoration, and every prodigality of ingenious invention, that can be thought of by those who encumber their necessities with superfluous accommodation; if they are as numerously attended; if their equipages are as splendid; if they regale at every table with as much or more variety of plenty than ever; if they are clad in as expensive and changeful a diversity according to the their tastes and modes; if they are not deterred from the pleasures of the field by the charges, which the Government has widely turned from the culture to the sports of the field; if the theatres are as rich and as well filled and greater, and at a higher price than ever; (and, what is more important than all) if it is plain from the treasures which are spread over the soil, or confided to the winds and the seas, that there are as many who are indulgent to their propensities of parsimony, as others to their voluptuous desires, and that the pecuniary capital grows undi-minishing;[45] on what ground are we authorized to say, that a nation, gambol-ling in a sea of superfluity, is undone by want? With what face can we pretend,

---

45 *Many [...] undiminishing*: Burke would appear to have in mind Adam Smith's preference for
    parsimony over prodigality in the accumulation of capital.

that they who have not denied any one gratification to any one appetite, have a right to please poverty in order to famish their virtues, and to put their duties on short allowance? That they are to take the law from an imperious enemy, and can contribute no longer to the honour of their king, to the support of the independence of their country, so the salvation of that Europe, which, if it falls, must crush them with its gigantic ruins? How can they affect to sweat, and stagger, and groan under their burdens, to whom the mines of Newfoundland, richer than those of Mexico and Peru, are now thrown in as a make-weight in the scale of their exorbitant opulence? How can they faint, and creep, and cringe, and prostrate themselves at the footstool of ambition and crime, who, during a short though violent struggle, which they have never supported with the energy of men, have amassed more to their annual accumulation, than all the well-husbanded capital, that enabled their ancestors, by long, and doubtful, and obstinate conflicts, to protect, and liberate, and vindicate the civilized world? But I do not accuse the people of England. As to the great majority of them, they have done whatever in their several ranks, and conditions, and descriptions, was required of them by their relative functions in society; and from those the great mass of mankind cannot depart, without the subversion of public order. They look up to that Government, which they obey that they may be protected. They ask to be led and directed, by those rulers, whom Providence and the laws of their country have set over them, to the attainment of their own safety, and welfare, and honour. They have again delegated the greatest trust, which they have to bestow, to those faithful representatives who have made their true voice heard against the disturbers and destroyers of Europe. They suffered, with unapproving acquiescence, solicitations to an unjust and usurping Power, whom they did not provoke, and whose hostile menaces they did not dread. When the exigencies of the public service could only be met by their voluntary zeal, they started forth with an ardour, which outstripped the desires of those, who had injured them by doubting, whether it might not be necessary to have recourse to compulsion. They have, in all things, reposed an enduring, but not an unreflecting confidence. That confidence demands a full return. It fixes a responsibility on the Ministers entire and undivided. The people stand acquitted, if the war is not carried on in a manner suited to its objects. If the public safety suffers any detriment, they are to answer it, and they alone. Its armies, its navies, are given to them without stint or restriction. Its treasures are poured out at their feet. Its constancy is ready to second in all their efforts. They are not to fear a responsibility for acts of manly adventure. The responsibility which they are to dread, is, lest they should show themselves unequal to the expectation of a brave people. The more doubtful may be the constitutional and economical questions, upon which they have received so marked a support, the more loudly they are called upon to support this great war, for the success of which their country is willing to supersede considerations of no slight importance. Where I speak of responsibility, I do not mean to exclude the species of it, which the legal powers of the country have a right finally to exact from those who abuse a public trust; but high as this is, there is a responsibility which attaches on them, from which the whole legitimate power of the kingdom cannot absolve them; there is a responsibility to conscience and to glory; a responsibility to the existing world, and to that posterity, which men of their eminence cannot avoid for glory or for shame; a responsibility to a tribunal, at which, not only Ministers, but Kings and Parliaments, but Nations themselves, must one day answer.

2.9   J. R. McCulloch, *A Discourse on Political Economy; Containing an Outline of a Course of Lectures on the Principles and Doctrines of that Science* (Edinburgh, 1824), pp. 2–5, 17–19, 98–100.

This extract, and the following one by Piercy Ravenstone, present contrasting views of the new science of 'Political Economy' that had constituted itself during the first two decades of the nineteenth century, under the influence first of Adam Smith, then of Thomas Malthus and David Ricardo. It is noteworthy that, in 1750, David Hume had no name for this field of study, and had to refer to his economics essays with the awkward term 'discourses on commerce, luxury, money, interest, &C'; *he also had to be suitably defensive about the intellectual propriety of such a topic. As the McCulloch extract shows, by the 1820s 'political economy' no longer had to be defined, and ambitious claims could be made for its position as the most important of human sciences.*

John Ramsay McCulloch (1789–1864) was an influential practitioner and more especially teacher of Political Economy; the Discourse on Political Economy *is a published version of lectures he was delivering to students at Edinburgh and London at the time. In the introductory lecture, from which passages are extracted here, McCulloch endows wealth and the desire to acquire it with near-magical powers, claiming they are 'almost omnipotent'; apart from providing the necessities of life, they stimulate individuals to greater attainment in the Arts as well as commerce, they raise civilisations like Venice and Holland from the sea, share the produce of the world between nations, and bind competing nations together for commercial advantage. In commerce, then, people come to a realisation of lack, and strive to replenish it, two experiential processes of the sublime. None of this is particularly new, and had been pointed out by any number of eighteenth-century thinkers. What is perhaps new is the confidence with which McCulloch assesses Political Economy's role in making these things happen. There is 'astonishment' that such an object of knowledge has hitherto not been considered worthy of study, as contrasted with subjects like Astronomy, given that Political Economy is seen as the key to understanding how best to facilitate the kind of perpetual improvement that commerce can bring about. The province of Political Economy is, in McCulloch's hands, a constantly expanding one, which in time will provide, 'the means of giv-ing a satisfactory solution of almost all the important problems in the science of wealth' and will 'ensure the continued advancement of the society in the career of improvement'. A grand project, then, but one that is required by the transcendent claims of economic progress, and one that looks sublimely forward to the solutions to be provided in the future.*

The consumption of wealth is indispensable to existence; but the eternal law of Providence has decreed that wealth can only be procured by industry – that man must earn his bread by the sweat of his brow. This twofold necessity renders the production of wealth a constant and principal object of the exertions of the vast majority of the human race; has subdued the natural aversion of man from labour; given activity to indolence; and armed the patient hand of industry with zeal to undertake, and patience to overcome, the most irksome and disagreeable tasks.

When wealth is thus necessary, when the desire to acquire is sufficient to induce us to submit to the greatest privations, the science which teaches the means by which its acquisition may be most effectually promoted – by which we may be enabled to obtain the greatest possible amount of wealth with the least possible difficulty – must certainly deserve to be carefully studied and meditated. There is no class of persons to whom this knowledge can be considered as either extrinsic or superfluous. The prices of all sorts of commodities – the profits of the manufacturer and merchant – rent of the landlord – the wages of the day-labourer – and the incidence and effect of taxes and regulations, all depend on principles which Political Economy can alone ascertain and elucidate.

Neither is the acquisition of wealth necessary only because it affords the means of subsistence: without it we should never be able to cultivate and improve our higher and nobler faculties. Where wealth has not been amassed, the mind being constantly occupied in providing for the immediate wants of the body, no time is left for culture; and the views, sentiments, and feelings of the people, become alike contracted, selfish and illiberal. The possession of a decent competence, or the being able to indulge in other pursuits than those which directly tend to satisfy our animal wants and desires, is necessary to soften the selfish passions; to improve the moral and intellectual character, and to ensure any considerable proficiency in liberal studies and pursuits. And hence, the acquisition of wealth is not desirable merely as the means of procuring immediate and direct gratifications, but as being indispensably necessary to the advancement of society in civilization and refine-ment. Without the tranquillity and leisure afforded by the possession of accumu-lated wealth, those speculative and elegant studies which expand and enlarge our views, purify our taste, and lift us higher in the scale of being, can never be success-fully prosecuted. A poor people are never refined, nor a rich people ever barba-rous. It is impossible to name a single nation which has made any distinguished figure either in philosophy or the fine arts, without having been at the same time celebrated for its wealth. The age of Pericles and Phidias[46] was the flourishing age

---

46 *Pericles*: Athenian statesman (c.495–429 BC) during the city's 'Golden Age', who used Athens' wealth to promote learning and the Arts; *Phidias*: sculptor (c. 480–430 BC), patronised by Pericles.

of Grecian, as the age of Petrarch and Raphael[47] was of Italian commerce. The influence of wealth is, in this respect, almost omnipotent. It raised Venice from the bosom of the deep, and made the desert and sandy islands on which she is built, and the unhealthy swamps of Holland, the favoured abodes of literature, science, and art. The number and eminence of our philosophers, poets, scholars and artists, have ever increased proportionally to the increase of the public wealth, or to the means of rewarding and honouring their labours.

The possession of wealth being thus indispensable to individual existence and comfort, and to the advancement of nations in civilization, it may justly excite astonishment, that so few efforts should have been made to investigate its sources; and that the study of Political Economy is not even yet considered as forming a principal part in a comprehensive system of education. A variety of circumstances might be mentioned, as occasioning the unmerited neglect of this science; but of these the institution of *domestic slavery* in the ancient world, and the darkness of the period when the plan of education in the universities of modern Europe was first formed, seem to have had the greatest influence.

[*McCulloch reviews the prejudices against industry and its study from Greece to the Middle Ages*]

To arrive at a true knowledge of the laws regulating the production, distribution, and consumption of wealth, the economist must draw his materials from a very wide surface. He should study man in every different situation – he should have recourse to the history of society, arts, commerce and civilization – to the works of philosophers and travellers – to every thing, in short, that can throw light on the causes which accelerate or retard the progress of civilization: He should mark the changes which have taken place in the fortunes and condition of the human race in different regions and ages of the world: He should trace the rise, progress and decline of industry: And, above all, he should carefully analyse and compare the effects of different institutions and regulations, and discriminate the various circumstances wherein an advancing and declining society differ from each other. Such investigations, by disclosing the real causes of national opulence and refinement, and of poverty and degradation, furnish the economist with the means of giving a satisfactory solution of almost all the important problems in the science of wealth, and of devising a scheme of public administration calculated to ensure the continued advancement of the society in the career of improvement.

Such inquiries cannot fail to excite the deepest interest in every ingenuous mind. The laws by which the motions of the celestial bodies are regulated, and over which man cannot exercise the smallest influence or control, are

47 *Petrarch*: Francesco Petrarca (1304–74), Italian poet and scholar; *Raphael*: Raffaello Sanzio (1483–1520), Italian artist.

yet universally allowed to be noble and rational objects of study. But the laws which regulate the movements of human society – which cause one people to advance in opulence and refinement, at the same time that another is sinking into the abyss of poverty and barbarism – have an infinitely stronger claim on our attention; both because they relate to objects which exercise a direct influence over human happiness, and because their effects may be, and in fact are, continually modified by human interference. National prosperity does not depend nearly so much on advantageous situation, salubrity of climate, or fertility of soil, as on the adoption of measures fitted to excite the inventive powers of genius, and to give perseverance and activity to industry. The establishment of a wise system of public economy can compensate for every other deficiency: It can render regions naturally inhospitable, barren and unproductive, the comfortable abodes of an elegant and refined, a crowded and wealthy population; but where it is wanting, the best gifts of nature are of no value; and countries possessed of the greatest capacities of improvement, and abounding in all the materials necessary for the production of wealth, with difficulty furnish a miserable subsistence to hordes distinguished only by their ignorance, barbarism, and wretchedness. [...]

This pursuit of individual advantage is admirably connected with the good of the whole. By stimulating industry, rewarding ingenuity, and by using the most efficaciously the particular powers bestowed by nature, commerce distributes labour most effectively and most economically; while, by increasing the general mass of necessary and useful products, it diffuses the general opulence, and binds together the universal society of nations by the common and powerful ties of mutual interest and reciprocal obligation. Commerce has enabled each particular state to profit by the inventions and discoveries of every other state. It has given us new tastes and new appetites, and it has also given us the means and the desire of gratifying them. The progress of domestic industry has been accelerated by the competition of foreigners. Commerce has either entirely removed, or greatly weakened, a host of the most unworthy prejudices. It has shown, that nothing can be more illiberal, irrational, and absurd, than that dread of the progress of others in wealth and civilization that was once so prevalent, and it has shown that the true glory and real interest of each particular people will be more certainly advanced by emulating and outstripping each other in the career of science and civilization, than by labouring to attain a barren pre-eminence in the bloody and destructive art of war.

2.10 Piercy Ravenstone (pseud.), *Thoughts on the Funding System and its Effects* (London, 1824), pp. 1–9, 15–17, 25–7.

In the early 1820s an author whose true identity is still unclear published two extraordinary critiques of the new science of Political Economy and the economic realities it sought to describe and defend. A Few Doubts as to the Correctness of Some Opinions Generally Entertained on the Subjects of Population and Political Economy *was published in 1821, followed by* Thoughts on the Funding System and its Effects *(1824). The main argument of* Thoughts on the Funding System *is that the 'funding system' as developed in Britain in the eighteenth century – that is to say, paying for government expenditure and issuing currency by taking out loans through the Bank of England – puts wealth and hence power firmly in the hands of the financiers who provide the loans, because money paid in taxes will end up paying the interest they charge. Capital creates a new kind of serfdom, with an entire population effectively forced to pay a 'tribute' to a small number of capitalists; hence the funding system is a new way of extracting surplus value from the labourer. In advancing this argument, Ravenstone makes the point that, while the political economists explicitly deplore war and the national debt thereby accrued, the growth of the funds in the eighteenth century in fact aided the interests of commerce because it allowed the pool of capital to grow; his analysis, but not his evaluation, thus has more in common with that of Thomas Mortimer than with Hume, Smith or Ricardo.*

Ravenstone attacks Political Economy in two main ways that are almost identical to the two strands of McCulloch's praise for it. Firstly, Ravenstone deplores the increasing complexity of the social and economic system, which brings individuals more often into conflict, and has given rise to a 'a new species of property' – capital held in funds – that has 'no tangible being'. This imaginary wealth – imaginary because based on credit and beliefs about future accumulation – changed the way people thought about wealth, because the rapid growth that resulted appeared to be perpetual and boundless. Secondly, the body of knowledge known as Political Economy developed as an attempt to understand and advance this accumulation, and, because born out of this economic climate, became an abstract, mysterious discipline that laid great claim to scienticity but in fact was deliberately obscure in order to dupe the gullible, and become the intellectual support for oppression. In significant ways, the debate about Political Economy being presented here is a debate about aesthetic preferences. McCulloch is impressed by the acceleration of growth, ever more complex systems of trade and manufacture, and the ability to imagine sublime greatness in the future, while Ravenstone prefers the beautiful simplicity of former economic systems and the tangibility of the material products of labour. Equally, McCulloch advocates the growing authority and potentially awesome powers of Political Economy as a discipline, while Ravenstone fears its abstraction and obscurity. Taken together these two texts demonstrate how two different attitudes to modern economic 'progress' turn on contrasting understandings of the aesthetics of the sublime.

The events of the last hundred years, the changes they have wrought in the mode of existence of every nation of Europe, and the complexity they have introduced into all the relations of society, have given to the science of political economy an importance to which it could never before pretend. As the classes into which nations are divided have been multiplied, as the space allotted to the motions of each individual have been more circumscribed, their different interests have brought men more frequently into collision, and it has required no small share of skill to state and regulate the pretensions of each. It is not, therefore, to be wondered at, however much it may be matter of regret, that in discussions so intricate and often so perplexed, the true principles should be lost sight of on which society is formed, and which alone, by the general happiness they produce, can make amends for its laws and restrictions, and the abridgment of natural freedom that it necessarily brings in its train. [...]

In a country where land is the only property, and its rents and the profits which arise from their expenditure the only source of revenue, as there can be no mystery, as there is no room for contrivance, men are not very solicitous to inquire into the causes of the wealth of nations, nor into the best manner of disposing of their savings. As they see that all productions are of a perishable nature, and have no value but what they derive from consumption, [...] they do not see how it is possible for accumulation to take place. Where there is no fund in which savings can be laid up, to save seems in reality to waste. What is not consumed can be thrown away. True wisdom, they think, and they think rightly, can only exist in well-regulated enjoyment: their industry can never be well employed but when it adds to their comforts.

Such is necessarily the state of every people who have created no public debt: such was the condition of all the nations of Europe before their governments had thought of the ingenious expedient of mortgaging the public revenues. They lived day to day, enjoying the good whilst they had it, and opposing nothing to extraordinary difficulties when they came but extraordinary privations. [...]

The funding system, by creating a new and undefinable species of property, which neither held of the land nor yet of the industry of the country, which had no local existence, no tangible being, not only overthrew the whole scheme of society, but gave a new turn to men's ideas. No bounds could be assigned to a nation's wealth when new fortunes might be created without taking away from those that already existed. The power of accumulation bestowed on individuals appeared to be conferred to the whole community. Where wealth grew with such rapidity, there seemed no difficulty in anticipating its growth, and supplying the wants of today with the means of to-morrow. The scheme could not be but agreeable to all the stirring spirits to whom it opened the road to fortune. Others without any interest were led away with the charm of words. The borrowing from posterity, as it was called, was so happy an expression, it was so full of vagueness and uncertainty, that it could not but generate confusion, and give birth to a thousand absurdities in reasoning. When men had once persuaded themselves that they could spend immediately what was to exist hereafter, they could have no difficulty in believing that they could save what had already ceased to exist. One false consequence led to another. Though they were usually adventurers who grew rich by these revolutions of fortune, yet as men saw capital everywhere fastening on industry to share in the produce of its labour, they concluded that it was capital that gave all its activity to industry. Though they saw fortunes raised during wars, which were again dissipated in times of peace, they chose, in deference to the common sense of mankind, but in defiance of their own principles, to consider war as a destroyer of capital, which could only be accumulated by the arts of peace.[48]

These reasonings proceeding from false premises, as they could not fail to involve in a labyrinth of perplexities all those who had no other guide than common sense, soon raised political economy to the rank of a science. From that moment, as might be expected, every day added to the darkness with which it was surrounded, every new treatise only sunk it deeper in obscurity. They who though uninitiated in its mysteries have been accustomed to watch the progress of science, cannot but be aware how readily learned men in their inquiries content themselves with words, and what a natural abhorrence they have of common sense. As their chief object is to distinguish themselves from the great herd of men who are busied with things, they delight in abstractions, they choose words for their province. Certain cabalistical[49] terms are introduced into the sciences, which are to silence all inquiries. It is not expected that the adept should understand them, it is enough that he can repeat them. No useful invention owes its birth to science; it seems the business of learned men to disguise under hard names, and to render obscure the simple discoveries of genius. [...]

[Political economy] seems to treat of the every-day occurrences of life; its terms are in common use; its language is that which is familiar in the world. The man who has spent all his days in getting and spending money easily fancies himself competent to decide on the nature of wealth and its consumption. He seems to be only generalizing his own experience, and embodying his own reflections. In an age of literary pretension, where every man is obliged, at least in appearance, to know something, political economy has accordingly become the study of all those who felt themselves unequal to other pursuits. It was the peaceful province of acrostic[50] land where they whose courage cowered before higher enterprise might yet hope to acquire a comfortable renown. No fiery dragons were placed to guard its treasures – no fearful monsters rendered dangerous their approach; there was nothing in the adventure to dishearten the most recreant knight.

The wonderful has irresistible charms for ignorance. Narrow minds cannot conceive the simplicity of true knowledge; nothing seems to them worth knowing that is not strange and mysterious. [...] Learned words with them sanctify

---

48 *Though [...] peace*: Ravenstone's argument is that, despite the fact that the cycle of war and peace during the eighteenth century had given rise to and perpetuated the funding system (as illustrated by Thomas Mortimer), political economists dishonestly denied this reality and generally bemoaned the national debt; Ravenstone returns to this subject later.

49 *cabalistic*: secret, partisan or conspiratorial.

50 *acrostic*: a short poem in which there is an encoded meaning; usually, the first letters of each line spell a significant word. Ravenstone's meaning appears to be that political economy is something of a trivial plaything or riddle for the weak-minded. Both the terms 'cabalistic' and 'acrostic' are Hebraic in origin, and refer originally to secret Jewish practices, suggesting perhaps a hint of anti-Semitism in the critique political economy.

the greatest absurdities; they readily yield their assent to propositions, when veiled under the garb of science, which in their natural state would stagger their belief. [...]

Political economy thus treated became perverted in all her principles. She was made the close ally of self-interest and corruption; it was in the armoury of her terms that tyranny and oppression found their deadliest weapons. She has oftener been called in as an auxiliary, when abuses were to be accounted for and justified than when their origin was to be detected and their remedy suggested. The most oppressive governments have been those which have most earnestly cultivated this science, for it has tended to give stability to misrule, by lending it the support of system, and shrouding its deformities under the semblance of wisdom. The doctrine of capital and its effects is indeed the most injurious to society that ever was broached. To teach that the wealth and power of a nation depend on its capital, is to make industry ancillary to riches, and to make men subservient to property. Where such a system is allowed to prevail, the greater part of the people must be, under whatever name disguised, *adscripti glebae*.[51] Their situation will be without comfort and hope, they will be doomed to toil, not for their own benefit, but for that of their masters. All rights will belong to the rich, all duties will be left to the poor. The people will be made to bow their necks beneath the yoke of the harshest rules, the aristocracy of wealth. [...]

As this doctrine of capital and the wonderful effects of accumulation are the basis of all modern political economy, as it is the key-stone which holds all the discordant parts of the funding system, it will not be a waste of time to examine it in detail. If it can be shown that it is not possible for a nation either to save or to anticipate its revenues; if it can be shown that all that is produced must be consumed at the very time of production, and that nothing can be consumed till it has first been produced; the whole merits and demerits of the funding system will stand confessed before us. [...]

Property is in reality but a rent charge on productive Industry. It cannot increase the quantity of industry, for the very condition of its existence is a superabundance of produce. As consumption is the purpose for which it is created, to that alone it can be devoted. As it increases with every increase of population and every improvement in the management of labour, it is continually outgrowing the natural wants of those to whom providence has assigned the right of living in idleness on the labours of their fellow creatures. The lord of boundless empires cannot in his own person consume more than the poorest of his subjects. The same quantity of food will satisfy his hunger; he does not require more clothing to protect him from the inclemency of the weather. He is compelled, therefore, to imagine artificial wants, to hire others to help in consuming his superfluities. This is the origin of all manufactures: they owe their existence to the necessity which the rich feel of consuming by the means

---

51 *adscripti glebae*: (Latin) 'tied to the land', that is, serfs. The dominance of capital thus creates a new kind of serfdom.

of others that part of the produce of the earth which is too much for their own consumption; none of them contribute to the existence of man, they are only conversant with his artificial wants. They cannot add to the wealth of a people, they only furnish easier means of expenditure. Their amount is dependent on the success of productive industry. They are the superfluities of the cultivator which reward the manufacturer and enable him to live. If each man's labour were but enough to procure his own food, there could be no property, and no part of a people's industry could be turned away to work for the wants of the imagination. In every case, however, accumulation is equally impossible. As consumption is the only purpose of production, it necessarily regulates its amount, for it gives it all its value. The labour that is employed on useless things is entirely thrown away. They who are so occupied might as well be idle; they have in reality only been busy about nothing. Houses that there were none to inhabit would only encumber the earth: corn that there were none to eat, clothes that there were none to wear, would soon become the prey of the weevil and the moth. Instead of adding to men's wealth, they would only increase their plagues. To hoard is the wisdom of a jackdaw; to multiply his enjoyments, that of a reasonable creature.

But whilst the uselessness of saving what perishes in the moment of accu-mulation be admitted, there will be those who, whilst they allow the inability of trade and manufactures to increase a nation's property, will contend that there are other objects of a less perishable nature, whose use is of all times and all countries; that hoards of the precious metals may be made to any amount without losing any of their value. This scheme is, however, as bottomless as the other. The government of a state may indeed place itself in the situation of the idle men; by drawing to itself all the revenues of the country it may annihilate their existence; it may determine that all who are not occupied with the industry of production shall be employed in working for gold or silver, either directly, or if the country has no mines, in producing objects that may be exchanged with those nations that have. It is clear that a country directing all its industry to such a purpose might amass a treasure of almost any conceivable magnitude. Its amount might render trifling even Dr. Price's most visionary conceptions.[52] Nor would the industry of the country receive any check whilst this abstraction of capital was going forward. Every man would be employed either in producing the necessaries of life or the means of purchasing gold and silver. The demand of the state would supply the want of individual consumption: the riches of the nation would make up for the poverty of private persons. As there would be no idle men, as the industry of all would be in constant activity, the amount of production would greatly exceed that of other nations where a large portion of the people are only employed in consumption, and its wealth, as it would not be consumed, would become almost boundless. But such is the fallacy of all human

---

52 *Dr. Price's [...] conceptions*: meaning Price's writing on the astonishing effects of compound interest, which had become well known by this time (see Note 30 above).

reasoning, that this accumulation, which on the principles of political economy should make a nation great and powerful, would only deprive the people of all comforts without adding to the power of the state. All this excess of industry would be only labour lost. Gold and silver, even more than other objects, as they administer only to the artificial wants of men, have but a conventional value. As they cannot themselves be applied to any useful purpose, their worth depends entirely on the means which people have of indulging in fancies. So long as they are only produced in proportion to the artificial wants of society, their value is estimated by the labour it has cost to procure them. The gold which it has taken ten days' labour to raise will exchange against the cloth which it has occupied the weaver ten days to make. Increase, however, the precious metals beyond what the state of society demands, and they become of no more value than stones. None will give the necessaries of life for a superabundance of super-fluities. A country thus overloaded with treasure would be in the situation of a besieged town, where the inhabitants may be dying of hunger whilst every bank is overflowing with gold and silver. An enormous hoard in the hour of danger would be found wholly inoperative to defend a country. As soon as it came to be used, it would destroy its own value. As all the surplus industry of the country will have been employed in its acquisition, there will be nothing against which it can exchange. Rub off the high polish which the imagination of avarice gives to the precious metals, and they shew but dross. To hoard them up serves but, like all other accumulation, to display their worthlessness [...]

Whoever on the principles of modern political economy examines the history of every national debt, the circumstances under which it has been created, and the manner in which it has grown, cannot but be forcibly struck with some strange inconsistencies. The conclusions are always at variance with the principles. Nothing ever happens as we are taught to expect it. Peace is supposed to be the time when capital increases with most rapidity; war is always looked on as destructive of its growth. Yet it is always at the breaking out of hostilities, when the hoards of peace are yet entire, when capital is looking in vain for employment, that a government finds the greatest difficulty in making a loan. The more it spends, the more it is supposed to have wasted the national resources, the more easily it borrows. Its credit rises with its extravagance.[53] The means of the nation grow the fastest which are destroyed with most rapidity. What was impossible to the wealth of a people, becomes easy to their poverty. In the last year of the last war, after all the exhaustion of twenty years of boundless extravagance, sixty millions were borrowed with greater ease than six in the first. Whatever the government wanted was always found; the means of the lender grew in exact proportion to the borrower's wants. To unravel

---

53 *Its ... extravagance*: As many noted during the eighteenth century, funding of the national debt was structured by a cycle of low-price stock at high rates of interest during war (making it easy for the government to borrow), and high-price stock at low rates of interest during peace. Thomas Mortimer illustrates how this provided investment opportunities and formed an apparently virtuous cycle.

this mystery, so puzzling to science, will not be difficult to common sense. If, instead of spinning theories, we attend to facts, we shall see that the expenditure always preceded the loan; that the nation in borrowing only changed the description of debts which had been already contracted; that the sum borrowed did not on an average exceed one third of what was spent; that whenever, as in the year 1797, it was attempted to exceed this proportion, so great distress was immediately felt by the monied men that when, as in that year, the contractors were called on to advance more than their profits, they were only enabled to do it by persuading the bank to exchange its bullion for their anticipation of future gains, an exchange which caused the failure of that establishment;[54] that the price of every article for the service of the government was greatly enhanced; that enormous fortunes were made by all those who in any way were concerned in supplying its wants. If we weigh all these circumstances carefully, we are irresistibly brought to the conclusion, that the real expenses of the war were, as they must always be, really defrayed by the funds raised from taxes, and that the stock created went only to satisfy the gains of the contractors, and the jobs and peculation[55] which so profusely attended the expense of the war. We shall be forced to conclude, what indeed reasoning would equally lead us to expect that they were only imaginary debts, that were or could be satisfied with an imaginary payment.

2.11   Thomas De Quincey, *Suspiria de Profundis, being a Sequel to the Confessions of an English Opium Eater,* in *Blackwood's Edinburgh Magazine* 57 (April 1845), pp. 497–501.

Suspiria de Profundis *('Sighs from the deep') is the second part in an autobiographical trilogy, of which the first and best known is* Confessions of an English Opium Eater *(1821–2). A major theme of these works is how events early in De Quincey's life impact upon adulthood, in a way that is analogous to, but also sharply different from, Wordsworth's practice in* The Prelude. *In De Quincey's autobiographical writing, it is the traumas of youth, and resultant disorders and neuroses that are brought to the fore. The passage extracted below serves as a good example of this; he was in debt, sometimes seriously so, for most of his adult life, and he finds an incident from his childhood when his problematic psychological relationship with money begins. The story of the small debt to a bookseller becomes the subject of a paranoid fantasy when De Quincey is told of 'a general history of navigation' whose volumes might grow to 15,000, or indeed an infinite number, given the extent of the seas and*

---

54 *failure of that establishment*: in 1797 there had been a run on the Bank of England because of fears about the level of debt unfunded by taxation; the crisis was eased when Pitt persuaded Parliament to introduce new taxes.

55 *peculation*: appropriation of public funds by government officials, with a strong implication of dishonest misappropriation.

possible voyages that could be made on them. Because of the contemporary practice of
subscribing to books before they had been released, the young boy develops a fantasy
of numberless cartloads of books being delivered, with demands for payment with
menaces from the bookseller. In an analogy typical of De Quincey, the accrual of
debt, which increases geometrically with every new charge of interest that is made,
is compared to the production of, and desire for knowledge, whose completion and
satisfaction are never possible. Hence the relationship between debt and knowledge
is a mode of the sublime, because of the ever-expanding magnitude of the object and
its belittling, shaming power over the subject. In a final analogy, De Quincey turns
his imagined public shaming in the matter of the debt to the bookseller, in a way
that is both shameful and glorious, into a transhistorical parable of sin, guilt and
punishment.

The new intercourse with my guardian,[56] and the changes of scene which it
naturally led to, were of use in weaning my mind from the mere disease which
threatened it in case I had been left any longer to my total solitude. But out
of these changes grew an incident which restored my grief, though in a more
troubled shape, and now for the first time associated with something like
remorse and deadly anxiety. I can safely say that this was my earliest trespass,
and perhaps a venial one – all things considered. Nobody ever discovered it; and
but for my own frankness it would not be known to this day. But that I could
not know; and for years, that is from seven or earlier up to ten, such was my
simplicity, that I lived in constant terror. This, though it revived my grief, did
me probably great service; because it was no longer a state of languishing desire
tending to torpor, but of feverish irritation and gnawing care that kept alive
the activity of my understanding. The case was this; – It had happened that
I had now, and commencing with my first introduction of Latin studies, a large
weekly allowance of pocket-money, too large for my age, but safely entrusted to
myself, who never spent or desired to spend one fraction of it upon anything
but books. But all proved too little for my colossal schemes. Had the Vatican,
the Bodleian, and the Bibliothèque du roi[57] been all emptied into one collection for my private gratification, little progress would have been made towards
content in this particular craving. Very soon I had run ahead of my allowance,
and was about three guineas deep in debt. There I paused; for deep anxiety now
began to oppress me as the course in which this mysterious (and indeed guilty)
current of debt would finally flow. For the present it was frozen up; but I had
some reason for thinking that Christmas thawed all debts whatsoever, and set
them in motion towards innumerable pockets. Now my debt would be thawed
with all the rest; and in what direction would it flow? There was no river to

---

56 *guardian*: effectively the young Thomas's tutor; his studies had been interrupted by the death of his
    sister Elizabeth in 1792, when De Quincey was seven; it is to grief over this death that De Quincey
    refers in the following sentence.
57 *Vatican, the Bodleian, and the Bibliothèque du roi*: Great library collections in Rome, Oxford and Paris
    respectively.

carry it off to sea; to somebody's pocket it would beyond a doubt make its way; and who was that somebody. This question haunted me forever. Christmas had come, Christmas had gone, and I heard nothing of the three guineas. But I was not easier for that. Far rather I would have heard of it; for this indefinite approach of a loitering catastrophe gnawed and fretted my feelings. No Grecian audience ever waited with more shuddering horror for the anagnorisis of the Oedipus,[58] than I for explosion of my debt. Had I been less ignorant, I should have proposed to mortgage my weekly allowance for the debt, or to form a sinking fund for redeeming it; for the weekly sum was nearly five per cent on the whole debt. But I had a mysterious awe of ever alluding to it. This arose from my want of some confidential friend; whilst my grief pointed continually to the remembrance – that so it had not always been. But was not the bookseller to blame in suffering a child scarcely seven years old to contract such a debt? Not in the least. He was both a rich man, who could not possibly care for my trifling custom, and notoriously an honourable man. Indeed the money which I myself spent every week in books, would reasonably have caused him to presume that so small a sum as three guineas might well be authorized by my family. He stood, however, on plainer ground. For my guardian, who was very indolent, (as people chose to call it,) that is, like his melancholy ward, spent all his time in reading, often enough would send me to the bookseller's with a written order for books. This was to prevent my forgetting. But when he found that such a thing as 'forgetting' in the case of a book, was wholly out of the question for me, the trouble of writing was dismissed. And thus I became factor-general[59] on the part of my guardian, both for his books, and for such as were wanted on my own account in the natural course of my education. My private 'little account' had therefore in fact flowed homewards at Christmas, not (as I anticipated) in the shape of an independent current, but as a little tributary rill that was lost in the waters of some important river. This I now know, but could not then have known with any certainty. So far, however, the affair would gradually have sunk out of my anxieties as time wore on.

[*De Quincey describes some of the multi-volume works to which he has subscribed.*]

But there was another work left more indefinite as to its ultimate extent, and which from its nature seemed to imply a wider range. It was a general history of navigation, supported by a vast body of voyages. Now, when I considered with myself what a huge thing the sea was, and that so many thousands of captains, commodores, admirals, were eternally running up and down it, and scoring lines upon the face so rankly, that in some of the main 'streets' and 'squares' (as one might call them) their tracks would blend into one undistinguishable blot, – I began to fear that such a work tended to infinity. What was little England to

---

58 *anagnorisis of the Oedipus*: revelations at the end of Sophocles' play *Oedipus Tyrannus*.
59 *factor-general*: mercantile agent or deputy.

the universal sea? And yet that went perhaps to fourscore parts. Not enduring the uncertainty that now besieged my tranquillity, I resolved to know the worst; and on a day ever memorable to me I went down to the bookseller's. [...] Never did human creature, with his heart palpitating at Delphi for the solution of some killing mystery, stand before the priestess of the oracle,[60] with lips that moved more sadly than mine, when now advancing to a smiling young man at the desk. His answer was to decide, though I could not exactly know that, whether for the next two years I was to have an hour of peace. He was a handsome, good-natured young man, but full of fun and frolic; and I dare say was amused with what must have seemed to him the absurd anxiety of my features. I described the work to him, and he understood me at once: how many volumes did he think it would extend to? There was a whimsical expression perhaps of drollery about his eyes, but which, unhappily, under my preconceptions, I translated into scorn, as he replied, – 'How many volumes? Oh! really I can't say, maybe a matter of 15,000, be the same more or less.' 'More?' I said in horror, altogether neglecting the contingency of 'less.' 'Why,' he said, 'we can't settle these things to a nicety. But considering the subject, (ay, that was the very thing which I myself considered,) 'I should say, there might be some trifle over, as suppose 400 or 500 volumes, be the same more or less.' What, then, here there might be supplements to supplements – the work might positively never end. On one pretence or another, if an author or publisher might add 500 volumes, he might add another round 15,000. Indeed it strikes one even now, that by the time the one-legged commodores and yellow admirals of that generation had exhausted their long yarns, another generation would have grown another crop of the same gallant spinners. I asked no more, but slunk out of the shop, and never again entered it with cheerfulness, or propounded any frank questions as heretofore. For I was now seriously afraid of pointing attention to myself as one that, by having purchased some numbers and obtained others on credit, had silently contracted an engagement to take all the rest, though they should stretch to the crack of doom. Certainly I had never heard of a work stretching to 15,000 volumes; but still there was no natural impossibility that it should; and if, in any case, in none so reasonably as one upon the inexhaustible sea. Besides, any slight mistake as to the letter of the number, could not affect the horror of the final prospect. I saw by the imprint, and I heard, that this vast work emanated from London, a vast centre of mystery to me, and the more so, as a thing unseen at any time by my eyes, and nearly 200 miles distant. I felt the fatal truth, that here was a ghostly cobweb radiating into all the provinces from the mighty metropolis. I secretly had trodden upon the outer circumference, had damaged or deranged the fine threads, – concealment or reparation there could be none. Slowly, perhaps, but surely, the vibration would travel back to London. The

---

60 *priestess of the oracle*: in the Oracle at Delphi, Apollo's prophecies were spoken by a priestess (known as the *Pythia*), who would fall into a trance-like state allowing the god to take possession of her spirit.

ancient spider that sat there at the centre would rush along the network through all latitudes and longitudes, until he found the responsible caitiff,[61] author so much mischief. Even, with less ignorance than mine, there was something to appal a child's imagination by which any elaborate work could disperse itself, could levy money, could put questions and get answers – all in profound silence, nay, even in darkness – searching every nook of town, and of every hamlet in so populous a kingdom. I had some dim terrors, also, connected with the Stationers' Company.[62] I had often observed them in popular works threatening unknown men with unknown chastisements, for offences equally unknown; nay, to myself, absolutely inconceivable. Could I be the mysterious criminal, pointed out, as it were, in prophecy? I figured the stationers, doubtless all powerful men, pulling at one rope, and my unhappy self hanging at the other end. But an image, which seems now even more ludicrous than the rest, at that time was the most connected with the revival of my grief. It occurred to my subtlety, that the Stationers' Company, or any other company, could not possibly demand the money until they had delivered the volumes. And they would have no pretence for not accomplishing this delivery in a civil manner. Unless I should turn out to be no customer at all, at present it was clear that I had a right to be considered a most excellent customer; one, in fact, who had given an order for fifteen thousand volumes. Then rose up before me this great opera-house 'scena' of the delivery. There would be a ring at the door. A waggoner in the front, with a bland voice, would ask for, 'a young gentleman who had given an order to their house.' Looking out, I should perceive a procession of carts and wagons, all advancing in measured movements; each in turn would present its rear, deliver its cargo of volumes, by shooting them, like a load of coals, on the lawn, and wheel off to the rear, by way of clearing the road for its successors. Then the impossibility of even asking the servants to cover with sheets, or counterpanes, or tablecloths, such a mountainous, such a "star-y-pointing"[63] record of my past offences lying in so conspicuous a situation! Men would not know my guilt merely, they would see it. But the reason why this form of the consequences, so much more than any other, stuck by my imagination was, that it connected itself with one of the Arabian nights which had particularly interested myself and my sister. It was that tale, where a young porter, having his ropes about his person, had stumbled into the special 'preserve' of some old magician.[64] He finds a beautiful lady imprisoned, to whom (and not without prospects of success) he recommends

---

61 *caitiff*: captive.
62 *Stationers' Company*: the Worshipful Company of Stationers, a livery company of the City of London, that protected the interests of booksellers, printers and related tradesmen.
63 *'star-y-pointing'*: Milton, 'On Shakespeare', l. 4.
64 *It was that tale [...] some old magician*: what follows is a version of the 'Tale of the Second Calender', possibly from *The Arabian Nights Entertainments* (London, 1792), i, pp. 82–90. The main differences are De Quincey's 'ventriloquised' defence of the porter's innocence, and that the 'porter' is in fact a prince disguised as a calender (i.e. one involved in the rolling process in paper or cloth production).

himself as a suitor, more in harmony with her years than a withered magician. At this crisis the magician returns. The young man bolts, and for that day successfully; but unluckily he leaves his ropes behind. Next morning he hears the magician, too honest by half, enquiring at the front door, with much expression of indolence, for the unfortunate young man who had lost his ropes in his own zenana.[65] Upon this story I used to amuse my sister, by ventriloquizing to the magician from the lips of the trembling young man – 'Oh, Mr Magician, these ropes cannot be mine! They are far too good. And one wouldn't like, you know, to rob some other poor young man. If you please, Mr Magician, I never had money enough to buy so beautiful a set of ropes.' But argument is thrown away upon a magician, and off he sets on his travels with the young porter – not forgetting to take the ropes along with him.

   Here now was the case, that had once seemed so impressive to me in a mere fiction from a far-distant age and land, literally reproduced in myself. For what did it matter whether a magician dunned one with old ropes for his engine of torture, or Stationers' Hall with 15,000 volumes, (in the rear of which there might also be ropes?) Should I have ventriloquized, would my sister have laughed, had either of us but guessed the possibility that I myself, and within one twelve months, and, alas! standing alone in the world as regarded confidential counsel, should repeat within my own inner experience the shadowy panic of the Bagdat intruder upon the privacy of magicians? It appeared, then, that I had been reading a legend concerning myself in the Arabian Nights. I had been contemplated in types a thousand years before on the banks of the Tigris. It was horror and grief that prompted that thought.

---

65 *zenana*: women's quarters in an Indian or Persian house; a harem.

3

Mind

As was the case with the study of political economy, the modern disciplines of psychiatry and psychology were in the process of being constituted during the period covered in this anthology (the term 'psychiatry' was coined in 1808 by the German doctor Johann Geil). Under the rubric of a new 'science of mind', these disciplines developed out of the enquiry into the relationship between thought and sense perception by philosophers like John Locke (1632–1704) and David Hume (1711–76), whose *Enquiry Concerning Human Understanding* (1748) called for a 'mental geography, or delineation of the distinct parts and powers of the mind' (I, viii). The discourse on the sublime was an important early component of this new 'geography' since the developing study of sublime effect was, in essence, the study of the interaction between the mind and the sublime object, or phenomenon. As the eighteenth century progresses, however, the relationship between the discourse on the sublime and the science of mind becomes more complex and multifaceted as writers across a range of genres and disciplines routinely use the tropes of the sublime to represent the 'parts and powers' of the mind, to borrow Hume's phrase. Hence, not only does the discourse on the sublime become part of the terminology of the new science of mind, but that science, in turn, contributes to the discourse on the sublime by generating a new model of the mind as sublime spectacle.

This process of reciprocal formation is particularly visible in four distinct lines of enquiry within the science of mind. The first and earliest of these is the study of 'genius': theorists like Young and Duff rely upon the language of the sublime to characterise genius, affirming not only that genius is conversant with and capable of producing sublime effect, but also configuring genius itself as an example of the sublime. A similar relationship can be perceived in the second significant locus of interaction between the discourse on the sublime and the science of mind: discussions of mental illness. The study of mental illness underwent a paradigm shift during the eighteenth century, as the traditional emphasis on physiological causes (imbalance of the four humours) and associated remedies (purging, bleeding, etc.) gave way to a new moral or psychological approach to diagnosis and treatment, an approach heralded by William Battie's seminal *Treatise on Madness* (1758), which links mental illness to a deluded imagination.[1]

---

1 See, for example, Roy Porter, *Mind forg'd manacles: A History of Madness in England from the Restoration to the Regency* (London: Athlone, 1987).

But despite this new scientific approach, with its emphasis on rational analysis, accounts of mental illness continue to describe both the asylum and the individual patient, in terms taken directly from the discourse on the sublime, as a scene of horror. Likewise, many influential figures involved in the treatment of the mentally ill note precisely the difficulty of introducing rational, empirical method to such an ostensibly chaotic environment as the asylum or the mind of a mentally ill patient; even for a skilled physician like Philippe Pinel, the study of mental illness involves, at least in part, a dizzying confrontation with the sublime.

The third significant locus of interaction between the science of mind and the discourse on the sublime concerns the impressive claims made for the science of mind by some of its practitioners. In his *Enquiry Concerning Human Understanding*, for example, Hume suggests that the science of mind, 'if cultivated with care', could eventually 'discover, at least in some degree, the secret springs and principles, by which the human mind is actuated in its operations' (I, ix). Following Hume's hint, a number of writers imagine that the systematic examination of one's own mental processes is capable of granting a sublime intellectual independence from traditional forms of knowledge and authority, effectively configuring the practice of the science of mind as a revolutionary process which breaks down the barriers of custom and authority. But for others, such intense self-examination is a deeply traumatic process, a terrifying confrontation with the limitations and uncertainties of human knowledge. Still others represent this intellectual independence as a threatening form of egotism, grounded in a materialist rejection of traditional morality, linking it to the seductive sublimity of figures like Satan and Napoleon. As with the study of mental illness, then, the tropes of the sublime are routinely used to figure the praxis, achievements and hazards of the science of mind.

The final locus of interaction between the science of mind and the discourse on the sublime which we consider here involves the use of imagery drawn from the discourse on the natural sublime to describe both the mind itself and various mental processes. In his *Enquiry Concerning Human Understanding*, Hume had envisaged the new science of mind as a 'mental geography' (I, viii). In practice, however, while phrenologists like Gall and Spurzheim did attempt to produce quasi-scientific 'maps' of the mind, numerous descriptions eschewed the sober, scientific language of a 'geography' in favour of images of mountains and abysses, torrents and storms, palaces and ruins. Wordsworth's 'Prospectus' to *The Recluse* is only one example of the manner in which 'the mind of man' emerges from these descriptions less as a discrete object of study than as a sublime *terra incognita*, comparable, in many respects, to the 'exotic' territories encountered by many European travellers and explorers. Once again, then, the discourse on the sublime and the science of mind are inextricably intertwined: the tropes of the sublime become a vital part of the vocabulary of the science of mind, while that science generates a new image of the mind as sublime spectacle.

3.1 Edward Young, *Conjectures on Original Composition*, 2nd edition (London, 1759), pp. 9–11, 37–9, 52–6.

Edward Young (1683–1765) is now principally remembered for his multi-volume poem The Complaint: or Night Thoughts on Life, Death, and Immortality *(1742–6), an extended meditation on a series of philosophical questions.* Night Thoughts *was hugely popular in its day, and is now routinely cited as a key text of eighteenth-century graveyard poetry, and as an important precursor of some Gothic and romantic-period writing. However, Young's extant works cover a wide range of subjects and genres, including poetry, drama, political prose, literary criticism and religious sermons. The* Conjectures, *a significant if neglected text in the history of critical theory, assesses the role of originality and moral instruction in literature, valuing authors who imitate 'Nature' and 'divine truth' above those who merely imitate other 'Authors', particularly the classical Greek and Roman authors lionised by eighteenth-century neo-classicists. Originality, for Young, is the mark of authenticity, a true expression of the diversity of human nature. In the extract given here, Young characterises 'the mind of a man of genius' in terms borrowed directly from the discourse on the sublime: this 'mind' is an explicitly sublime spectacle, rising 'as the sun from chaos', possessing an 'uncontrolled' and 'unconfined' 'creative power', and conversant with 'infinite objects' and 'divine truth'.*

The mind of a man of genius is a fertile and pleasant field, pleasant as Elysium, and fertile as Tempe;[2] it enjoys a perpetual spring. Of that spring, *Originals* are the fairest flowers: *Imitations* are of quicker growth, but fainter bloom. *Imitations* are of two kinds; one of nature, one of authors: The first we call *Originals*, and confine the term *Imitation* to the second. I shall not enter into the curious enquiry of what is, or is not, strictly speaking, *Original*, content with what all must allow, that some compositions are more so than others; and the more they are so, I say, the better. *Originals* are, and ought to be, great favourites, for they are great benefactors; they extend the republic of letters, and add a new province to its dominion: *Imitators* only give us a sort of duplicate of what we had, possibly much better, before; increasing the mere drug[3] of books, while all that makes them valuable, *knowledge* and *genius*, are at a stand. The pen of an *original* writer, like *Armida*'s wand,[4] out of a barren waste calls a blooming spring: Out of that blooming spring an *Imitator* is a transplanter of laurels, which sometimes die on removal, and always languish in a foreign soil [...]

---

2 *Elysium … Tempe*: Elysium is the paradise of Greek and Roman myth; in classical literature, the valley of Tempe, in northern Thessalia (Greece), was sacred to Apollo and the muses.

3 *the mere drug of books*: 'books of little or no value' (see *OED*: 'drug' n.2: 'a commodity which [...] has lost its value').

4 *Armida's wand*: Armida is a sorceress in Torquato Tasso's *Jerusalem Delivered* (1581).

But here a caution is necessary against the most fatal of errors in those automaths,[5] those self-taught philosophers of our age, who set up genius, and often, mere *fancied* genius, not only above human learning, but divine truth. I have called genius wisdom; but let it be remembered, that in the most renowned ages of the most refined heathen wisdom (and theirs is not Christian), 'their world by wisdom knew not God, and it pleased God by the foolishness of preaching to save those that believed'.[6] In the fairyland of fancy, genius may wander wild; there it has a creative power, and may reign arbitrarily over its own empire of chimeras.[7] The wide field of nature also lies open before it, where it may range unconfined, make what discoveries it can, and sport with its infinite objects uncontrolled, as far as visible nature extends, painting them as wantonly as it will. But what painter of the most unbounded and exalted genius can give us the true portrait of a seraph?[8] He can only give us what by his own, or others' eyes, has been seen; though that indeed infinitely compounded, raised, burlesqued, dishonoured, or adorned. In like manner, who can give us divine truth unrevealed? Much less should any presume to set aside divine truth when revealed, as incongruous to their own sagacities. — Is this too serious for my subject? I shall be more so before I close [...]

Since it is plain that men may be strangers to their own abilities, and by thinking meanly of them without just cause, may possibly lose a name, perhaps immortal, I would find some means to prevent these evils. Whatever promotes virtue, promotes something more, and carries its good influence beyond the *moral* man. To prevent these evils, I borrow two golden rules from *ethics*, which are no less golden in *Composition*, than in life. 1. *Know thyself*; 2ndly, *Reverence thyself*. [...] Of ourselves it may be said, as Martial says of a bad neighbour: *Nil tam propre, proculque nobis*.[9] Therefore dive deep into the bosom; learn the depth, extent, bias, and full sort of thy mind; contract full intimacy with the stranger within thee; excite and cherish every spark of intellectual light and heat, however smothered under former negligence, or scattered through the dull, dark mass of common thoughts; and collecting them into a body, let thy genius rise (if a genius thou hast) as the sun from chaos; and if I should say, like an *Indian*, *Worship it*, (though too bold) yet should I say little more than my second rule enjoins, vis. *Reverence thyself*.

That is, let not great examples, or authorities, browbeat thy reason into too great a diffidence of thyself. Thyself so reverence, as to prefer the native growth of thy own mind to the richest import from abroad; such borrowed riches make us poor. The man who thus reverences himself, will soon find the world's

---

5 *automaths*: 'autodidacts', that is, self-taught individuals.

6 The quotation is adapted from 1 Corinthians 1:21.

7 *chimeras:* in Greek myth, the chimera was a monster with the head of a lion, body of a goat, and tail of a serpent. Cp. De Carbonnières' reference to the 'chimeras' of the 'imagination' (see Mountains).

8 *seraph*: angel.

9 *Nil ... nobis*: 'Nothing is closer to, or further from us'. Adapting Martial, *Epigrams*, I, lxxxvi ,10: 'Quisquam est tam propre tam proculque nobis'.

reverence to follow his own. His works will stand distinguished; his the sole property of them; which property alone can confer the noble title of an *author*; that is, of one who (to speak accurately) *thinks*, and *composes*; while other invaders of the press, how voluminous and learned soever, (with due respect be it spoken) only *read*, and *write*.

This is the difference between those two luminaries in literature, the well-accomplished scholar, and the divinely-inspired enthusiast; the *first* is, as the bright morning star; the *second*, as the rising sun. The writer who neglects those two rules above will never stand alone; he makes one of a group, and thinks in wretched unanimity with the throng. Encumbered with the notions of others, and impoverished by their abundance, he conceives not the least embryo of new thought; opens not the least vista through the gloom of ordinary writers, into the bright walks of rare imagination, and singular design; while the true genius is crossing all public roads into fresh untrodden ground; he, up to the knees in antiquity, is treading the sacred footsteps of great examples with the blind veneration of a bigot saluting the papal toe, comfortably hoping full absolution for the sins of his own understanding, from the powerful charm of touching his idol's infallibility.

3.2　Jean Jacques Rousseau, *Émile, ou, de l'Éducation* (1762), transl. M. Nugent, 2 vols (London, 1763), II, pp. 13–15.

This extract from Rousseau's influential and controversial novelistic treatise on education is taken from the 'Profession of faith of a Savoyard vicar', the centrepiece of Book IV. By way of illustrating the best means of educating children about religious matters, Émile's narrator describes the case of a priest from the French Alps who is defrocked for breaching his vow of celibacy and who subsequently undergoes a spiritual and existential crisis, which he finally resolves through rational observation of the natural world. The 'Profession' provoked outrage when Émile first appeared, but is now generally recognised as one of the most important eighteenth-century discussions of natural religion, and a significant influence on romantic-period attitudes to nature. The 'Profession' also deploys what would become a key trope of romantic-period writing about the mind (e.g. Godwin): the ability of the individual mind, in a period of trauma, to break through the constraints of custom and arrive at a sublime intellectual and existential independence. This practical application of the science of mind is in keeping with the praxis of enlightenment rationalism, but is also consistently represented as attended by extreme anxiety and often, as in Émile, as the product of an encounter with the natural sublime (in this case, the priest's Alpine home).

Very little experience of this kind carries a reflective mind a great way. Observing by melancholy examples, a general subversion of the ideas I had conceived of justice, and honesty, and of all human duty, I gradually began to lose some of the opinions I had imbibed; those which remained, being insufficient to form a body capable of supporting itself, by degrees the evidence of the principles began to vanish; and being reduced at length to a total ignorance and want of thought, I sunk exactly into your situation; with this difference, that my incredulity, being the fruit of a much riper age, was formed with greater difficulty, and must have been far more difficult to remove.

I was in that very disposition of uncertainty and doubt, which Descartes[10] requires for an inquiry after truth. This is a painful situation; but it is of short continuance; vice or indolence only can engage us to resign ourselves up to it. My heart was not so debauched, as to find any pleasure in it; and nothing so greatly preserves the habit of reflection, as to find more content in ourselves, than in our fortune.

I therefore began to contemplate the wretched fate of mortals, fluctuating in this ocean of human opinions, without either helm or compass, without any other guide than an inexperienced pilot, who knows not the right course, nor from what point he sailed, nor to what port he is steering. I said to myself: I love the truth; I have been inquiring after it in vain; let me see it, and I will firmly embrace it; why should it lie concealed from a heart formed to adore it?

Though I have often experienced great hardships, yet I never led a life so disagreeable as that which I passed during those times of perturbation and anxiety, when incessantly wandering from one doubt to another, all the benefit I received from my long meditations, was blind uncertainty, and a heap of contradictions in regard to the cause of my existence, and the rule of human duty.

I cannot comprehend how it is possible to be a sceptic by system, and *bona fide*.[11] Either there are no such philosophers, or they are the most wretched of all mankind. Suspension and doubt in regard to matters which it behoves us to know,[12] is too violent a state for the human mind: the resistance it makes, does not last long; it determines one way or other, whether we will or no; and it chooses rather to be imposed upon, than not to believe at all.

What added very much to my perplexity, was that being educated in a church[13], which takes upon her to determine everything, and will not permit her members to doubt, the rejection of one single point made me reject all the rest; and the impossibility of assenting to so many absurd decisions, unhinged my belief even in regard to those, which were not subject to the same absurdity. By being ordered to believe everything, I was prevented from giving my assent to anything, and I knew not where to stop.

---

10 *Descartes*: René Descartes (1596–1650), a French philosopher, whose *Discourse on Method* (1637) and *Meditations on First Philosophy* (1641) are founding texts of Enlightenment rationalism, and whose statement 'I think therefore I am' has become one of the best-known philosophical aphorisms.

11 *bona fide*: Latin, meaning 'in good faith', that is, honestly.

12 *which it behoves us to know*: 'which it is desirable or necessary for us to know'.

13 *a church*: meaning the Catholic religion.

I consulted the philosophers, searched their books, examined into their different opinions; but found them all conceited and dogmatical even in their pretended scepticism, extremely ignorant, proving nothing, and laughing at one another; in this they all agreed, and it seemed to be the only point in which they had reason on their side. Victorious whenever they attack, but weak and spiritless, when they act upon the defensive. If you weigh their reasons, they have none but to destroy; if you reckon voices, each stands by himself; and they agree only to dispute: to listen to these was not the way to get rid of my uncertainty.

I perceived very plainly that the insufficiency of the human understanding is the first cause of that prodigious diversity of sentiments; and pride the second. We have no way to measure this immense machine, no way to calculate its various relations: we know not its first laws, nor its final cause; we do not even know ourselves; we are ignorant of our nature, and of our active principle;[14] we can scarcely tell whether man be a simple or compound being;[15] on all sides were are surrounded with impenetrable mysteries; they are beyond the scale of sensible beings; we think we have understanding enough to pierce through them, but it is all imagination. In this visionary world everyone pursues which route he pleases, but nobody can tell whether his be the right one or not. And yet we fain would know[16] and penetrate into everything. The only point of which we are ignorant, is that we are incapable of knowledge. We had rather be determined by chance, and believe what does not really exist, than acknowledge that none of us can see into the reality of things. Though we are but an inconsiderable part of a great whole, the bounds of which surpass our comprehension, and which its Maker has resigned to our foolish disputes, yet we are vain enough to determine the nature of that whole, with its relations in regard to us.

3.3   William Duff, *An Essay on Original Genius*, 2nd edition (London, 1767), pp. 163–9.

In this extract from Book II, Section III of his Essay, *the Scottish Reverend William Duff (1732–1815) discusses 'original genius in poetry'. Duff, like Young before him, describes 'original genius' in language drawn from the discourse on the sublime, defining it as 'breaking through' or 'overleaping' the formal and thematic constraints of eighteenth-century, neo-classical aesthetics ('the legal restraints of criticism'). 'Original genius', according to Duff, is characterised by an 'irregular greatness' and 'fiery impetuousity' of 'the Imagination', wholly distinct from 'the dull uniform tenor of common sentiments'. 'Genius', in other words, is both a sublime spectacle in itself ('like the flight of an eagle*

---

14 *our active principle:* that is, what animates us, or gives us life.

15 *a simple [...] being:* that is, whether man is simply a material organism, or a blend of body and soul.

16 *yet we fain would know:* 'yet we would be glad to know'.

[…] the course of a comet) and 'naturally' conversant with the sublime, the 'wonderful', 'grand', 'awful', and 'magnificent'.

An *irregular greatness* of Imagination is sometimes supposed to imply a mixture of great beauties and blemishes, blended together in any work of Genius; and thus we frequently apply it to the writings of Shakespeare, whose excellencies are as transcendent, as his faults are conspicuous. Without rejecting this sense altogether, or denying that an original author will be distinguished by his imperfections as well as by his excellencies, we may observe, that the expression above-mentioned is capable of a juster and more determinate meaning than that just specified. It may, we think, be more properly understood to signify that native grandeur of sentiment which disclaims all restraint, is subject to no certain rule, and is therefore various and unequal. In this sense principally we consider the expression, and are under no difficulty in declaring, that an irregular greatness of Imagination, as thus explained, is one remarkable criterion of exalted and original Genius. A person who is possessed of this quality, naturally turns his thoughts to the contemplation of the grand and wonderful, in nature or in human life, in the visible creation, or in that of his own fancy. Revolving these awful and magnificent scenes in his musing mind, he labours to express in his compositions the ideas which dilate and swell his Imagination; but is often unsuccessful in his efforts. In attempting to represent these, he feels himself embarrassed; words are too weak to convey the ardour of his sentiments, and he frequently sinks under the immensity of his own conceptions. Sometimes indeed he will be happy enough to paint his very thought, and to excite in others the very sentiments which he himself feels: he will not always however succeed so well, but, on the contrary, will often labour in fruitless attempt; whence it should seem that his composition will upon certain occasions be distinguished by an irregular and unequal greatness.

Whether this quality is to be ascribed to the cause above-mentioned in particular; or whether it is the effect of that fiery impetuosity of Imagination, which, breaking through the legal restraints of criticism, or overleaping the bounds of authority and custom, sometimes loses sight of the just and natural, while it is in pursuit of the new and wonderful, and, by attempting to rise above the sphere of humanity, tumbles from its towering height; or lastly, whether it is to be ultimately derived from the unavoidable imperfection of the human faculties, which admit not of perpetual extension, and are apt to flag in a long though rapid flight; whichsoever of these may cause the phenomenon above-mentioned, or whether all of them may contribute to produce it, certain it is, that an irregular greatness of Imagination, implying unequal and disproportioned grandeur, is always discernible in the compositions of an original Genius, however elevated, and is therefore an universal characteristic of such a Genius.

It deserves however to be observed, that the imperfection here suggested, is a natural effect and a certain proof of an exuberant Imagination. Ordinary minds seldom rise above the dull uniform tenor of common sentiments, like those animals that are condemned to creep on the ground all the days of their life; but the most lawless excursions of an original Genius, like the flight of an eagle, are towering, though devious; its path, as the course of a comet, is blazing though irregular; and its errors and excellencies are equally inimitable.

We observed that original Genius is likewise distinguished by a *wildness* of Imagination. This quality, so close allied to the former, seems also to proceed from the same causes; and is at the same time an infallible proof of a fertile and luxuriant fancy. *Wildness* of imagery, scenery and sentiment, is the *pastime* of a playful and sportive imagination; it is the effect of its exuberance. This character is formed by an arbitrary assemblage of the most extravagant, uncommon, and romantic ideas, united in the most fanciful combinations; and is displayed in grotesque figure, in surprising sentiments, in picturesque and enchanting description. The quality of which we are treating, wherever it is discovered, will afford such a delicious entertainment to the mind, that it can scarce ever be satisfied with a banquet so exquisitely prepared, satiety being prevented by a succession of dainties, ever various and ever new.

3.4 John Thelwall, *The Peripatetic: or, Sketches of the Heart, of Nature and Society; in a Series of Politico-Sentimental Journals, in Verse and Prose, of the Eccentric Excursions of Sylvanus Theophrastus; Supposed to be Written by Himself* (London, 1793), pp. 163–5.

A close friend of the young Coleridge and Wordsworth, John Thelwall (1764–1834) was a prominent member of the English reform movement during the 1790s and a defendant, along with other leading radicals Thomas Hardy and John Horne Tooke, in the notorious Treason Trials of 1794, when Pitt's government attempted to silence its key political opponents (Thelwall and the others were eventually acquitted). Thelwall published a number of important political pamphlets and some considerably less influential poetry, including his 1795 Poems written in Close Confinement, *composed while he was awaiting trial in the Tower of London. Thelwall's* Peripatetic – *the title refers to a school of classical Greek philosophy founded by Aristotle – is very much in the tradition of eighteenth-century didactic poems such as Erasmus Darwin's* Botanic Garden *(1791), which sought to make contemporary scientific theory – much of it challenging to the established orthodoxy of church and state – available to a wider audience. In this extract, Thelwall describes the sublime spectacle of the human anatomical system, under the control of the brain, 'whose subtle dictates all the frame command'. Although entirely materialist in scientific outlook, the passage is replete with imagery drawn from the discourse on the sublime.*

> See where the heart, life's awful reservoir!
> That pours to every part the vital store, —

Great seat of Passion, at whose proud control
Or slow, or wild the purple torrents roll —
(Now thrilling quick when, all the soul on fire,
Eyes the bright nymphs, and pants with warm desire,
Now creeping slowly thro' the sluggish veins
When chilling Fear, or drooping Sorrow reigns —)
This awful power, on whom high heaven conferr'd
Of life's great charge the first important third[17] —
Timid, and conscious of her charge, she flies
To pant and flutter far from human eyes;
While the soft lungs, in flexible membrane bound,
Like fond maternal wings embrace her round:
And, while the current through each channel swells,[18]
Woo the fresh zephyrs[19] to their countless cells:
And, ere again the imprison'd gales retire,
Draw from their souls the pure electric fire[20] —
The electric fire the passing streams impart
(Life's first great mover) to the swelling heart.
Should rude disaster these or that confound,
Life and Life's hope rapidly fly the wound:
Here 'scape the currents whence we life receive,
The zephyrs there by which those currents live.

But these to guard from ills that might assail,
Spread the strong ribs, their moving coat of mail,
And stretch'd around, with strong, but flexile[21] sweep,
At distance due each casual danger keep.

Nor less the brain – fair Reason's awful stand!
Whose subtle dictates all the frame command;
Doom'd each important function to sustain;

---

17 'The circulation of the blood being essential long before the functions of the lungs or brain are requisite' (Thelwall's note).

18 'In the human subject, and all the most perfect of the quadruped species, the whole mass of blood passes in every circulation through the lungs' (Thelwall's note).

19 *zephyrs:* the fresh air; from 'Zephyrus', the classical Greek name for the West Wind, supposedly a bringer of health.

20 'That the air in passing from the lungs, loses some part of its elementary composition is evident […] It is equally evident from the changes taking place in the colour and properties of the blood […] that something is imbibed from the air. Whether this be certain portions of the electric fluid, contained always in large quantities in the atmosphere, may, perhaps, be worth enquiry. The author hazards it only as a conjecture sufficiently probable for the foundations of a poetical allusion' (from Thelwall's note).

21 *flexile:* flexible, pliable.

Mysterious 'Lord of Pleasure and of Pain',[22]
Of Reason, Knowledge, Sense's varied sway,[23]
And Fancy's train – fantastic, grave, or gay.
Where vibrates sound, where splendid Vision lives,
Where Taste – where Smell her essence all receives,
And Touch, fine-thrilling, each impression gives!
From this, when injur'd, all tumultuous fly
The wond'rous train of sudden Sympathy:[24]
The Lungs, the Heart, their functions each disclaim:
Dies thro' each Nerve the paralytic frame!

3.5   William Godwin, *Things as They Are: or, The Adventures of Caleb Williams*, 3 vols (London, 1794), II, xii–xiii.

*Like Thelwall, Godwin (1756–1836) was an important figure in the English radi-
cal movement of the 1790s and his* Enquiry Concerning Political Justice *(1793,
1794, 1798) was a major influence on the political ideas of the young Coleridge
and Wordsworth, as well as on Byron and Percy Shelley (his son-in- law). Conceived
as a response to Edmund Burke's condemnation of the French Revolution in his*
Reflections *(1790), the* Enquiry *argues against the continuance of social institutions based on custom or tradition in opposition to public opinion, and insists on
the need for government to be accountable to the people. However, unlike many
other radicals, Godwin favoured gradual rather than revolutionary political change,
a position which (together with the high price of the* Enquiry) *may have saved him
from prosecution for treason. Godwin's quasi 'Gothic' novel* Caleb Williams *is a
fictional treatment of the political theories advanced in the* Enquiry. *Caleb is the
servant of Falkland, a man whom he greatly admires. However, when Caleb learns
that Falkland has committed murder in order to preserve his honour, he leaves his
service. Falkland, convinced that Caleb means to expose him, and still desperate
to preserve his honour, uses his social status to accuse, incriminate and pursue his
former servant, eventually leaving Caleb no choice but to expose him – an apparent warning from Godwin that aristocratic oppression of the masses may lead to
precisely the kind of violent retribution that it is intended to prevent. In the present
extract, Caleb, imprisoned and facing execution for an offence of which he is innocent, begins to explore the resources and abilities of his own mind, a process which
ultimately leads him to a sublime 'exultation' in the extent of his own mental
prowess. The episode is thus in the tradition that runs through to the romantic*

---

22 The quotation is from Samuel Johnson, *The Vanity of Human Wishes* (1749), p. 196.
23 *sway:* command.
24 'The sympathy between the Brain, Heart, and Lungs has long engaged the attention of Physiologists,
    it being evident, that no injury whatever can be done to the one, without the others being imme-
    diately affected' (Thelwall's note).

period from Rousseau's 'Savoyard Vicar', configuring the human mind as a sublime phenomenon.

Such were the reflections that haunted the first days of my imprisonment, in consequence of which they were spent in perpetual anguish. But after a time nature, wearied with distress, would no longer stoop to the burden; thought, which is incessantly varying, introduced a series of reflections totally different.

My fortitude revived [...] I found out the secret of employing my mind. I said, I am shut up for half the day in total darkness without any external source of amusement; the other half I spend in the midst of noise, turbulence and confusion. What then? Can I not draw amusement from the stores of my own mind? Is it not freighted with various knowledge? Have I not been employed from my infancy in gratifying an insatiable curiosity? When should I derive benefit from these superior advantages, if not at present? Accordingly I tasked the stores of my memory and my powers of invention. I amused myself with recollecting the history of my life. By degrees I called to mind a number of minute circumstances which but for this exercise would have been for ever forgotten. I repassed in my thoughts whole conversations, I recollected their subjects, their arrangement, their incidents and frequently their very words. I mused upon these ideas till I was totally absorbed in thought. I repeated them till my mind glowed with enthusiasm.[25] I had my different employments fitted for the solitude of the night in which I could give full scope to the impulses of my mind, and the uproar of the day in which my chief object was to be insensible to the disorder with which I was surrounded.

By degrees I quitted my own story, and employed myself with imaginary adventures. I figured to myself every situation in which I could be placed, and conceived the conduct to be observed in each. Thus scenes of insult and danger, of tenderness and oppression became familiar to me. In fancy I often passed the awful hour of dissolving nature. In some of my reveries I boiled with impetuous indignation, and in others patiently collected the whole force of my mind for some fearful encounter. I cultivated the powers of oratory[26] suited to these different states, and improved more in eloquence in the solitude of my dungeon, than perhaps I should have done in the busiest and most crowded scenes. At length I proceeded to as regular a disposition of my time as the man in his study who passes from mathematics to poetry, and from poetry to the law of nations in the different parts of a single day; and I seldom infringed upon my plan. Nor were my subjects of disquisition less numerous than his. I went over, by the assistance of memory

---

25 *enthusiasm*: an important concept in eighteenth-century and romantic-period philosophy, used to describe various forms of intense emotional response, especially the emotion produced by the encounter with the sublime.

26 *the powers of oratory*: here meaning 'eloquent speech'.

only, a considerable part of Euclid[27] during my confinement, and revived day after day the series of facts and incidents in some of the most celebrated historians. I became myself a poet; and while I described the sentiments cherished by the view of natural objects, recorded the characters and passions of men, and partook with burning zeal in the generosity of their determinations, I eluded the squalid solitude of my dungeon, and wandered in idea through all the varieties of human society. I easily found expedients, such as the mind seems always to require, and which books and pens supply to the man at large,[28] to record from time to time the progress that had been made.

While I was thus employed I reflected with exultation upon the degree in which man is independent of the smiles and frowns of fortune. I was beyond her reach, for I could fall no lower. To an ordinary eye I might seem destitute and miserable, but in reality I wanted for nothing. My fare[29] was coarse; but I was in health. My dungeon was noisome[30]; but I felt no inconvenience. I was shut up from the usual means of exercise and air; but I found the method of exercising myself even to perspiration in my dungeon. I had no power of withdrawing my person from a disgustful[31] society in the most cheerful and valuable part of the day; but I soon brought to perfection the art of withdrawing my thoughts, and saw and heard the people about me for just as short a time and as seldom as I pleased.

Such is man in himself considered; so simple his nature; so few his wants. How different from the man of artificial society! Palaces are built for his reception, a thousand vehicles provided for his exercise, provinces are ransacked for the gratification of his appetite, and the whole world traversed to supply him with apparel and furniture. Thus vast is his expenditure, and the purchase slavery. He is dependent on a thousand accidents for tranquillity and health, and his body and soul are at the devotion of whoever will satisfy his imperious cravings.

In addition to the disadvantages of my present situation, I was reserved for an ignominious death. What then? Every man must die. No man knows how soon. It surely is not worse to encounter the king of terrors[32] in health and with every advantage for the collection of fortitude, than to encounter him already half-subdued by sickness and suffering. I was resolved at least fully to possess the days I had to live, and this is peculiarly the power of the man who preserves his health to the last moment of his existence. Why should I suffer my mind to be invaded by unavailing regrets? Every sentiment of vanity, or rather of independence and justice within me, instigated me to say to my persecutor, You may cut off my existence, but you cannot disturb my serenity [...]

---

27 *Euclid*: third-century BC Greek mathematician, whose *Elements* is the founding text of Western geometry.
28 *the man at large*: that is, the free man.
29 *fare*: food.
30 *noisome*: 'disgusting'.
31 *disgustful*: meaning 'disgusting', not 'disgusted'.
32 *the king of terrors*: death; cf. Job 18:14.

In the midst of these reflections another thought, which had not before struck me, occurred to my mind. I exult, said I, and reasonably, over the impotence of my persecutor. Is not that impotence greater than I have yet imagined? I say, he may cut off my existence, but cannot disturb my serenity. It is true: my mind, the clearness of my spirit, the firmness of my temper, are beyond his reach; is not my life equally so, if I please? What are the material obstacles that man never subdued? What is the undertaking so arduous that by some has not been accomplished? And, if by others, why not by me? [...]The mind is master of itself; and is endowed with powers that might enable it to laugh at the tyrant's vigilance. I passed and repassed these ideas in my mind; and, heated with the contemplation, I said, No, I will not die!

3.6 William Wordsworth, 'Prospectus' to *The Recluse* (1799) 25–41, from *The Excursion* (London, 1814), p. xii.

When Wordsworth (1770–1850) published The Excursion *in 1814, he included a preface which explained that the poem was to be considered 'only a portion' of a larger, projected work called* The Recluse, *which was to be 'a philosophical poem, containing views of Man, Nature, and Society' (pp. vii, viii). The preface concludes with some seventy-seven lines of verse, probably composed in 1799, which Wordsworth hoped would 'be acceptable as a kind of* Prospectus *of the design and scope' of* The Recluse *(p. x). In language consciously echoing Milton's* Paradise Lost *(1667), Wordsworth states his intention to produce a secular epic, with the 'Mind of Man' as its subject. This short extract from the 'Prospectus' shares with much contemporaneous writing about the human mind a sense of the mind as sublime spectacle, in this case as sublime landscape, possessing heights and depths, and peopled by the gods and demons of classical and Christian myth. As for a number of writers who followed Hume's call for a 'mental geography', then, in this case too, the study of the mind is configured, at least in part, as a discourse on the sublime.*

> [...] Urania,[33] I shall need
> Thy guidance, or a greater Muse, if such
> Descend to earth or dwell in highest heaven!
> For I must tread on shadowy ground, must sink
> Deep – and, aloft ascending, breathe in worlds
30   To which the heaven of heavens is but a veil.[34]
> All strength – all terror, single or in bands,

---

33 *Urania*: in classical myth, the muse of the heavens; also invoked by Milton in *Paradise Lost* (e.g. vii, 1).

34 *the heaven of heavens*: the home, in *Paradise Lost*, of God and the angels (e.g. vii, 12), as distinguished from the visible heavens (i.e. the night sky).

That ever was put forth in personal form –
Jehovah[35] – with his thunder, and the choir
Of shouting Angels, and the empyreal thrones[36] –
35   I pass them unalarmed. Not Chaos, not
The darkest pit of lowest Erebus,[37]
Nor aught of blinder vacancy, scooped out
By help of dreams – can breed such fear and awe
As fall upon us often when we look
40   Into our Minds, into the Mind of Man –
My haunt, and the main region of my song.

3.7   Philippe Pinel, *Traité médico-philosophique sur l'aliénation mentale; ou la manie* (1801), translated as *A Treatise on Insanity* by David Daniel Davis (London, 1806), pp. xv–vi, 1–5.

The French physician Philippe Pinel (1745–1826) was responsible for the treatment of mentally ill patients at the Bicêtre and Salpêtrière hospitals in southern Paris. Pinel was one of the pioneers of the so-called moral approach to mental illness, which emphasised the treatment and rehabilitation of patients through the identification and resolution of an underlying psychological basis of their condition (in severe emotional trauma, etc.), rather than through archaic, pseudo-medical practices like purging, bleeding, etc. Davis, a highly rated obstetrician and member of the London College of Medicine, produced the first English translation of Pinel's influential Treatise. *In the first of the two extracts given here, Davis, in his translator's introduction, uses the language of the discourse on the sublime to describe the 'calamitous and interesting' spectacle of the mentally ill, comparing the mind of the patient to 'the ruins of a once magnificent edifice'. The second extract, from Pinel's own 'general plan' of his* Treatise, *deploys similar imagery, with Pinel noting the difficulty of imposing rational methodology upon the sublime 'chaos and confusion' of the asylum.*

[*from Davis's 'Introduction'.*]

Of all the afflictions to which human nature is subject, the loss of reason is at once the most calamitous and interesting. Deprived of this faculty, by which man is principally distinguished from the beasts that perish, the human form is frequently the most remarkable attribute that he retains of his proud distinction. His character, as an individual of the species, is always perverted; sometimes

---

35 *Jehovah*: Old Testament name for God; Wordsworth here appears to conflate Jehovah with Zeus, the chief god in Greek mythology, associated with thunder and lightning.

36 *empyreal*: heavenly. Cp. *Paradise Lost* ii, 430: 'O progeny of heaven, empyreal thrones'.

37 *Erebus*: a dark part of the underworld in Greek mythology; sometimes synonymous with hell.

annihilated. His thoughts and actions are diverted from their usual and natural course. The chain which connected his ideas in just series and mutual subserviency, is dissevered. His feelings for himself and others are new and uncommon. His attachments are converted into aversions, and his love into hatred. His consciousness even is not unfrequently alienated; insomuch, that with equal probability he may fancy himself a deity, an emperor, or a mass of inanimate matter. Once the ornament and life of society, he is now become a stranger to its pleasures or a disturber of its tranquillity. Impatient of restraint, and disposed to expend the unusual effervescence of his spirits in roving and turbulence, coercion of the mildest kind adds fury to his delirium, and colours with jealousy or suspicion every effort of friendly or professional interest in his fate. His personal liberty is at length taken from him; and taken from him perhaps by his nearest relative or dearest friend. Retaining his original sensibility, or rendered more acutely sensible by opposition to his will and deprivation of his usual gratifications, co-operating with a morbid excitement of his nervous functions, he gives himself up to all the extravagances of maniacal fury, or sinks inexpressibly miserable into the lowest depths of despondence and melancholy. If the former, he resembles in ferocity the tiger, and meditates destruction and revenge. If the latter, he withdraws from society, shuns the plots and inveiglements which he imagines to surround him, and fancies himself an object of human persecution and treachery, or a victim of divine vengeance and reprobation. To this melancholy train of symptoms, if not early and judiciously treated, idiotism, or a state of the most abject degradation, in most instances, sooner or later succeeds. The figure of the human species is now all that remains to him, 'and like the ruins of a once magnificent edifice, it only serves to remind us of its former dignity and grandeur',[38] and to awaken our gloomiest reflections – our tenderest regret for the departure of the real and respectable man.

The history of this formidable disorder is necessarily and intimately connected with that of the human mind in general. The physical and metaphysical opinions entertained of it by theologists and physicians of different countries bear due correspondence to the prevailing doctrines, prejudices, and fashions of their respective times. However our thinking faculty may be connected with the operations of the body, the apparent remoteness of its nature, from the generally acknowledged properties of matter, have determined many philosophers, and especially those of antiquity, to detach its history from the other pursuits of the naturalist, and to ascribe its phenomena to the agency of an indwelling principle, perfectly distinct in its essence, and infinitely more exalted in its origin and destination [...]

[*from Pinel's 'General Plan of the Work'.*]

---

38 No single source for this quotation has been identified, though the imagery and sentiment is ubiquitous in eighteenth- and early nineteenth-century writing about the sublime.

Nothing has more contributed to the rapid improvement of modern natural history, than the spirit of minute and accurate observation which has distinguished its votaries. The habit of analytical investigation, thus adopted, has induced an accuracy of expression and a propriety of classification, which have themselves, in no small degree, contributed to the advancement of natural knowledge. Convinced of the essential importance of the same means in the illustration of a subject so new and so difficult as that of the present work, it will be seen that I have availed myself of their application, in all or most of the instances of this most calamitous disease, which occurred in my practice at the Asylum de Bicêtre. On my entrance upon the duties of that hospital, everything presented to me the appearance of chaos and confusion. Some of my unfortunate patients laboured under the horrors of a most gloomy and desponding melancholy. Others were furious, and subject to the influence of a perpetual delirium. Some appeared to possess a correct judgement upon most subjects, but were occasionally agitated by violent sallies of maniacal fury; while those of another class were sunk into a state of stupid idiotism and imbecility. Symptoms so different, and all comprehended under the general title of insanity, required, on my part, much study and discrimination; and to secure order in the establishment and success to the practice, I determined upon adopting such a variety of measures, both as to discipline and treatment, as my patients required, and my limited opportunity permitted. From systems of nosology, I had little assistance to expect, since the arbitrary distributions of Sauvages and Cullen were better calculated to impress the conviction of their insufficiency than to simplify my labour.[39] I, therefore, resolved to adopt that method of investigation which has invariably succeeded in all the departments of natural history, vis. to notice successively every fact, without any other object than that of collecting materials for further use; and to endeavour, as far as possible, to divest myself of the influence, both of my own prepossessions and the authority of others.

With this view, I first of all took a general statement of the symptoms of my patients. To ascertain their characteristic peculiarities, the above survey was followed by cautious and repeated examinations into the conditions of individuals. All our new cases were entered at great length upon the journals of the house. Due attention was paid to the changes of the seasons and the weather, and their respective influences upon the patients were minutely noticed. Having a peculiar attachment for the more general method of descriptive history, I did not confine myself to any exclusive mode of arranging my observations, nor to any one system of nosography. The facts which I have thus collected are now submitted to the consideration of the public, in the form of a regular treatise.

Few subjects in medicine are so intimately connected with the history and philosophy of the human mind as insanity. There are still fewer, where there are so many errors to rectify, and so many prejudices to remove. Derangement

---

39 *nosology* [...] *Cullen*: during the eighteenth century, François Boissier de Sauvages (1706–67) and William Cullen (1710–90) pioneered the science of nosology, the classification of diseases.

of the understanding is generally considered as an effect of an organic lesion of the brain, consequently as incurable; a supposition that is, in a great number of instances, contrary to anatomical fact. Public asylums for maniacs have been regarded as places of confinement for such of its members as are become dangerous to the peace of society. The managers of those institutions, who are frequently men of little knowledge and less humanity,[40] have been permitted to exercise towards their innocent prisoners a most arbitrary system of cruelty and violence; while experience affords ample and daily proofs of the happier effects of a mild, conciliating treatment, rendered effective by steady and dispassionate firmness. Availing themselves of this consideration, many empirics[41] have erected establishments for the reception of lunatics, and have practised this very delicate branch of the healing heart with singular reputation. A great number of cures have undoubtedly been affected by those base born children of the profession; but, as might be expected, that have not in any degree contributed to the advancement of science by any valuable writings. It is on the other hand to be lamented, that regular physicians have indulged in a blind routine of inefficient treatment, and have allowed themselves to be confined within the fairy circle of antiphlogisticism,[42] and by that means to be diverted from the more important management of the mind. Thus, too generally, has the philosophy of this disease, by which I mean the history of its symptoms, of its progress, of its varieties, and of its treatment in and out of hospitals, been most strangely neglected.

3.8 Robert Gray (attrib), *The Theory of Dreams*, 2 vols, (London, 1808) I, pp. iii–vi; II, pp. 54–60, 73–4.

Robert Gray (1762–1834), biblical scholar and Bishop of Bristol (1827–34), is now principally remembered for being the father of the first Anglican Bishop of Cape Town, and for his very public opposition to the Reform Bill of 1831, which provoked an angry crowd to burn down his residence during riots following the Bill's defeat in October 1831. The Theory of Dreams, attributed to Gray, is a kind of precursor of Freudian and Jungian psychotherapy, in which Gray offers a taxonomy of dreams, compiled from dreams represented in classical and Christian literature, as well as from some contemporaneous sources. On the basis of this taxonomy, Gray conducts, as the full title announces, 'an inquiry [...] into the powers and faculties of the human mind'. In the extracts given here, Gray represents these 'powers and faculties' as a sublime spectacle, eulogising the ability of the mind to transcend the limitations of sensation, and to

---

40 'The English legislature has taken some cognisance of the crying evils which formerly existed in this country, as they now do in France, from the indiscriminate toleration of empyrical lunatic establishments. More however might and ought to be done' (Translator's Note).

41 *empirics*: physicians whose practices are derived from experience rather than theory (*OED* B.n.).

42 *antiphlogisticism*: the reduction of inflammation.

overcome the mental 'harassment and affliction' occasioned by contemporary political turmoil. The Theory thus parallels the conservative psychology of Wordsworth's and Coleridge's later work.

[*from 'Preface'.*]

The author of the following little work begs leave to enter his caveat against all sarcastic strictures on the title of his book, and requests that he may not be accused, as was Vigilantius, (for the sake of the play upon his name probably) by St. Jerome,[43] of writing in waking slumbers; because at a time so awful as the present, when every day teems with great events, and the fate of empires, he has employed his thoughts on dreams; for, in truth, the fearful importance of the scenes which now interest the attention of mankind, as they only harass and afflict the mind, affording it no prospect of speedy relief, lead him to have recourse to speculative inquiries, with a view of receding from gloomy reflections [...]

[*from 'On the Nature and Efficient Cause of Dreams' (II, xiv).*]

As dreams usually obtain when the senses are closed against external objects, they must be considered as the work of the mind, sketches of the fancy, deriving its materials and objects from experience. It is the preeminent glory of the mind that it can thus subsist, as it were, in a separate state, independently of the body, which in none of its regular functions, is removed from the superintendence and control of the mind.

It is true, that whatever ideas the mind may enjoy are originally acquired through the senses before they become steeped[44] in forgetfulness, all of them being formed from the observation of earthly circumstances, and not appearing to be innate.[45] The images, however combined in extravagant pictures, and in whatever manner acquired, are composed of the representation of real objects, and are called up at pleasure by the mind [...] every dream originates in some sensation, yet the independent energies of the mind are sufficiently displayed in the preservation of the successive phantoms, and in the continuance of reflection long after the sensation is excited. The scenes which pass in review before us in sleep are sometimes composed of images which are produced immediately by corporeal impressions, not sufficiently strong to destroy the enchantment of

---

43 *Vigilantus* [...] *Jerome:* Vigilantius was an Italian priest whose criticism of the Catholic Church was condemned by St. Jerome (347–420) in his *Contra Vigilantium* (406). The Latin root of 'Vigilantius' means 'wakeful', hence 'the play upon his name'.

44 *steeped:* immersed.

45 *innate:* eighteenth-century British and French philosophy frequently distinguishes between 'acquired' and 'innate' ideas: ideas which the mind acquires through experience, and ideas with which it is born. The empirical tradition rejects the notion of innate ideas, arguing that all ideas are learned through experience.

sleep [...]. Dreams are, however, more often produced by sensation or motion of the brain, excited when we were awake, and continued [...] after the removal of the object. Although the powers of the mind are not limited to the contemplation of the image first introduced, but range in the wide scope of their observation to the view of every particular with which they are acquainted, and call up in the concatenation[46] of their reflections, often extending to the most remote and forgotten images long since committed to memory. Hence it is that we are so little able to trace any affinity between the subjects of our dreams and the sensations of recent impression. The links which connect the successive ideas of the mind, either waking or sleeping, being in general so imperceptibly fine, as to be traced with difficulty.

Allowing then that dreams are sometimes prompted by immediate or recent sensations, they must in general be considered as the creation of the mind, existing, as it were, in an abstracted state, though still capable of being easily summoned to attention by the body. The sympathy and reciprocal influence which subsist between them are never destroyed, and the mutual interchange of feeling is quickly communicated. There is perhaps never a total insensibility; the moment when vigilance sinks into oblivious indifference can never be accurately marked; no one, at least, hath ever yet noted the moment which precedes sleep [...]

Considering dreams then principally as the productions of the mind ruminating[47] on its own stores, we perceive that the imagination is ever in a state of vigilance; that it can paint and recall to its own view those scenes of nature and of life which it hath admired [...]. That the mind retains its full and native energies in sleep, its powers of memory, and of reasoning, is evident from the circumstances of somnambules, or sleep-walkers, in which the will directs the body, though in state of somnolency,[48] often guiding it by an accurate recollection of accustomed circumstances and local particulars, and acting, as it seems, by its own vigour as an ethereal spirit moving a passive machine. It then appears indeed capable of performing some things better than when its attention is diverted by the senses to external objects; it seems left to its own reflections, and free to apply its own views. In some case it has been known to solve difficulties better than when awake [...]

[*from 'On the Operation of the Mind in the Production of Dreams' (II, xv)*]

It is an idea to which we have before adverted, that those faculties of the mind often display themselves with greater energy when the body is sepulchred in sleep, and when the spirit is as it were released from 'the earthly tabernacle

---

46 *concatenation:* connection.
47 *ruminating:* meditating.
48 *a state of somnolency:* sleep.

which weigheth down the mind that museth on many things'.[49] – They seem to expiate with uncontrolled freedom, to unfold new powers of intelligence and fancy, to range with sudden and excursive flights, in which the horizon of the prospect is varied and enlarged, and the scattered scenes of memory collected into one point of view; objects are grouped with rapid observation, our action seems uncircumscribed, and we glide in visionary celerity[50] from scene to scene with the imperceptible flight of the eagle soaring through the trackless air [...]

It may perhaps be argued, that whatever excellency of thought and reflection is displayed by the mind in sleep, it is the excellency of the lesser faculties, not of reason [...] and Mr. Locke[51] indeed represents dreams as not under the rule and conduct of the understanding; but it may still be maintained, that however the fancy may appear to predominate over the judgement, and however the mind may be deluded into a belief of the reality of those fictitious scenes which it forms [...] yet that the superior powers of the mind are often exercised in sleep with considerable effect, and its faculties of judgement and discrimination manifested in a chain of reasoning. Much of the incongruity, which is supposed to prove the suspension of reason, and much of the wild discordancy of representation which appears to prevail, may arise from the defect of memory when we awake, that does not retain the impression of images which have passed across the mind in light and rapid succession; and which, therefore, exhibit but a partial and imperfect sketch of the picture that engaged the attention in sleep.

3.9 Francis Jeffrey, Review of Dugald Stewart's *Philosophical Essays* (1810), in *The Edinburgh Review* (November, 1810), pp. 167–80.

Dugald Stewart (1753–1828), disciple of Thomas Reid (1710–96), was one of the key philosophers of the Scottish Enlightenment. Stewart's Elements of the Philosophy of the Human Mind *(1792, 1814, 1822) and* Philosophical Essays *(1810), which develop and expand Reid's work, are core texts of the so-called common sense philosophy, which sought to refute both the idealism of Berkeley and the scepticism of Hume by appealing, at least in part, to universally accepted or 'common sense' truths (critics, of course, were quick to point out that these supposedly self-evident truths are precisely the kind of preconceptions that philosophy ought to scrutinise). Francis Jeffrey (1773–1850) was co-founder and editor of the influential,* Whig Edinburgh Review. *In this extract from his review of Stewart's*

---

49 Wisdom IX, 15 (Gray's Note).

50 *celerity:* speed.

51 *Mr Locke:* John Locke (1632–1704), English philosopher and political theorist, whose *Essay Concerning Human Understanding* (1690) exerted a profound influence on eighteenth-century British philosophy.

Essays, Jeffrey remarks upon the ongoing, exponential increase in the range of human knowledge, essentially registering the emergence of what we would now call disciplinarity, *a process which he configures as at once empowering and overwhelming for the individual. The 'philosophy of mind', Jeffrey suggests, will be a notable casualty of this process, because the 'universal hurry' of increasing disciplinarity militates against the 'solitude and silence' required for the study of the mind. Hence Jeffrey uses the tropes of the sublime, here, to describe the shifting contours of the western episteme.*

The studies to which Mr. Stewart has devoted himself have lately fallen out of favour with the English public;[52] and the nation which once placed the name of Locke immediately under those of Shakespeare and of Newton, and has since repaid the metaphysical labours of Berkeley and Hume with such just celebrity, seems now to be almost without zeal or curiosity as to the progress of the Philosophy of the Human Mind [...]

The progress of knowledge has given birth, of late years, to so many arts and sciences, that a man of liberal curiosity finds both sufficient occupation for his time, and sufficient exercise for his understanding, in acquiring a superficial knowledge of such as are the most inviting and most popular; and, consequently, has much less leisure, and less inducement than formerly, to dedicate himself to those abstract studies which call for more patient and persevering attention. In older times, a man had nothing for it, but either to be absolutely ignorant and idle, or to take seriously to theology and the school logic [...] Nowadays, however, the necessary qualification is prodigiously raised, – at least in denomination; and a man can scarcely pass current in the informed circles of society, without knowing something of political economy, chemistry, mineralogy, geology, and etymology, – having a small notion of painting, sculpture, and architecture, with some sort of taste for the picturesque, – and a smattering of German and Spanish literature, and even some idea of Indian, Sanskrit, and Chinese learning and history, – over and above some little knowledge of trade and agriculture; with a reasonable acquaintance with what is called the philosophy of politics, and a far more extensive knowledge of existing parties, factions, and eminent individuals, both literary and political, at home and abroad, than ever was required in any earlier period of society. The dissipation of time and of attention occasioned by these multifarious occupations, is, of course, very unfavourable to the pursuit of any abstract or continued study; and even if a man could, for himself, be content to remain ignorant of many things, in order to obtain a profound knowledge of a few, it would be difficult for him, in the present state of the world, to resist the impulse and the seductions that assail him from without. [...]

In the mean time, the misfortune is, that there is no popular nor royal road to the profounder and more abstract truths of philosophy; and that these are apt,

52 *the English public*: perhaps a significant qualification given that Stewart, like many of the other philosophers mentioned in Jeffrey's review, was Scottish.

accordingly, to fall into discredit or neglect, at a period when it is labour enough for most men to keep themselves up to the level of that great tide of popular information, which has been rising, with such unexampled rapidity, for the last forty years. [...]

If the philosophy of mind has really suffered more, from this universal hurry, than all her sister sciences of the same serious complexion, we should be inclined to ascribe this misfortune, partly to the very excellence of what has been already achieved by her votaries, and partly to the very severe treatment which their predecessors have received at their hands. Almost all the great practical maxims of this mistress of human life, such as the use of the principle of Association in education,[53] and the generation and consequences of Habits in all periods of life, have been lately illustrated in the most popular and satisfactory manner; and rendered so clear and familiar, as rules of practical utility, that few persons think it necessary to examine into the details of that fine philosophy by which they may have been first suggested, or brought into notice. There is nothing that strikes one as very important to be known upon these subjects which may not now be established in a more vulgar and empirical manner, – or which requires, in order to be understood, that the whole process of a scientific investigation should be gone over. By most persons, therefore, the labour of such an investigation will be declined; and the practical benefits applied – with ungrateful indifference to the sources from which they were derived. Of those, again, whom curiosity might still tempt to look a little closer upon this great field of wonders, no small part are dismayed at the scene of ruin which it exhibits. The destruction of ancient errors, has hitherto constituted so very large a part of the task of modern philosophers, that they may be said to have been employed rather in throwing down, than in building up, and have as yet established very little but the fallacy of all former philosophy. Now, they who had been accustomed to admire that ancient philosophy, cannot be supposed to be much delighted with its demolition; and, at all events, are naturally discouraged from again attaching themselves to a system, which they may soon have the mortification of seeing subverted in its turn. In their minds, therefore, the opening of such a course of study is apt only to breed a general distrust of philosophy, and to rivet a conviction of its extreme and irremediable uncertainty: while those who had previously been indifferent to systems of error, are displeased with the labour of a needless refutation; and disappointed to find, that, after a long course of inquiry, they are brought back to that very state of ignorance from which they had expected it would relieve them. [...]

The philosophy of mind is distinctly defined, by Mr. Stewart himself, to be that which is employed 'on phenomena of which we are conscious'; its peculiar object and aim is stated to be, 'to ascertain the laws of our constitution, in so far as they can be ascertained, by attention to the subjects of our consciousness';

---

53 *the principle of Association*: a key concept in eighteenth-century empirical philosophy, used to explain the manner in which ideas and sense impressions become linked in the mind.

and, in a great variety of passages, it is explained, that the powers by which all this is to be effected, are, reflection upon our own mental operations, and the faculty of calm and patient attention to the sensations of which we are conscious. But, if this be the proper province and object of the philosophy of mind, what benefit is the student to receive from observing the various effects of manners and situation, in imparting a particular colour or bias to the character of the savage and the citizen, 'the prejudiced clown, and factitious man of fashion'? The observation of such varieties is, no doubt, a very curious and a very interesting occupation of a student of philosophy. It is an occupation which can only be effectually pursued, in the world, by travelling, and intercourse with society; and, at all events, by vigilant observation of what is shown to us, by our senses, of the proceedings of our fellow men. The philosophy of mind, however, is to be cultivated in solitude and silence – by calm reflection on *our own* mental experiences, and by patient attention to the subjects of our own consciousness.

3.10 Samuel Taylor Coleridge, *The Statesman's Manual* (London, 1816), Appendix C, pp. ix–x.

In his Statesman's Manual, *Coleridge (1772–1834) makes important arguments about both the limits of philosophical rationalism and the need for a wide-ranging reform of British cultural values. Ultimately, however, and as its full title suggests,* The Statesman's Manual; or, The Bible the Best Guide to Political Skill and Foresight: A Lay Sermon, Addressed to the Higher Classes of Society, With an Appendix, Containing Comments and Essays Connected to the Study of the Inspired Writings *is a very difficult and deeply conservative text, which essentially proposes the resolution of the social and political divisions of early nineteenth-century Britain through a return to traditional Christian spirituality. The present extract exemplifies the strengths and weaknesses of the* Manual. *Coleridge begins by evaluating the rival claims of 'reason and religion', suggesting that the exercise of the former without the balancing effect of the latter conducts to an extreme form of materialistic individualism, which Coleridge links here to Satan (or, at least, to Milton's portrait of Satan in* Paradise Lost*) and to political tyrants. It is the tropes of the Gothic and religious sublimes, in other words, that Coleridge deploys in this psychological profile of the minds of those whom he considers to be the enemies of liberty and spirituality.*

But neither can reason or religion exist or coexist as reason and religion, except as far as they are actuated by the WILL (the platonic Θυμός), which is the sustaining, coercive and ministerial power, the functions of which in the individual correspond to the officers of war and police in the ideal Republic of Plato.[54] In

---

54 *the ideal Republic of Plato*: the utopian community, ruled by philosophers, imagined by the Greek philosopher Plato in his *Republic*, composed c. 380 BC.

its state of immanence (or indwelling) in reason and religion, the WILL appears indifferently, as wisdom or as love: two names of the same power, the former more intelligential,[55] the latter more spiritual, the former more frequent in the Old, the latter in the New Testament. But in its utmost abstraction and consequent state of reprobation, the Will becomes satanic pride and rebellious self-idolatry in the relations of the spirit to itself, and remorseless despotism relatively to others; the more hopeless as the more obdurate by its subjugation of sensual impulses, by its superiority to toil and pain and pleasure; in short, by the fearful resolve to find in itself alone the one absolute motive of action, under which all other motives from within and from without must be either subordinated or crushed.

This is the character which Milton has so philosophically as well as sublimely embodied in the Satan of his *Paradise Lost*. Alas! too often has it been embodied in *real* life! Too often has it given a dark and savage grandeur to the historic page! And wherever it has appeared, under whatever circumstances of time and country, the same ingredients have gone to its composition; and it has been identified by the same attributes. Hope in which there is no Cheerfulness; Steadfastness within and immoveable Resolve, with outward Restlessness and whirling Activity; Violence with Guile; Temerity with Cunning; and, as the result of all, Interminableness of Object with perfect Indifference of Means; these are the qualities that have constituted the COMMANDING GENIUS! These are the Marks, that have characterised the Masters of Mischief, the Liberticides,[56] and mighty Hunters of Mankind, from NIMROD to NAPOLEON.[57] And from inattention to the possibility of such a character as well as from ignorance of its elements, even men of honest intentions too frequently become fascinated. Nay, whole nations have been so far duped by this want of insight and reflection as to regard with palliative admiration, instead of wonder and abhorrence, the Molocks of human nature,[58] who are indebted, for the far larger portion of their meteoric success, to their total want of principle, and who surpass the generality of their fellow creatures in one act of courage only, that of daring to say with their whole heart, 'Evil, be thou my good!'[59] – All *system* so far is power; and a *systematic* criminal, self-consistent and entire in wickedness, who entrenches villainy within villainy, and barricades crime by crime, has removed a world of obstacles by the mere decision, that he will have no obstacles, but those of force and brute matter.

---

55 *intelligential:* intellectual (*OED* 1).

56 *Liberticides*: literally, 'murderers of liberty' (meaning enemies of freedom).

57 *mighty hunters* [...] *Napoleon*: Genesis 10:9 describes the Babylonian king Nimrod as 'a mighty hunter before the Lord', and this epithet was sometimes taken to mean that he was a tyrant responsible for many deaths. Napoleon I's 15-year reign as consul and then emperor of France brought war to much of western Europe.

58 *Molocks*: in various ancient cultures, Moloch is identified as a brutal god, demanding human sacrifices; Moloch also features as one of the fallen angels in Milton's *Paradise Lost*.

59 *Evil* [...] *my good!*: Lucifer's words in *Paradise Lost* iv, p. 110.

3.11 Johann Caspar Spurzheim, *Phrenology: or, the Doctrine of the Mind*, 3rd edition (London, 1825), pp. 207–9.

Spurzheim (1776–1832) was onetime pupil, assistant and friend of Franz Joseph Gall (1758–1828), the celebrated German physician who pioneered the study of phrenology, or brain localisation: the idea that specific intellectual, emotional and moral aptitudes are linked to distinct physical regions of the brain. It was actually Spurzheim who coined the term 'phrenology' (Gall described the practice as 'cranioscopy'), and it was Spurzheim's writings which were largely responsible for the spread of Gall's theories across Europe. In this extract from his Phrenology, *Spurzheim examines the physiological basis of poetic genius, which he links to sublime mental states ('exaltation', 'rapture', etc.). Following Gall, Spurzheim locates the 'organ' that he believes to be responsible for these states, 'the organ of Ideality', above the temples, beside the 'organ' of 'marvellousness', and suggests that all great poets have this 'cerebral part [...] much developed'.*

That a poet must be born, has passed into a proverb, and education is generally acknowledged inadequate to produce poetic talents. Children sometimes exhibit such powers previous to all instruction, and there is the greatest difference among adults in the capacity. Pope says of himself, 'I lisped in numbers for the numbers came'.[60] Those who study the phenomena of insanity, know that the talent of poetry is often excited and developed by this diseased condition. 'Several facts', says Pinel, 'seem so extraordinary, that they stand in need of the most respectable testimonies, in order to be admitted. I speak of the poetical enthusiasm which characterises certain fits of mania when verses are recited, which are by no means the result of reminiscence alone'.[61] Pinel mentions several of his own observations, and quotes the case of a girl from Van Swieten,[62] who, during her fits of mania, showed a rare facility in making verses, though previous to her illness she had been employed in manual labour, and had never had her understanding cultivated by education.

Before we left Vienna, Dr. Gall had looked for an organ of poetry, and even observed that the heads of great poets were enlarged above the temples in a direction backward and upward [...] but he spoke guardedly on this point at that time. Since we commenced our journey, however, we have multiplied observations and accumulated facts to such an amount, that Dr. Gall now admits an organ of poetry as quite certain.

---

60 *'I lisped [...] came'*: Pope, *An Epistle to Dr. Arbuthnot* (1734), pp. 127–8.

61 'Second edition, p. 111' (Spurzheim's note). The reference is to Philippe Pinel's *Traité médico-philosophique sur l'aliénation mentale; ou la manie* (1801).

62 *Van Swieten*: Gerard Van Swieten (1700–72), a Dutch physician and personal doctor of Maria Theresa, Empress of Austria.

It is true, that all great poets, both of ancient and modern times, Homer, Pindar, Euripides, Sophocles, Terence, Ovid, Horace, Ariosto, Torquato Tasso, Shakespeare, Milton, Lord Byron, Schiller, Goëthe, Wieland, Racine, Corneille, Voltaire, etc. etc., have the cerebral part, indicated above, much developed. It seems to me, however, that there is no peculiar or single faculty of poetry in the widest acceptation of that term. We must therefore determine the essential of every kind of poetry, which I am inclined to attribute to this organ as its special faculty, whilst the species of poetry produced depends on the combination of this with the other faculties of the individual poet. It cannot be the faculty of versification for some authors, J. J. Rousseau, Buffon,[63] and many others, write in prose, and yet their expressions are highly poetical; while others make verses which contain no tinge of poetic feeling. Still less it is the faculty of rhyming, since among the ancients rhyme was entirely unknown, and among the moderns, poetry is not always in rhyme.

Now all great poets have this part of the brain much developed, but all who have it large are not necessarily great poets, though they be found of poetical conceptions. Women illustrate this point; they often possess the organ much developed; are fond of poetry; but seldom excel in its composition.

I think that the poetic turn of mind results from a peculiar mode of feeling, a certain manner of viewing the world and events. A plain, unadorned description of things as they are cannot be called poetry; exaltation, imagination, inspiration, rapture, and warmth in the expressions, are requisite to constitute compositions worthy of the name; all is represented in exaggerated terms, in a state of perfection, such as it ought to be. Poets picture forth a factitious and imaginary world. Thus I admit a sentiment which vivifies the other faculties, and impresses a peculiar character called poetical or ideal. It may be combined with both the affective and intellectual faculties,[64] and aspires to imaginary perfection or completion in everything. It produces the sublime in the arts, makes enthusiasts of us in friendship, virtue, painting, music, or any other direction which our natural feelings or talents take.

The organ of this sentiment is placed by the side of marvellousness, and the two frequently act together, particularly in mythology. Poetry is often embellished by the addition of the mysterious and supernatural. I have collected many facts on this organ, and am quite certain that its function corresponds to the manner of feeling just now described. The degree of exaltation experienced by poets varies according to its greater or smaller development.

Too great activity of the sentiment is a frequent cause of unhappiness, since it makes us look for a state of things, which as it does not exist, we cannot find. I call its organ that of Ideality.

---

63 *Buffon*: George Louis Leclerc, Comte de Buffon (1707–88), whose influential, 35-volume *Histoire Naturelle, Générale et Particulière* (1749–88) and *Les époques de la nature* (1788) pioneered the scientific study of natural history.

64 *the affective [...] faculties*: distinct regions of the brain, according to phrenology.

3.12   Thomas De Quincey, *Suspiria de Profundis,* in *Blackwood's Edinburgh Magazine* (June 1845), pp. 742–3.

In this extract from his quasi-autobiographical Suspiria de Profundis *('sighs from the depths'), De Quincey describes the model of the mind upon which the reconstruction of his life is premised.*[65] *Anticipating both the Freudian concept of the unconscious and more recent notions of depth psychology, De Quincey compares the mind to a palimpsest: a manuscript upon which successive layers of text have been superimposed, but which nevertheless remain decipherable. So, De Quincey says, the past experiences of our lives remain 'sleeping' in the mind and can be recovered in moments of extreme physical or emotional trauma. This, for De Quincey, is a sublime revelation of the power of the mind, an 'astonishing' proof of 'the grandeur of human unity', which confirms the potential of the science of mind envisioned by eighteenth-century philosophy.*

What else than a natural and mighty palimpsest is the human brain? Such a palimpsest is my brain; such a palimpsest, O reader!, is yours. Everlasting layers of ideas, images, feelings, have fallen upon your brain softly as light. Each succession has seemed to bury all that went before. And yet in reality not one has been extinguished. And if, in the vellum palimpsest, lying amongst the other *diplomata*[66] of human archives or libraries, there is anything fantastic or which moves to laughter, as oftentimes there is in the grotesque collisions of those successive themes, having no natural connexion, which by pure accident have consecutively occupied the roll, yet, in our own heaven-created palimpsest, the deep memorial palimpsest of the brain, there are not and cannot be such incoherencies. The fleeting accidents of a man's life, and its external shows, may indeed by irrelate[67] and incongruous; but the organizing principles which fuse into harmony, and gather about fixed predetermined centres, whatever heterogeneous elements life may have accumulated from without, will not permit the grandeur of human unity greatly to be violated, or its ultimate repose to be troubled in the retrospect from dying moments, or from other great convulsions.

Such a convulsion is the struggle of gradual suffocation, as in drowning; and, in the original Opium Confessions,[68] I mentioned a case that nature communicated to me by a lady[69] from her own childish experience [...] she had completed her ninth year, when playing by the side of a solitary brook, she fell into one of its deepest pools. Eventually, but after what lapse of time nobody ever knew, she was saved from death by a farmer, who, riding in some distant lane, had

---

65 For details about the composition and publication of the *Suspiria*, see Money p. 86–7.
66 *diplomata*: official documents.
67 *irrelate*: unrelated (OED 1; which cites this passage as the first usage).
68 *the original Opium Confessions*: De Quincey's own *Confessions of an English Opium-Eater,* first published in the *London Magazine* in 1821.
69 *a lady*: usually identified as De Quincey's mother.

seen her rise to the surface; but not until she had descended within the abyss of death, and looked into its secrets, as far, perhaps, as ever human eye *can* have looked that had permission to return. At a certain stage of this descent, a blow seemed to strike her – phosophoric radiance[70] sprang forth from her eye-balls; and immediately a mighty theatre expanded within her brain. In a moment, in the twinkling of an eye, every act – every design of her past life lived again – arraying themselves not as a succession, but as parts of a coexistence [...] her consciousness became omnipresent at one moment to every feature in the infinite review.

[...] the true point for astonishment is not the *simultaneity* of arrangement under which the past events of life – though in fact successive – had formed their dread line of revelation. This would be but a secondary phenomenon; the deeper lay in the resurrection itself, and the possibility of resurrection, for what had so long slept in the dust. A pall, deep as oblivion, had been thrown by life over every trace of these experiences; and yet suddenly, at a silent command, and the signal of a blazing rocket sent up from the brain, the pall draws up, and the whole depths of the theatre are exposed. Here was the greater mystery: now this mystery is liable to no doubt; for it is repeated, and ten thousand times repeated by opium, for those who are its martyrs.

Yes, reader, countless are the mysterious handwritings of grief or joy which have inscribed themselves successively upon the palimpsest of your brain; and, like the annual leaves of aboriginal forests, or the undissolving snows of the Himalaya, or light falling upon light, the endless strata have covered up each other in forgetfulness. But by the hour of death, but by fever, but by the searchings of opium, all these can revive in strength.[71] They are not dead, but sleeping. In the illustration imagined by myself, from the case of some individual palimpsest, the Grecian tragedy had seemed to be displaced, but was *not* displaced, by the monkish legend; and the monkish legend had seemed to be displaced, but was *not* displaced, by the knightly romance. In some potent convulsion of the system, all wheels back into its earliest elementary stage. The bewildering romance, light tarnished with darkness, the semi-fabulous legend, truth celestial mixed with human falsehoods, these fade even of themselves as life advances. The romance has perished that deluded the boy. But the deep, deep tragedies of infancy, as when the child's hands were unlinked for ever from his mother's neck, or his lips for ever from his sister's kisses, these remain lurking below all, and these lurk to the last. Alchemy there is none of passion or disease that can scorch away these immortal impresses.

---

70 *phosphoric radiance*: the chemical element phosphorus burns brightly on contact with air; in
   De Quincey's day, the term referred to any luminous substance.
71 *But by*: comprising the two senses of 'however by' and 'only by'.

4

Gothic

Perhaps the best way of understanding the late eighteenth century's interpretation of, and infatuation with, the Gothic, is as a fascination with the hidden or obscure. The mystery of that which is just beyond view, either at the political or psychological level, draws the curious individual from their safe, stable existence, into a riskier world of fantasy, desire and fear, wagering that a return will be possible once the light of knowledge has been shone into the darkness. Such was the hunger of the reading public for Gothic culture's ability to articulate this kind of investigation, that most magazine issues were likely, by the end of the eighteenth century, to carry an example of the Gothic tale. This section presents extracts from a number of Gothic fragments, tales and longer works of fiction, that proliferated in the popular and literary press, demonstrating the attraction of Gothic writers and readers to experience usually hidden from view.

Three mechanisms for engagement with such sublime objects can, broadly speaking, be discerned in the following extracts. First, Gothic locations are typically historically and geographically distant, and are also either wild (mountains and forests), or dark enclosed spaces (dungeons). The wildernesses are usually described within the terms of the natural sublime exemplified elsewhere in this book. Mountains, to use the example of the extract from Radcliffe's *Mysteries of Udolpho*, appear to be never-ending, exciting awe and fear in the subject, while in the same moment arousing the imagination to awareness of such grandeur. Equally, the darkness of the dungeon, although enclosed, prevents the clear visibility of things outside the self, leading the imagination to try to fill the void with fantasy. Such situations require individuals – both characters in the texts and their readers – to investigate aspects of themselves not usually seen, to peek beyond the self seen in everyday, civilised life. This leads to the second type of engagement with the sublime, which has to do with the psychoanalytic (or proto-psychoanalytic) nature of Gothic writing. More than a century before such vocabulary was in place, eighteenth-century Gothic can be seen as a mode of investigating the unconscious, those nameless and often prohibited urges on the edge of experience. In the anonymous 'Triumph of Love', for example, the unnamed narrator's journey into his darker desires is expressed as a journey into a deep cave where, in seeing a man mad with grief for his past life of dissipation, he is confronted with his own desires. Similarly, 'Edwy' explores the experience of alienation by describing a Saxon pilgrim in an invaded land who is unable to find his way home. Such texts can be seen as attempts to grasp, by turning into narrative, experience that is usually beyond reach.

However, such attempts can never fully be realised; rather, they form part of a cyclical process of investigation leading to discovery of things that turn out to contain within them more mystery, which in turn needs to be investigated. Far from obscurantist celebrations of superstition, eighteenth-century Gothic offers numerous texts which document an insatiable desire for rational enquiry. At the level of narrative, highly episodic texts like Smollett's *Ferdinand Count Fathom*, or 'Leonto and Almeria', are structured as a series of enigmas or problems in need of resolution, but whose solution leads only to further mysteries. Fundamentally, the hidden is attractive because it *is* hidden, and asks the participants in Gothic – readers and characters – to investigate. So the typical Gothic heroine runs towards the object of her fears, enacting precisely what the readership is doing, but is rarely satisfied by what she finds; the boundaries of knowledge are forever expanding even as the subject moves towards the horizon, beyond which always lies the imagined sublime object.

4.1   Tobias Smollett, *The Adventures of Ferdinand Count Fathom*, 2 vols (London, 1754), I, chps 21–2, pp. 128–33.

*Ferdinand Count Fathom is the highly episodic story of the eponymous charac-
ter's journey across Europe from Vienna to London, and of his various adventures in
Britain. This passage, in which Ferdinand becomes lost in a forest and subsequently
finds a body in the cottage in which he takes refuge, has received attention partly
because of Aikin's mention of it in her influential essay, 'On the Pleasure Derived from
the Objects of Terror' (see pp. 127–30 below), but also because Smollett predicts many
of the Gothic effects that were practised more programmatically during the latter half
of the century. The darkness of the forest hides any number of potential threats in the
mind of the protagonist, and his response shifts from the imagining of hidden dangers
to a very physical experience of a nervous system close to collapse. Out of such mental
and physical terror comes a resolution to act, leading to his resolution to seek safety
in the cottage. This in turn holds a still greater terror, from which extreme of physical
and imaginary terror he has to extract himself once again. Such a cycle of imagined
threat, terror, and rational action leading to further threat was a familiar structure of
the Gothic sublime once the genre became established from* The Castle of Otranto
onwards.

[Ferdinand] departed from the village that same afternoon, under the auspices of his conductor, and found himself benighted in the midst of a forest, far from the habitations of men. The darkness of the night, the silence and solitude of the place, the indistinct images of the trees that appeared on every side, 'stretching their extravagant arms athwart the gloom',[1] conspired, with the dejection of spirits occasioned by his loss, to disturb his fancy, and raise strange phantoms in his imagination. Although he was not naturally superstitious, his mind began to be invaded with an awful horror, that gradually prevailed over all the consolations of reason and philosophy; nor was his heart free from the terrors of assassination. In order to dissipate these disagreeable reveries, he had recourse to the conversation of his guide, by whom he was entertained with the history of divers travellers who had been robbed and murdered by ruffians, whose retreat was in the recesses of that very wood.

In the midst of this communication, which did not at all tend to the elevation of our hero's spirits, the conductor made an excuse for dropping behind, while our traveller jogged on in expectation of being joined again by him in a few minutes. He was, however, disappointed in that hope; the sound of the other horse's feet by degrees grew more and more faint, and at last altogether died away. Alarmed at this circumstance, Fathom halted in the middle of the road, and listened with the most fearful attention; but his sense of hearing was saluted with nought but the dismal sighings of the trees, that seemed to foretell an approaching storm. Accordingly, the heavens contracted a more dreary aspect, the lightning began to gleam, and the thunder to roll, and the tempest, raising its voice to a tremendous roar, descended in a torrent of rain.

In this emergency, the fortitude of our hero was almost quite overcome. So many concurring circumstances of danger and distress might have appalled the most undaunted breast; what impression then must they have made upon the mind of Ferdinand, who was by no means a man to set fear at defiance! Indeed, he had well-nigh lost the use of his reflection, and was actually invaded to the skin, before he could recollect himself so far as to quit the road, and seek for shelter among the thickets that surrounded him. Having rode some furlongs into the forest, he took his station under a tuft of tall trees, that screened him from the storm, and in that situation called a council within himself, to deliberate upon his next excursion. He persuaded himself that his guide had deserted him for the present, in order to give intelligence of a traveller to some gang of robbers with whom he was connected; and that he must of necessity fall a prey to those banditti, unless he should have the good fortune to elude their search, and disentangle himself from the mazes of the wood.

Harrowed with these apprehensions, he resolved to commit himself to the mercy of the hurricane, as of two evils the least, and penetrate straightforwards through some devious opening, until he should be delivered from the forest. For this purpose he turned his horse's head in a line quite contrary to the direction of the high road which he had left, on the supposition that the robbers would pursue that track in quest of him, and that they would never dream of his deserting the highway, to traverse an unknown forest, amidst the darkness of such a boisterous night. After he had continued in this progress through a succession

---

1 John Armstrong, *The Art of Preserving Health: A Poem* (1744) I, p. 744.

of groves, and bogs, and thorns, and brakes, by which not only his clothes, but also his skin suffered in a grievous manner, while every nerve quivered with eagerness and dismay, he at length reached an open plain, and pursuing his course, in full hope of arriving at some village, where his life would be safe, he descried a rush-light at a distance, which he looked upon as the star of his good fortune, and riding towards it at full speed, arrived at the door of a lone cottage, into which he was admitted by an old woman, who, understanding he was a bewildered traveller, received him with great hospitality. [...]

He was accordingly ushered up by a sort of ladder into an apartment furnished with a standing-bed, and almost half filled with trusses of straw. He seemed extremely well pleased with his lodging, which in reality exceeded his expectation; and his kind landlady, cautioning him against letting the candle approach the combustibles, took her leave, and locked the door on the outside.

Fathom, whose own principles taught him to be suspicious, and ever upon his guard against the treachery of his fellow-creatures, could have dispensed with this instance of her care, in confining her guest to her chamber, and began to be seized with strange fancies, when he observed that there was no bolt on the inside of the door, by which he might secure himself from intrusion. In consequence of these suggestions, he proposed to take an accurate survey of every object in the apartment, and, in the course of his inquiry, had the mortification to find the dead body of a man, still warm, who had been lately stabbed, and concealed beneath several bundles of straw.

Such a discovery could not fail to fill the breast of our hero with unspeakable horror; for he concluded that he himself would undergo the same fate before morning, without the interposition of a miracle in his favour. In the first transports of his dread, he ran to the window, with a view to escape by that outlet, and found his flight effectually obstructed by diverse strong bars of iron. Then his heart began to palpitate, his hair to bristle up, and his knees to totter; his thoughts teemed with presages of death and destruction; his conscience rose up in judgment against him, and he underwent a severe paroxysm of dismay and distraction. His spirits were agitated into a state of fermentation that produced a species of resolution akin to that which is inspired by brandy or other strong liquors, and, by an impulse that seemed supernatural, he was immediately hurried into measures for his own preservation.

What upon a less interesting occasion his imagination durst not propose, he now executed without scruple or remorse. He undressed the corpse that lay bleeding among the straw, and, conveying it to the bed in his arms, deposited it in the attitude of a person who sleeps at his ease; then he extinguished the light, took possession of the place from whence the body had been removed, and, holding a pistol ready cocked in each hand, waited for the sequel with that determined purpose which is often the immediate production of despair. About midnight he heard the sound of feet ascending the ladder; the door was softly opened; he saw the shadow of two men stalking towards the bed, a dark lantern being unshrouded, directed their aim to the supposed sleeper, and he that held it thrust a poniard to his heart; the force of the blow made a compression on the chest, and a sort of groan issued from the windpipe of the defunct; the stroke was repeated, without producing a repetition of the note, so that the assassins concluded the work was effectually done, and retired for the present with a design to return and rifle the deceased at their leisure.

Never had our hero spent a moment in such agony as he felt during this operation; the whole surface of his body was covered with a cold sweat, and his nerves were relaxed with an universal palsy. In short, he remained in a trance that, in all probability, contributed to his safety; for, had he retained the use of his senses, he might have been discovered by the transports of his fear. The first use he made of his retrieved recollection, was to perceive that the assassins had left the door open in their retreat; and he would have instantly availed himself of this their neglect, by sallying out upon them, at the hazard of his life, had he not been restrained by a conversation he overheard in the room below, importing, that the ruffians were going to set out upon another expedition, in hopes of finding more prey. They accordingly departed, after having laid strong injunctions upon the old woman to keep the door fast locked during their absence; and Ferdinand took his resolution without farther delay [...]

4.2   Horace Walpole, *The Castle of Otranto* (London, 1765), ch. 1, pp. 21–6.

The Castle of Otranto *is usually, and probably correctly, thought of as the first novel in the modern Gothic tradition. Purporting to have been translated from an Italian manuscript found in the house of a 'Catholic family in the North of England', it concerns the attempts of Manfred, the usurping Prince of Otranto, to hold on to power in the face of a series of prophecies foretelling his doom, and attempts by the younger protagonists to resist his autocratic power.*

Perhaps Walpole's major innovation as the originator of a mode of writing is his use of an exotic and sinister setting, in this case an Italian castle, in which gloom works as part of an apparatus to obscure truths about men and things, so that solutions to mysteries can gradually be revealed. Clearly, the heightened emotion, sometimes verging on hysteria, created by suspense, provides the reader with something of a cheap thrill. But this thrill is part of a more interesting process: the astonishment felt by characters and readers at these hyperbolised experiences leads the imagination to construe meanings for events, which have in turn to be realised by rational enquiry. But the revelations brought up by such enquiry turn out to bring up more mysteries, in a cyclical process that has its final reference in the sublime. In this passage, Manfred has just attempted to force the young Isabella, who was to be Manfred's late son's bride, to marry him, but Isabella has managed to escape. Walpole focuses on the workings of Isabella's mind as she imagines the meanings of the sensory information coming to her. The sequence ends with her meeting

*the prisoner, who provides temporary salvation but whose identity turns out to be
another enigma to be unravelled.*

That Lady [Isabella], whose resolution had given way to terror the moment
she had quitted *Manfred*, continued her flight to the bottom of the principal
staircase. There she stopped, not knowing whither to direct her steps, nor how
to escape from the impetuosity of the Prince [Manfred]. The gates of the castle
she knew were locked, and guards placed in the court. Should she, as her heart
prompted her, go and prepare *Hippolita*[2] for the cruel destiny that awaited her,
she did not doubt but *Manfred* would seek her there, and that his violence would
incite him to double the injury he meditated, without leaving room for them
to avoid the impetuosity of his passions. Delay might give him time to reflect
on the horrid measures he had conceived, or produce some circumstance in her
favour, if she could, for that night at least, avoid his odious purpose. – Yet where
conceal herself! how avoid the pursuit he would infallibly make throughout
the castle! As these thoughts passed rapidly through her mind, she recollected a
subterraneous passage which led from the vaults of the castle to the church of
St. *Nicholas*. Could she reach the altar before she was overtaken, she knew even
Manfred's violence would not dare to profane the sacredness of the place; and she
determined, if no other means of deliverance offered, to shut herself up forever
among the holy virgins, whose convent was contiguous to the cathedral. In this
resolution, she seized a lamp that burned at the foot of the staircase, and hurried
towards the secret passage.
    The lower part of the castle was hollowed into several intricate cloisters; and
it was not easy for one under so much anxiety to find the door that opened into
the cavern. An awful silence reigned throughout those subterraneous regions,
except now and then some blasts of wind that shook the doors she had passed,
and which, grating on the rusty hinges, were re-echoed through that long labyrinth of darkness. Every murmur struck her with new terror;— yet more she
dreaded to hear the wrathful voice of *Manfred* urging his domestics to pursue her.
She trod as softly as impatience would give her leave,— yet frequently stopped,
and listened to hear if she was followed. In one of those moments she thought
she heard a sigh. She shuddered, and recoiled a few paces. In a moment she
thought she heard the step of some person. Her blood curdled: she concluded it
was *Manfred*. Every suggestion that horror could inspire rushed into her mind.
She condemned her rash flight, which had thus exposed her to his rage in a
place where her cries were not likely to draw anybody to her assistance. Yet the
sound seemed not to come from behind: if *Manfred* knew where she was, he
must have followed her: she was still in one of the cloisters, and the steps she
had heard were too distinct to proceed from the way she had come. Cheered
with this reflection, and hoping to find a friend in whoever was not the prince,
she was going to advance, when a door that stood ajar, at some distance to the

2 *Hippolita*: Manfred's current wife.

left, was opened gently; but ere her lamp, which she held up, could discover who opened it, the person retreated precipitately on seeing the light.

Isabella, whom every incident was sufficient to dismay, hesitated whether she should proceed. Her dread of Manfred soon outweighed every other terror. The very circumstance of the person avoiding her, gave her a sort of courage. It could only be, she thought, some domestic belonging to the castle. Her gentleness had never raised her an enemy, and conscious innocence made her hope that, unless sent by the prince's order to seek her, his servants would rather assist than prevent her flight. Fortifying herself with these reflections, and believing, by what she could observe, that she was near the mouth of the subterraneous cavern, she approached the door that had been opened; but a sudden gust of wind, that met her at the door, extinguished her lamp, and left her in total darkness.

Words cannot paint the horror of the princess's situation. Alone, in so dismal a place, her mind impressed with all the terrible events of the day, hopeless of escaping, expecting every moment the arrival of *Manfred*, and far from tranquil on knowing she was within reach of somebody, she knew not whom, who for some cause seemed concealed thereabouts; all these thoughts crowded on her distracted mind, and she was ready to sink under her apprehensions. She addressed herself to every saint in heaven, and inwardly implored their assistance. For a considerable time she remained in an agony of despair. At last, as softly as was possible, she felt for the door, and having found it, entered trembling into the vault from whence she had heard the sigh and steps. It gave her a kind of momentary joy to perceive an imperfect ray of clouded moonshine gleam from the roof of the vault, which seemed to be fallen in, and from whence hung a fragment of earth or building, she could not distinguish which, that appeared to have been crushed inwards. She advanced eagerly towards this chasm, when she discerned a human form standing close against the wall.

She shrieked, believing it the ghost of her betrothed *Conrad*. The figure, advancing, said in a submissive voice, be not alarmed, lady, I will not injure you.

4.3 Anna Laetitia Aikin, 'On the Pleasure Derived from Objects of Terror' in J. & A. L. Aikin, *Miscellaneous Pieces, in Prose* (London, 1773), pp. 119–27.

This essay on the aesthetics of terror, was one of the first theoretical explorations of Gothic effect, and had a powerful influence on that genre of writing during the 50 years following its publication. It appeared first in a slim volume of critical essays which Aikin (1743–1825) – better known after her marriage as 'Mrs. Barbauld' – published with her brother John, and was republished at least ten times up until 1820.

The paradox that the essay attempts to resolve is well stated in the title, and Aikin considers a number of aesthetic strategies to this end. She first rules out those 'scenes of misery' in which we enjoy the moral sentiment of empathy with those who are suffering, concentrating instead on 'objects of pure terror': examples from trag-edy, and from the 'Gothic romance' and 'Eastern tale', are given. The first solution suggested by Aikin has to do with narrative suspense: the reader, sometimes despite their better judgment, endures the terrible in order to satisfy the craving to know what lies beyond. This explanation, Aikin argues, suggests a lower form of aesthetic experience, because it is involuntary on the part of the reader and manipulative on the part of the writer. Higher experiences of terror, on the other hand, are entertained voluntarily by the sophisticated reader, because they recognise from experience that anything surprising – be it positive or negative – causes an expansion of the imagina-tive powers; a sense of jubilation at this state ensues, which confounds the mind's empirical perception of terror. In arguing this, Aikin offers a defence of the sensa-tionalism and hysterics of Gothic by pointing to the pleasurable imaginative activity that it stimulates, as the reader is progressively pointed towards as yet undiscovered objects.

That the exercise of our benevolent feelings, as called forth by the view of human afflictions, should be a source of pleasure, cannot appear wonderful to one who considers that relation between the moral and natural system of man, which has connected a degree of satisfaction with every action or emotion productive of the general welfare. The painful sensation immediately arising from a scene of misery, is so much softened and alleviated by the reflex sense of self-approbation attending virtuous sympathy, that we find, on the whole, a very exquisite and refined pleasure remaining, which makes us desirous of again being witnesses to such scenes, instead of flying from them with disgust and horror. It is obvious how greatly such a provision must conduce to the ends of mutual support and assistance. But the apparent delight with which we dwell upon objects of pure terror, where our moral feelings are not in the least concerned, and no passion seems to be excited but the depressing one of fear, is a paradox of the heart, much more difficult of solution.

The reality of this source of pleasure seems evident from daily observation. The greediness with which the tales of ghosts and goblins, of murders, earth-quakes and shipwrecks, and all the most terrible disasters attending human life, are devoured by every ear, must have been generally remarked. Tragedy, the most favourite work of fiction, has taken a full share of those scenes; it has, 'supt full with horrors'[3] – and has perhaps been more indebted to them for public admiration than to its tender and pathetic parts. The ghost of Hamlet, Macbeth descending into the witches' cave, and the tent scene in Richard, command as forcibly the attention of our souls as the parting Jaffeir and Belvedera,[4] the fall

---

3 *'supt full with horrors'*: *Macbeth*, V, v, 13.
4 *Jaffeir and Belvedera*: characters in Thomas Shadwell, *The Humours of the Army* (1713).

of Wolsey,[5] or the death of Shore.[6] The inspiration of *terror* was by the ancient critics assigned as the peculiar province of tragedy; and the Greek and Roman tragedians have introduced some extraordinary personages for this purpose: not only the shades of the dead, but the furies, and other fabulous inhabitants of the infernal regions. Collins, in his most poetical ode to Fear, has finely enforced this idea.

> Tho gentle pity claim her mingled part,
> Yet all the thunders of the scene are thine.[7]

The old Gothic romance and the Eastern tale, with their genii, giants, enchantments and transformations, however a refined critic may censure them as absurd and extravagant, will ever retain a most powerful influence on the mind, and interest the reader independent of all peculiarity of taste. Thus the great Milton, who had a strong bias to these wildnesses of the imagination, has with striking effect made the stories 'of forests and enchantments drear' a favourite subject with his *Penseroso*; and had undoubtedly their awakening images strong upon his mind when he breaks out:

> Call up him the left half-told
> The story of Cambuscan bold; &c.[8]

How are we then to account for the pleasure derived from such objects? I have often been led to imagine that there is a deception in these cases; and that the avidity with which we attend is not a proof of our receiving real pleasure. The pain of suspense, and the irresistible desire of satisfying curiosity, when once raised, will account for our eagerness to go quite through an adventure, though we suffer actual pain during the whole course of it. We rather choose to suffer the smart pang of a violent emotion than the uneasy craving of an unsatisfied desire. That this principle, in many instances, may involuntarily carry us through what we dislike, I am convinced from experience. This is the impulse which renders the poorest and most insipid narrative interesting when once we get fairly into it; and I have frequently felt it with regard to our modern novels, which, if lying on my table, and taken up in an idle hour, have led me through the most tedious and disgusting pages, while, like Pistol eating his leek,[9] I have swallowed and

---

5 *Wolsey*: in Shakespeare's *Henry VIII*.

6 *Shore*: mistress to Edward IV and the subject of a number of plays, including Thomas Heywood's *History of King Edward the Fourth* (1613) and Nicholas Rowe's *The Tragedy of Jane Shore* (1714).

7 William Collins, 'Ode to Fear' (1746), ll. 44–5.

8 Milton, 'Il Penseroso' [The brooding or melancholy person], ll. 109–10. Milton's reference is to Chaucer's unfinished *Squire's Tale*, an orientalist and fantastical story of the Tartar King Cambuscan and his family.

9 *Pistol eating his leek*: in *Henry V*, V, i, Pistol is forced by the Welshman Fluellen to eat a raw leek after he mocked the tradition of wearing leeks on St David's day.

execrated to the end. And it will not only force us through dullness, but through actual torture – through the relation of a Damien's execution,[10] or an inquisitor's act of faith. When children, therefore, listen with pale and mute attention to the frightful stories of apparitions, we are not, perhaps, to imagine that they are in a state of enjoyment, any more than the poor bird which is dropping into the mouth of the rattlesnake – they are chained by the ears, and fascinated by curiosity. This solution, however, does not satisfy me with respect to the well-wrought scenes of artificial terror which are formed by a sublime and vigorous imagination. Here, though we know before-hand what to expect, we enter into them with eagerness, in quest of a pleasure already experienced. This is the pleasure constantly attached to the excitement of surprise from new and wonderful objects. A strange and unexpected twist awakens the mind, and keeps it on the stretch; and where the agency of invisible beings is introduced, of 'forms unseen, and mightier far than we',[11] our imagination, darting forth, explores with rapture the new world which is open to its view, and rejoices in the expansion of its powers. Passion and fancy co-operating elevate the soul to its highest pitch; and the pain and terror is lost in amazement. Hence, the more wild, fanciful, and extraordinary are the circumstance of a scene of horror, the more pleasure we receive from it; and where they are too near common nature, though violently borne by curiosity through the adventure, we cannot repeat it or reflect on it, without an overbalance of pain. In the 'Arabian Nights' are many most striking examples of the terrible joined with the marvellous: the story of Alladin, and the travels of Sindbad, are particularly excellent. 'The Castle of Otranto'[12] is a very spirited modern attempt upon the same plan of mixed terror, adapted to the model of Gothic romance. The best conceived, and most strongly worked-up scene of mere natural horror that I recollect, is in Smollett's 'Ferdinand Count Fathom';[13] where the hero, entertained in a lone house in a forest, finds a corpse just slaughtered in the room where he is sent to sleep, and the door of which is locked upon him. It may be amusing for the reader to compare his feelings upon these, and from thence form his opinion of the justness of my theory.

4.4   Anon., 'The Triumph of Beauty', *in The European Magazine* (January, March, April 1782), pp. 10–12, 259–60.

Although this anonymous story ends up being a simple moralistic tale about the dangers of vice and the liberation of virtue, the heightened, often hysterical, mode of

---

10 *Damien's execution*: Robert-François Damiens was executed in Paris for his attempted assassination of Louis XV in 1757. Descriptions of the gruesome execution were widely circulated, often as evidence of French barbarity.

11 A misquotation of Pope, *Essay on Man* (1733–4), III, 251: 'power unseen, and mightier far than they'.

12 Horace Walpole. *Castle of Otranto* (1764); see pp. 125–7 above.

13 Tobias Smollett, *The Adventures of Ferdinand Count Fathom* (1753); see pp. 123–5 above.

narration, and the responses of the characters, reference the sublime in a way that belies the moralistic conclusion. The narrator is a sentimental English tourist in Tuscany, where he meets a stranger in a state of some distress. The 'terror and dismay' evoked by this meeting inevitably have the effect of engaging his curiosity, and, unsatisfied by the locals' superstitious explanation of the stranger as a ghost, he goes to search out the truth. Journeying deeper into a labyrinthine hideout, the narrator is told a tale of the stranger's former life as an aristocratic libertine, whose disastrous scheming leads to his demise and ultimate penitence without hope of redemption. Rather like Coleridge's ancient mariner, he is doomed forever to tell his tale as a warning to others. His listener soon understands the relevance of the tale to his own life, and resolves to leave behind his ways of sexual licence. At this point, we realise that the stranger is an exaggerated representation of the narrator's own desires: in Gothic hyperbole, the narrator sees himself, and the journey to the place of abjectness has been one into his own mind. In this there is a clear parallel with the journey of Radcliffe's protagonist, Emily, in The Mysteries of Udolpho, *and with the 'bad' example of Emily's future life personified by Signora di Laurentini. Through an expanding process of terror, bewilderment and rational enquiry, the narrator finds an answer to those problems by a further surrender of self, to an orthodox idea of love that transcends individual desire.*

Omnia vincit amor, & nos cedamus amori.[14]

A Passion for solitude and rural pleasure induced me to pass the finest months of autumn in the most delightful and romantic parts of Tuscany. In one of my excursions I was bewildered in an adjacent forest; in vain I endeavoured to find the path that would conduct me to the villa of my friend. In this situation night came suddenly on, and created those alarms which result from being exposed to the dangers of some savage prowler. Chance conducted me through an avenue, at the end of which I found a large extensive plain covered with yews, beeches, and venerable oaks. On an eminence was seen the ruins of an uninhabited castle where a majestic linden[15] reared its towering branches over the mouldering battlements. An ancient chapel, which had as yet escaped the ravages of time, the clattering of a neighbouring mill, the hollow rumbling of the winds, and the melancholy murmurings of a waterfall, spread around this lonesome scene a gloomy horror. I heard the piercing accents of a human voice; I hastened to the spot whence it came and there beheld the mournful complainer, clothed in black prostrate on the ground, his hands lifted up to heaven, his hair dishevelled, and a countenance expressing all the bitterness of woe.

---

14 Virgil, *Eclogues*, X, 69: 'Love conquers all; and we must surrender to love.'
15 *Linden*: tree of the genus *tilia*, or 'lime tree', traditionally a symbol of love.

I approached him with respect, and inquired my way to Prato;[16] he made no reply, preserving the same posture and attitude: I repeated the question again and again with some importunity; at last he turned towards me, and, with deep sepulchral tone of voice, articulated,

'The days are for you – the nights for me – cease to disturb my meditations.'

Terror and dismay seized my soul; astonished at my timidity, I in vain attempted to resume my presence of mind – I thought I saw this being in darkness in bulk and hideousness – frightful spectres seemed to surround me – the air darkened an instant – a panic caught my senses – and a cold deadly sweat bedewed every limb. I fled the spot with the swiftest precipitancy, till I found myself at the brink of a precipice, which seemed to terminate in the regions of departed spirit: I paused; and looking which way to pursue my flight, a spire appeared before me, and, at my nearer approach, I saw the glimmerings of some scattered cottages. My fears were instantly dissipated, nor could I refrain smiling at my cowardice; nevertheless, what I had seen and heard impressed on my mind a sensation of the blackest melancholy.

[*The following day.*]

An irresistible curiosity prompted me to return to the very scene I had quitted in my fright: ashamed of my pusillanimity, I was firmly resolved to brave every danger: and, in this determination, I, the following evening, quitted my reverend host, bending my steps towards the spot, which was now disarmed of all its terrors. I calmly contemplated the object when I found him in the same posture of sorrow and humility. The rays of light, emitted by the moon and stars, gave me an opportunity of watching all his actions.

Already the night was far advanced, yet I was determined not to quit my position till the denouement of this strange adventure. Some hours after, he arose from his kneeling, bathed the ground with his tears and kisses, and retreated through a kind of labyrinth, but with so slow and solemn a step as enabled me to follow at a proper distance. He soon descended into the bottom of the valley; at the end of it projected a little eminence covered with box and creeping ivies, and at the foot of which he instantly disappeared; I hastened my cautious steps, but could not discover the least trace of habitation. I still persevered in my search, and at last I found an aperture in the rock, into which I entered, but with much difficulty; and, as I advanced in this subterraneous passage, it became more and more spacious.

Is it possible, exclaimed I, that this can be the retreat of any human being? Is it even probable that a man voluntarily conceals himself in the very bowels of the earth? No, certainly no. In fact, I knew not what to think, and I began to lose that presence of mind necessary on such situations – I thought of returning back – I feared I had gone too far, and rashly exposed my life to some beast

---

16 *Prato*: medieval town close to Florence.

of prey retreated hither. The reiterated noises heard at some distance, which appeared to be coming nearer and nearer, which were dreadfully alarming. My courage, however, did not totally forsake me; I advanced till a piece of rock opposed my passage. On farther examination I found it suspended by a kind of equilibrium; for it easily gave way, and, with its fall, the cavern resounded with a tremendous noise.

A sudden light, joined to a frightful spectacle, now opened to my view, and exhibited on every side an image of religious horror. Here this ghastly inhabitant was extended upon a large stone, hewn out in the form of a coffin, and absorbed in so profound a reverie, that even the clamour I had occasioned did not excite the least emotion. I drew nearer to this unhappy mortal with a kind of dread, mixed with a feeling of the tenderest compassion; and, on closer inspection, I saw the strongest impressions of despair and grief had furrowed his livid cheeks, which wore every mark of an extreme wretchedness; nevertheless there still remained some faint traces of youth and comeliness. His eyelids half open – his looks fixed and haggard – one hand extended towards heaven, the other impressed on his heart, which throbbed with the pangs of a perturbed imagination. Around him hung, on scrolls rudely sculptured and in large characters, the most striking sentences from the sacred volumes.

As the assassin in his sleep pursues the bloody phantom of him whom he has murdered, starting from his bed awakes, so, in like manner, this living corpse was roused from his reverie, exclaiming,

Wretched body! when wilt thou return to dust? O death, where is thy sting? O grave, where is thy victory? His frame trembled with the excruciating torments of his mind, while the big starting tears, or rather drops of blood, rolled down his pallid cheeks – the picture was too distressing to behold in silence – I ran to console his miseries. 'Pardon, oh pardon, the powerful interest you have inspired; I have sympathised in your agonies; deign therefore to tell me what terrible calamity has made you so singularly wretched?'

Surprise and astonishment were seen in every feature of his face. 'What destiny', exclaimed he, 'what destiny is more rigorous! I have fled the society of men. You discovered a retreat that I would have concealed from all human nature. What new enemy of my fatal existence has conducted you to this lonely and deserted cell?'

'No enemy, but the suggestions of a compassionate tender heart. It was I who addressed you the other evening; it was I whose voice knew not how to respect your solitude. Your words struck me to the soul; they incited an unconquerable propensity to learn your fate; to offer you my friendship, and give you every possible consolation.'

'Consolation can never enter the sepulchre I inhabit; it is sacred to groans, sighs, and fruitless lamentations – I have consecrated it to penitence and tears.'

'But remember that the Deity condemns a penitence too austere, and rejects the vows which have for their object the destruction of our being.'

'A life contrary to what I now experience, would be an offence towards heaven and human nature; yet I welcome the voice which invites affliction to lift up her languishing head. But my fate is fixed and my resolution cannot be shaken; nevertheless, I will unfold the shocking tale, provided you will swear religiously to keep it as a profound secret, as also the place of my retirement: that you spare me all manner of superfluous advice, and that you leave this cavern never to enter it again.'

'My eagerness to hear the history of so extraordinary a character induced me to comply with his injunctions. He then gave me the following narrative.

[*The stranger starts on the story of how, during his dissipated youth, he resolves to seduce a novice nun named Cecilia by entering her convent dressed as a woman. Finally, he enters her cell while she is asleep.*]

A taper at the farther end of the room threw a feeble light on the alcove, in which lay for the last time the tranquil Cecilia; this light, faint as it was, disclosed to my longing eyes, a multitude of charms. O what a fascinating spectacle is that of beauty and innocence in the arms of sleep! Unhappily I was too great a slave to my passions to revere the temple of chastity; I saw nothing but what served to inflame my senses, my eyes rioted in forbidden pleasures, – my burning kisses lighted up new fires in the bosom of this angelic maid – this discovery bereft me of every consideration – and heaven was witness to my criminal delights.

The lost Cecilia beheld me with amazement, terror and distraction – I with difficulty stifled her cries against her brutal ravisher – I threw myself at her feet, and conjured her to look upon me as unhappy mortal, – an unhappy mortal, whose audacity had but too justly incurred her hatred and indignation. 'Who,' said I, 'could behold such ravishing attractions, and not pant to possess them? Let me conjure you to make the avowal of your passion; and if the words of the most tender and devoted of lovers can efface the crime dictated by the acuteness of his feelings, suffer me to add, that heaven condemns this tyranny exercised on susceptible hearts: break then the chain imposed by ignorance, prejudice, and cruelty – in a speedy flight I shall become less culpable in your eyes – embrace the fortune of your adorer – this is to follow the sweet invitation of nature, and the sure road to future happiness. Let us fly these prison walls – Let us fly to the land of liberty, where –

'Cease, vile seducer, said the distracted Cecilia, this pitiful harangue inspires me with that contempt which I have for your person and sentiments – think rather to finish the abominable work, by not suffering me to live, after you have robbed me of what is dearer than life itself.'

Tears sparkling with the fire of indignation ran trickling down her animated cheeks, and her stifled sighs announced the extreme agitation of her mind. She seemed to struggle against the most visible despair: she remained for some minutes in the profoundest reverie; at last a more than human courage brightened up in her countenance.

'The crime is consummated, said she, (endeavouring to conceal the horror I had inspired) haste, take me from the spot which is now become insupportable.'

At these words, joy and ravishment took place to that stupor of astonishment into which I was before plunged. Without losing an instant of time, I ran back to my chamber, dressed myself in the clothes of my sex, and adopting every precaution which prudence suggested, I effected our escape in the most perfect security.

[they escape, but Cecilia throws herself into a river and drowns. The stranger is arrested and banished from the area.]

I no sooner learnt this circumstance, than I not only resolved to quit my native country, but to shun the society of the whole world. This project engrossed all my thoughts, and I feigned every necessary preparative for my going abroad; in this interval I meditated on making my retreat hither, which I have ever since consecrated to penitence and tears. To effect this, I disguised myself in a dress suitable to the horrors of my mind, and this cave I devoted as my future asylum; from whence I never ventured out, but when an universal darkness reigned; then I visited the place where you first heard my fruitless plaints. There I seemed to hear her shade reproach me for my perfidy; but far from being dismayed at this phantom of the imagination, I was even pleased to contemplate it, which I thought wandered incessantly about me. I even prostrated myself before her, and endeavoured to appease her moans with inarticulate sounds, sighs and tears. Every night these woods, these recesses are responsive to my bitter wailings; and my only luxury is the luxury of woe. There, I asked, what are the pleasures of a sublunary mortal? And I answered, they are like the rays of sun sporting on the deep, which are obscured by the first passing cloud.

I see, added he, in you, Sir, the appearance of youth, health and cheerfulness; but you have as yet made but a few steps into the career of life, a life which at first offers a series of iterated delights. But be not deceived by such fallacious appearances! Guard against the inclinations incident to youth; for if you once suffer them to blind your reason, you are from that moment treading upon precipices which will lead you to inevitable destruction.

It is here, Sir, pointing to his heart, it is here spring all the evils incident to human nature: we carry with us the seeds of misfortune, vice and crime – a thousand objects, a thousand circumstances, nay some trifling incident may lay a train of accumulated wretchedness. This heart of mine, has been my only enemy – my woeful history shows it with a vengeance! Let my misfortunes then serve as a terrible lesson – and remember the important truth, that the road to happiness is never to be found but in an uniform control of the passions.'

Here ended the recital of a tale, which had filled my soul with the tenderest compassion. I had sworn to obey his injunctions, and therefore silently retired from this scene of singular distress.

The day began to re-animate every creature, and opened a new world to my ideas. I now for the first time, reflected on the train of evils resulting from a criminal indulgence of the passions. I even saw those objects which before I used to consider as the highest bliss, in a point of view which called up a sentiment of pity. I entered a pretty village on the banks of the spreading Po,[17] and by its numerous flocks, and hilarity of its inhabitants, I pictured the return of the golden age.[18] Among a troop of blooming damsels was one in particular, who appeared to be a perfect beauty. She wore a hat ornamented with flowers, which half discovered a pair of eyes that darted fire. I was struck with the elegancy of her figure, her animated countenance, her fine complexion, and the delicate whiteness of her bosom – never did the Egyptian Queen, when drinking costly pearls,[19] dying with love and voluptuousness, display half the charms of this artless creature; nor could I figure Venus more attractive, when in her Idalian groves she caressed her favourite Adonis.[20] I approached her with respect – she glanced a timid look, and instantly retired. My eyes followed the object that had fascinated my senses. I was going to follow her, when I was stopped by the recollection of the virtuous and affectionate Julia.

What, exclaimed I, what violence am I about to commit against the most lovely and the best of women! O no, I cannot injure thee in thought. I have only given way to the surprise of my senses – my heart is incapable of an infidelity. A beauty has made a forcible impression on my feelings, but it is because she has thy charms, thy features, and thy attractions. No, my Julia; never will I cloud the serenity of thy brow with that demon jealousy. Thy empire over my heart is not to be shaken. My tenderness and assiduous attentions will justify thy happy confidence. I will fly to thy fond arms, and expiate my momentary error in thy endearing caresses. Then shall I hear the tender solicitudes which my absence has occasioned. In pronouncing this soliloquy I hastened my steps, and soon after joyously reached the villa of my friend, determined to abridge my visit, that I might return to the bosom of love, ease and tranquillity.

4.5   Anon., 'Edwy: An Ancient Gothic Tale', in *Walker's Hibernian Magazine* (August, 1788), pp. 408–9.

These passages, reprinted here in full, are extracts from a full-length novel, published three years later under the authorial name 'A Lady', as Edwy, Son of Ethelred the Second: An Historical Tale. *Their first publication was doubtless*

---

17 *Po*: major river in northern Italy. The geography here is very inaccurate; at its nearest point, the Po flows at least 60 miles outside the border of Tuscany.

18 *golden age*: here the pastoral golden age as depicted in Virgil's *Georgics*.

19 *Egyptian* [...] *pearls*: Cleopatra drank a concoction of pearls and vinegar as she died (Pliny the Elder, *Natural History*, IX, 119–21).

20 *Venus* [...] *Adonis*: Venus, Roman goddess of love and beauty, lived in Idalium in Cyprus; Adonis was her lover.

meant to publicise the forthcoming novel, but they can also be seen as examples of the 'Gothic fragment' sub-genre, which had become a popular form in magazines of the period. The studied incompleteness of the fragments means of course that they are more concerned with atmospheric and psychological effect than with narrative shape and closure, and can be seen as purely aesthetic exercises in Gothic, without the encumbrances of plot and characterisation. Further, the status of the text as a fragment also informs its construction of the sublime. In completed narratives, the bewilderment and terror occasioned by mystery prompts rational enquiry and action, and in authors like Radcliffe, leads to the ultimate resolution of enigmas in rational terms. In 'Edwy', on the other hand, the untameable power of sublime mystery cannot be foreclosed: we are presented with a protagonist, 'a Pilgrim' on some kind of lonely journey, but without history, and cut off from all understanding of what is happening around him or any means of acquiring such knowledge; the pilgrimage cannot be successfully completed. In the first of the two episodes, we find Edwy lost in a wilderness, an evocation of the sublime as alienation. In the second episode, the sense of a journey reaching its conclusion is more pronounced, but each point of hope disperses as the protagonist is led on, only to be frustrated by a new challenge and disappointment. The magazine publication of Gothic fragments such as these suggests a public appetite for the unresolved sublime, with its power to make the subject work ceaselessly to replenish the lack that it is the work of the sublime to negotiate.

On a gloomy day, toward the end of the Autumnal Equinox, when thick and louring[21] clouds had obscured the sun, a Pilgrim, with slow and unsteady steps less than from fatigue than from heaviness of heart, was met as he crossed a wide extended plain, by a troop of young men in the gay garb of war; – they passed without heeding him; and he heard one of them say – 'This is no day for our sport, we will put it off to another when the sun will gild the arms of the victor with his beams. – this gloomy day seems to portend, our sportive fight would end in blood.' The Pilgrim stopped as two of the knights passed him, and the words – My brothers! burst from his lips: he turned, and stood looking at them until they were hid from his sight by the hills that environed the plain on one side, as deep wood did on the other: – When he could see them no longer, he cast himself on the ground, and again repeated – 'My brothers! surely it was they? But a wretch like me, was not deemed worthy of their notice; or perhaps they remember not the features of the unfortunate Edwy. Let me not forget I have kindred, whom I count on as friends; and let me seek among strangers an asylum, denied me in my native land, and in my own blood.'

The Pilgrim remained some time in silence, while the deserted and gloomy look of the surrounding objects, and the black and heavy clouds that overspread the skies increased the weight on his spirits, and the sorrow that oppressed him. A cold damp wind blew from the mountains, and the trees of the forest groaned

---

21 *louring*: lowering.

to the blast: It blew the withered leaves along the plain; – everything wore the look of desolation. At last, as if frighted, he started from the earth on which he sat, and turned towards the hills which lay on the right, and which had hid the little troop that were passed from his sight: – 'If I can recover their view, he said, though at a distance, they may guide me to a place inhabited, where I may find shelter from the coming storm.' Saying this he began to move, but intent on the ill-fortune that every where pursued him, he walked heedlessly on until he found himself entangled in the hills, and knew not how to get free of them. Had his mind been more at ease, the wild variegated beauty of everything might have charmed him, but he was too sad to taste vernal delights. And finding himself faint and exhausted by fasting and fatigue, he stopped by the side of a clear brook that watered a dell, formed by the hill, and drinking a draught from the stream, he laid himself under the shelter of a rock which formed a sort of arch – and sleep – though it generally flies the wretched, soon closed his eyes; but it did not shut out those gloomy thoughts that tormented him waking. They continued to harass him during his slumber, which was broken and uneasy. After tossing from side to side, he at length started up unrefreshed, though by the increasing gloom he found he had slept some time. The clouds now wore a terrible appearance, they were streaked with a fiery red, which portended a thunder storm! He arose, casting his eyes on all sides; the plain he had passed, the gloomy torrent on one side, the surrounding hills among which he was entangled, and to the right a wide and desolate view of the ocean, which from the top of one of the hills he had climbed, he saw dashing against the rocky shore at their feet, were the only object[s] that presented themselves to the eyes of the forlorn Pilgrim. Looking toward the ocean, he thought the sky began to brighten, though each moment of remaining light was precious, as he had no hope of getting free of the labyrinth he was in, but by making use of it; yet he wasted those precious moments, and stood intensely viewing that bright spot, until the sun just going to set showed for a moment his last beams, then sinking from his sight, his hopes of getting free of the place he was in, sunk with it.

What now will betide thee? he said, descending the hill. The rock under whose shelter he had slept was in sight, he bent his steps, and again casting himself on the same spot that he had lately pressed, he could not contain his sorrowful thoughts, but again gave them utterance. – Alas, said he, in a voice broken by sighs, 'Why, oh Heaven, was I sent into this world, where no one owns or seems connected with me? Ah why, since it was thy pleasure to bestow existence on me, why curse me with a feeling of my sordid fate? Why was I not the son of a labouring hind? Then had I toiled for bread, and blessed thee?'

The above is an extract from the first book of Edwy. – The following is from the last.

The swelling passions which the sight of his native land had raised in the soul of Edwy, deprived him of all appetite, but finding himself faint with fasting, he hasted towards his dreary retreat, resolved when there, to taste some of the food which one of the mariners had given him in a basket. The building whose ruined battlements and dismantled windows were conspicuous enough to be discerned at a distance, was now not more than a quarter of a league off, the grey twilight was fading fast to darkness, and no moon or stars appeared. He kept his eyes steadily fixed on the object to which he was approaching, hoping to reach it ere the darkness which increased each moment, should shroud it from his sight. His haste made him make many false steps, which retarded his journey, and he began to fear he would be forced to pass the tempestuous night, houseless and cold, beneath the inclement sky among those dreary moors. This fear made him resolve to push forward with all his force; yet he made little way on account of his frequent stumbles. At last to his infinite joy, a light appeared in one of the towers of the building to which he was wending his steps, and soon after the tolling of a bell increased his satisfaction, he now began to hope, that notwithstanding the ruined appearance of the pile before him, it might be inhabited: the lights and the bell encouraged him to hope for it, but of what sort were the inhabitants was what he could not divine: not yet cared much about in his present emergency. A roof to cover him from the night; and a fire to warm his cold limbs was all he wished. The sound of the bell, and the dim twinkling of the light served to guide him aright, and in less than a quarter of an hour he arrived at the building; it was too dark to discern whether it was in so ruinous a condition as to exclude the hope of obtaining shelter in it. The bell whose slow toll continued still gave him hopes it was not uninhabited; and as he was bending his steps to that part of the building from which the sound proceeded, it suddenly ceased, and to his infinite sorrow the light from the top of the tower disappeared, and left the forlorn Edwy in total darkness. What to do, whither to betake him from the fury of the coming tempest which was ready to burst on his unsheltered head, now perplexed him. While he stood in vain looking for the appearance of the light in the place he had seen it before, a melancholy cry which passed over his head, without his being able to discern any object, in spite of reason, which made him reject the silly fears of midnight ghosts struck him with a momentary terror, and the silence which reigned broke only by the howling of the wind through the battlements and porches, added to the terror he could not help feeling. But what became of him, when somewhat, which appeared to have claws sharp as thorns, struck him on the face, uttering at the same time a short faint scream. His heart now beat fearfully and casting himself on his knees, he recommended himself to the protection of every Saint in heaven. His Earnestness in prayer, which took off his attention from the objects of terror around him, gave him time to recover; he began to breathe with more freedom. But not long after he heard something snoring at no great distance, and the same melancholy notes repeated. He now renewed his fervent supplications for a ray of light to guide him into some place of shelter. He arose, and with the assistance of his staff, endeavoured to grope for the entrance of the building, when a sudden flash of lightning made him again throw himself on his face. He renewed his devotions, until interrupted by a clap of thunder, which seemed to burst just over his head, while the hollow echoing of the vaults and empty dismantled walls of the desolate building increased, and prolonged the fearful sound; another followed, but it rolled to a greater distance, and a third seemed to die away: All was still again, save the howling winds. Edwy, during this interval, began to reflect, that the short light afforded by lightning's flash might have served to guide him to the entrance of the mansion before him; and he raised his face from the ground, in hope, that though the thunder had gone off, the lightning might still continue, and to his joy it did. Fixing his eyes steadily on the building, at last by the same short gleam, for which he so ardently wished, he discerned a low arched gateway and went towards it, waiting with breathless impatience for another flash. One burst from the clouds, and showed it just before him. He then let his staff fall within his arms, and groping with his hands, at last gained the entrance and went in.; but another flash let him see the roof in various places broken, and the wind which blew as piercing as without, showed the windows demolished and dismantled; he crept to a dark corner, and resting his back against the wall, was grateful for the slight shelter the place he was in afforded from the rain, which poured with violence through the broken roof. He was now again in total darkness, and in some time the wind died away, and the most fearful silence reigned around him. – Weak mortals – how hard to be contented! – The howling wind and the screams that had so much appalled him, would now have been music to his ears; it would have broke the horrid silence […]

4.6   Francis Walsh Jnr, 'Leonto and Almeria', in *The General Magazine and Impartial Review* (August 1789), pp. 342–8.

The following Gothic fragments present what is in some ways a fairly insipid narrative of a battle, a single combat and the efforts of a champion, Leonto, to rescue the heroine Almeria from the clutches of a magician. Its interest here is threefold. First, it begins with a defence of the genre of 'Gothic legends': the improbability of the action, far from being a fault, is the response of the 'old historians' to the far-fetched nature of their source material, which necessitated narrative expansion beyond the probable to arouse stronger passions, and resulted in tales, so it is argued, that stimulate the reader to the contemplation of greater things. Second, the successful outcome of Albert and Leonto's combat is frustrated, as human agency so often is in these tales, by supernatural interventions: a 'hovering army' comes to abduct Almeria, leaving the protagonists in awe at greater powers, and their human efforts confounded. Finally, the concluding fragment details Leonto's quest to rescue Almeria, in which he battles more or less blindly against a succession of unseen enemies. As in our extract from Smollett's Ferdinand Count Fathom, *the narrative is characterised by a cycle of obscured threat and desperation, countered by renewed hope, effort and achievement. Such a cycle, which is prominent in most Gothic tales of the period, references an understanding of the sublime as a play between bewilderment at, and resolution against, incomprehensibly greater forces.*

Notwithstanding all that has been urged against Gothic legends, I cannot help owning myself much attached to them. They were certainly written to stimulate youth to great and daring enterprises, and to inspire the mind with magnanimity. To produce such effects they were well calculated. And, notwithstanding that fabulous air, I am inclined to think they were mostly founded on historical facts. The ancient recorders of actions performed in remote ages laboured under many disadvantages. Superstition deformed, and ignorance maimed, everything which was handed down to them. The old historians were obliged (according to the taste of the age) to have recourse to marvellous relations of enchantments and necromancers. But, as they were sure of being disbelieved by the more enlightened part of mankind, if their works were calmly perused, they stretched their invention to the utmost to arouse their passions, and draw off the attention from probability and fix it on the captivating revels of imagination.

Such may, perhaps, be the effects of the story (or rather fragments of the story) of Leonto and Almeria. I found the manuscript among some old papers, and shall present to my readers such parts as I could make out.

[*The story starts with an account of a conflict between a virtuous king, Albert, and his ambitious rival Revelher. The youth Leonto is chosen as the champion for Albert's kingdom against the aggressor.*]

Albert, arrayed in his robes, attended by his council and the relations of youth, proceeded to the place of combat, where a stage was erected and covered with a purple cloth. At each extremity was a throne, and round each throne were seats for the council and arbitrators. The prince Revelher and his soldiers first ascended the stage, who were followed by the youthful Leonto and his aged father, venerable alike for his years and his virtues. His silver locks challenged respect, and his open countenance proclaimed him a friend to benevolence and to his country.

'My son,' said the venerable old man, checking the tear of parental anxiety which was starting in his eye, 'the fate of your country is entrusted to your hands. Be valiant, revenge her wrongs, and show yourself worthy of the honour conferred upon you. If an old man's prayer can avail, Heaven will succour us – Heaven will protect you! But oh! should fortune be averse, though the heart of thy aged father will burst, yet do thou, my child, avoid the deed of self-destruction, which has stained the memory of many a valiant hero; Live my boy, and look forward to Heaven's appointed time for the destruction of tyranny and deliverance of thy country; and remember that, as well as thy fortune, thy life belongs to that Power who alone has a right to fix its period. That Power, I trust, will see thee run thy race of glory; and I exult in the hope that an honest fame will enrol thee among the list of worthies which are to illuminate the memorials of ages yet to come.' He could add no more, but turned away to hide the gushing tear.

The worthy Albert was not less interested in Leonto's fate: with his own right hand he conducted them to the lists: – Adieu ,' said he, 'my hero! remember thy country, and forget not Almeria!'

Albert, and the arbiter for Ravelher, having ascended their thrones, the trumpets sounded, and Leonto threw down his gauntlet: – Ravelher sprang forward. They drew their weapons; – every eye was fixed upon them, and every heart throbbed with anxiety.

Ravelher pressed violently upon his antagonist, but the youth shifted his ground, and parried his thrusts with astonishing dexterity. The fury of each increased, and the arts of combat began to give way to impetuosity of youthful valour. Headstrong ardour and prudent recollection alternately propelled them to rashness, and checked their heedless fury. Blow was returned for blow, and wound repaid wound. The combat became every moment more and more interesting. The shields of both the combatants were severed, and they grasped their daggers in their left hands. The expectations of the two nations were now wound to their greatest height, when the sword of Revelher pierced the side of Leonto. The blood gushed from the wound – the youth staggered, and the army of the invader shouted, 'Victory! victory!'

Ravelher aimed his dagger at the breast of his foe, but by this he laid his left side unguarded; and Leonto, who had only staggered through stratagem, drove his poignard to his heart. And now the subjects of Albert rejoined, 'Victory! victory! the sword so long exercised in cruelty shall be exercised no more.'

In an instant, the noonday sky became darkened, hideous noises were heard, and shouts of soldiers alarmed the astonished Albert. He turned his eyes towards the city, and beheld lights in the air, proceeding from torches which an hovering army carried in their hands.[22] In a little time he beheld a troop, born upon the clouds, coming to the lofty turrets of his palace; and as they flew over his head, he heard the shrieks of his captive daughter. Leonto leaped from the stage, and would have pursued on earth the route which their passage through the air should direct; but in a moment the torches were extinguished, and all was utter darkness.

For two hours Albert and Leonto remained in this distressing situation. At length, Nicander, the magician, appeared above in his chariot drawn by dragons. 'Detested Albert,' said he, 'Nicander triumphs. Though Fate forbade me to aid Revelher, yet thus far is permitted, and I have revenged his fall.'

The sun again beamed forth, but the country was deserted; not a soldier of Ravelher's was to be seen. The wretched train proceeded towards the city; – all was horror and dismay!

---

22 *hovering army*: the idea of an airborne army is biblical, and there are a number of such interventions especially in the Old Testament. This episode recalls Elijah being taken up to Heaven by the famous 'chariots of fire' in 2 *Kings* 2:11.

Albert repented having proposed the combat; while Leonto mourned the fatal success which had reserved him for so much misery. In the midst of this distress and astonishment a soldier of Ravelher's was brought into the palace by the populace; a gleam of satisfaction enlivened the brow of Albert. Hope flattered Leonto that he should yet find his beloved Almeria. 'Slave,' said the monarch, 'where have your infernal magicians conveyed the princess?'

'Sir,' replied the soldier, 'I am a man inured to war; and therefore subject to the impulse of fear: but I am not lost to feeling. Your daughter is confined to the castle of the magician Nicander. To inform you of this, and to instruct you how the castle may be found, I have deserted from the camp of the tyrant. If among you one is found who has courage to encounter the dangers which surround the castle, and penetrate the innermost apartment, though no degree of courage can *insure* success, there is –

[*Here is another chasm in the manuscript; what follows seems to allude to the enchanted castle,*]

It was situated on a steep rock, and was illumined by innumerable lamps. Leonto pressed forward up the toilsome steep; the thought of Almeria supported him under the fatigue. Arrived at the summit he was permitted to rest; as he approached the castle, though no hand was visible, a huge club struck him with astonishing violence. Instantly the lights vanished. Leonto hewed his way in the dark through the hissing serpents which guarded the gate, while a noise like thunder issued from the castle. At length all was still again, and the knight preparing to force the hinges, of a sudden the gate opened, and Leonto, winding through a long dark passage, arrived at an apartment enlightened only by a self-suspended lamp. Looking round he saw nothing but sable walls distilling gore. A sullen groan tremulated the pavement, and the lamp fell to the ground – All was dark! numberless weapons now assailed the knight, but he fought his way through to another apartment illuminated by innumerable tapers. He looked around, but the confines of the room were concealed by a blue mist, which thickening presently obscured all the lights. The champion felt himself pulled forward by a rope which surrounded his body. Shouts reverberated from every part, while lights, of sullen faces, danced around him. Leonto felt himself dismayed. But in a moment his recollection returned; he severed the cord with his scimitar, and following his blows, struck a being whose cries made the castle shake from its foundation. He repeated the blow with added force, and a deluge of blood overwhelmed him; – at the same instant, a dismal groan gave the signal of dissolution, and the fall of the body convulsing the whole pile, a part of the building tumbled into ruins, and revealed the adjoining dome; in which was a table with mystic writing. The champion climbed over the ruins, and approached the table intent on the scroll; but suddenly a gigantic figure rushed upon him with his sword. Leonto avoided the weapon, and returned the attack, but without effect. Dreadful was the conflict which ensued! the champion of the magician wounded Leonto; but the wound only increased the fury of the hero; and after a hard struggle, he brought his foe to the earth, and severed his head from his body.

The magician now entered. Despair was in his look! With his incantations he endeavoured to disarm his adversary in vain! The dreadful hour of account was arrived. The demons of darkness neglected his call; and the champion of virtue smote off his head.

As the magician fell a peel of thunder shook the castle; the wainscot opened; and the daughter of Albert rushed into the arms of her brave deliverer.

[*This is all of the manuscript which is intelligible, but the sequel is obvious.*]

4.7   Mary Hays, 'The Vision of Cleanthe', in *Walker's Hibernian Magazine* (September, 1789), pp. 483–4.

The following is an early work by Hays (1759–1843), which was later republished in revised form in Letters and Essays, Moral and Miscellaneous *(1793). The protago-nist, Cleanthe (a variant of the Greek 'Cliantha', meaning 'glorious flower'), becomes lost in thought outside her home, and then literally lost in a forest, and has a number of visions. Taken together, these visions can be seen as an allegory of feminine sexual desire: Cleanthe is thinking about her beloved Alcanhor, then imagines two men fight-ing, before being ushered into a sexually-charged, 'Arabian' garden with Alcanhor, and being offered a liquor that, so it is promised, will bring her bliss. The fact that these visions are representative of specifically feminine desire adds a noteworthy twist to the use of the sublime in the Gothic. As exemplified by the preceding texts, Gothic's journey into unknown otherness and the escalation of mystery are components in the processes of self-discovery and self-mastery that the characters undergo: the dangers of bewilderment and self-destruction lead to a resolve to overcome such obstacles. Here, however, the escalation of fantasy has to be forestalled by a didactic voice from outside the discourse of the sublime, warning Cleanthe of the dangerous nature of her fanta-sies, and telling her to return to the safety of domesticity. If, as Barbara Freeman and others have argued, the eighteenth-century sublime is a masculine discourse aiming at articulating and ultimately controlling the experience of otherness in the sovereign subject, so the feminine sublime must confound such constructions.[23] Despite the pres-ence of the male lover in Cleanthe's garden, the vision of paradise is a feminine one, being oriental and inhabited by 'a train of young beauties' who praise her as the most beautiful. Alcanhor kneels, too, at Cleanthe's feet. The self-mastery (through humility) recommended by the moralistic voice at the end comes as something of an abrupt inter-ruption to the build-up of self-regarding sexual tension, finally taming the recalcitrance of the feminine sublime.*

---

23 Barbara Freeman, *The Feminine Sublime: Gender and Excess in Women's Fiction* (Berkeley: University of California Press, 1995).

Just as the sun was sinking below the horizon after a calm day in the autumnal season, the young and beauteous Cleanthe strayed into a thick forest that reared its awful shade behind the stately castle of the baron her father. The serenity of the evening – the plaintive cooings of the stock-dove – and the distant murmur of a water-fall – joined with the tender recollection of an absent lover, conspired to lull her into that pleasing train of ideas when the mind, abstracted from sensible objects, loses itself in distant and visionary pursuits. She was roused from this reverie by the sweet and melodious sounds of a lute, which at first swelled into the most sublime and elevated strains, and then, gradually dying away – was succeeded by a deep silence! – not a leaf stirring to interrupt the solemn repose! – The moon was rising, and cast a shadowy whiteness over the leafy umbrage which sheltered her. She started! and gazing round, perceived with terror she had wandered out of her knowledge, and of the various paths which presented themselves, was at a loss to conjecture which would conduct her to the peaceful, parental asylum she had unwarily quitted. In the midst of this perplexity her ears were assailed by the most mournful and piercing shrieks – a thick cloud covered the moon, out of which darted incessant flashes of lightning – the trees shook without a wind – and the howlings of savage beasts resounded on every side! A mortal paleness covered the cheeks of Cleanthe, her limbs trembled, a cold damp bedewed her face, and she sunk motionless on the ground. From this trance she was awakened by a clashing of swords, and saw approaching her two knights, richly caparisoned,[24] engaged in a fierce and desperate combat; – collecting her strength she arose, and, winged with fear, rushed precipitately into the thickest part of the forest, and espying at some distance a glimmering light like that of a lamp, ran towards it with mingled hope and apprehension! – as she advanced nearer she found it proceeded from the ruins of an ancient abbey; she entered trembling! and walking up a long aisle, at the end of which the light seemed suspended, she saw at the foot of an altar half destroyed by time, a woman spread on the floor, who appeared as if expiring, with eyes fixed, and features pale and ghastly: a stream of blood issued from her bosom, and her hand convulsively grasped a rusty and leaden hilted poignard! The timid Cleanthe, struck with amazement, gazed on her with unutterable anguish, unable to move either to assist, or to fly from the miserable wretch extended before her.

At length opening her eyes and fixing them on Cleanthe, 'whoever thou art, (said she in a sullen and hollow tone of voice), behold in me the fatal effects of heedlessness, vice, and criminal despair!' She ceased, and in convulsive pangs breathed her last! – No sooner had the guilty soul forsook the lacerated body than the light was extinguished! the earth trembled and shook, and loud peals of thunder, mixed with a noise like the roaring of cataracts, totally overwhelmed the spirits of the terrified maid, who screamed aloud and sank lifeless on the ground! – But how great was her astonishment when, after a few minutes, returning to life and recollection, she found herself in the most delicious garden, surrounded with all that could charm and delight the sense! The sun shone resplendently, and gilded

---

24 *caparisoned*: decked out, particularly in reference to riding tackle.

every object with his animating beams, the fervour of which was tempered by cool and refreshing breezes loaded with fragrant and odoriferous odours – all Arabia breathed in the gale! Groves of orange and myrtle, interspersed with thickets of roses, and beds of violets, flowers of every variegated scent and hue, and trees bending with fruit of the most beautiful and vivid bloom diversified the prospect! Soft music floated above, about, and underneath – every bower resounded with the voice of festivity, and all was pleasure, harmony and love! The terrors which had lately agitated the mind of Cleanthe subsided apace – her soul dissolved in softness; the roses were again flung over her cheek, and her eyes sparkled with hilarity and delight! She was rising to explore a scene so new and paradisiacal, when she saw approaching her, crowned with intermingled roses and myrtle, the brave and beauteous Alcanhor (for whom her gentle bosom had long sighed in secret); his air breathed delight, while more than mortal beauty seemed to animate his form! – He advanced, and kneeling at her feet poured out vows of tenderness and ardour – then seizing her hand, conducted her to a temple sacred to Loves and Graces. A train of young beauties crowded around, and with siren voices hailed her fairest of the throng! Her senses swam in pleasure, while half fainting she leaned on Alcanhor! A nymph, more lovely than the rest, quitting her companions, approached the enamoured pair, and presenting a bowl of an intoxicating mixture, 'drink, (said she) and partake of immortal felicity, or bliss that knows no period, or satiety!' – Her lover snatching the bowl, drank deep of its contents, and raising it to the lips of Cleanthe, she was about to taste, when a low voice sounded in her ears – *forbear!* – call to remembrance the ghastly figure, pavement dyed with blood, the convulsive pangs, the dying groans! heedlessness has already betrayed thee into danger – temptation is now plunging thee into vice! – despair! death! destruction follow! – *It ceased!* – Cleanthe started and dashed on the floor the fatal beverage! a loud shriek followed, succeeded by a hideous crash – and the whole vision faded away. Cleanthe looked around, and beheld the moon and stars glittering over her head, the waving foliage at the back of her father's castle, and welcome portico of his hospitable mansion. She rushed in, and in the soothings of parental affection, sought consolation and repose for her agitated spirits.

4.8 Ann Radcliffe, *The Mysteries of Udolpho*, 3 vols (London, 1794), II, ch. 5, pp. 165–74.

Ann Radcliffe's novels are amongst the most important works of eighteenth-century Gothic, and can be seen as the systematised and fully developed culmination of half a century of experimentation in the Gothic genre. The Mysteries of Udolpho, *Radcliffe's fourth and most popular novel, concerns the travails of the young heroine Emily St. Aubert, who is orphaned early in the piece, and is taken, more or less forcibly by her aunt's husband, Signor Montoni, to his castle in the Italian Apennines. The story consists of her adventures in, and escape from, Udolpho Castle, and of her subsequent return to her ancestral home in Gascogny, South-West France. The journey from France to Italy and back again is also a journey of personal discovery, with Emily ultimately resolving a series of mysteries concerning the life and legacy of her late father, and in the process developing from an overly-sensitive adolescent into a balanced and rational adult. In a number of ways, the narrative's movements to introduce and then resolve mysteries turn on Radcliffe's appropriation of the discourse of the sublime, which is sophisticated and self-conscious, but also, as the following extract demonstrates, problematic and at times contradictory.*

The extract exemplifies the emotional and political uses to which Radcliffe puts description of the natural landscape. A party composed of Emily St. Aubert, Signor Montoni (the villain of the piece) and Madame Montoni (Emily's aunt and recent bride to Montoni), and a number of servants, have left Venice and are travelling by coach to Montoni's castle, Udolpho, in the Apennines. Much of the novel is predicated on the associations resulting from the distinction between the pastoral and harmonious landscape of Emily's homeland (in Burkean terms, 'beautiful'), and the exciting but dangerous wildernesses through which she travels ('sublime'); during the first part of the novel she journeys through the Pyrenees and the Alps, where she experiences with joy – and only a small sense of danger – the imaginative expansion of the natural sublime. In the ascent through the Apennines to Udolpho, the reader is presented with Emily's familiar perception of mountains – they appear to be endless, afford literally and mentally expansive panoramas, and contrast pastoral scenes with the more rugged dangers of rocky terrains higher up. The view of the castle itself is couched in explicitly political language; it stands the 'sovereign' of the scene, is obscured by shadow, and appears in an imperial purple light. It is owned by the Italian aristocrat Montoni, whose name of course connotes mountains; upland sublimity is, then, closely associated with aristocratic and monarchical tyranny, which it is Emily's business to resist. However, Radcliffe's narrative very clearly encounters a difficulty, and there is a kind of backtracking in the comment that these scenes, 'had far less of the sublime, than had those of the Alps.' The association of the Apennine mountains with tyranny contradicts the former association of the natural sublime with political and personal liberation. Throughout, 'good' characters respond emotionally to scenery; in this extract, Madame Montoni's lack of sensibility is demonstrated by her being moved only grudgingly. Openness to the natural sublime demonstrates openness to personal and political critique and reform, as the perceptual horizon is constantly widened. Emily, for example, views a panorama with awe, but is nonetheless appreciative that her viewing position enables her to see what she lacks (her lover, Valancourt, and her freedom), as much as what is there. Thus Radcliffe's backtracking is illustrative of two divergent understandings – one conservative, the other progressive – of the political implications of the natural sublime.

As the travellers still ascended among the pine forests, steep rose over steep, the mountains seemed to multiply, as they went, and what was the summit of one eminence proved to be only the base of another.

At length, they reached a little plain, where the drivers stopped to rest the mules, whence a scene of such extent and magnificence opened below, as drew even from Madame Montoni a note of admiration. Emily lost, for a moment, her sorrows, in the immensity of nature. Beyond the amphitheatre of mountains, that stretched below, whose tops appeared as numerous almost, as the waves of the sea, and whose feet were concealed by the forests – extended the campagna[25] of Italy, where cities and rivers, and woods and all the glow of cultivation were mingled in gay confusion. The Adriatic bounded the horizon, into which the Po and the Brenta, after winding through the whole extent of the landscape, poured their fruitful waves. Emily gazed long on the splendours of the world she was quitting, of which the whole magnificence seemed thus given to her sight only to increase her regret on leaving it; for her, Valancourt[26] alone was in that world; to him alone her heart turned, and for him alone fell her bitter tears.

From this sublime scene the travellers continued to ascend among the pines, till they entered a narrow pass of the mountains, which shut out every feature of the distant country, and, in its stead, exhibited only tremendous crags, impending over the road, where no vestige of humanity, or even of vegetation, appeared, except here and there the trunk and scathed branches of an oak, that hung nearly headlong from the rock, into which its strong roots had fastened. This pass, which led into the heart of the Apennine, at length opened to day, and a scene of mountains stretched in long perspective, as wild as any the travellers had yet passed. Still vast pine-forests hung upon their base, and crowned the ridgy precipice, that rose perpendicularly from the vale, while, above, the rolling mists caught the sun-beams, and touched their cliffs with all the magical colouring of light and shade. The scene seemed perpetually changing, and its features to assume new forms, as the winding road brought them to the eye in different attitudes; while the shifting vapours, now partially concealing their minuter beauties and now illuminating them with splendid tints, assisted the illusions of the sight.

Though the deep valleys between these mountains were, for the most part, clothed with pines, sometimes an abrupt opening presented a perspective of only barren rocks, with a cataract[27] flashing from their summit among broken cliffs, till its waters, reaching the bottom, foamed along with unceasing fury; and sometimes pastoral scenes exhibited their 'green delights' in the narrow vales, smiling amid surrounding horror. There herds and flocks of goats and sheep, browsing under the shade of hanging woods, and the shepherd's little cabin, reared on the margin of a clear stream, presented a sweet picture of repose.

---

25 *campagna*: Italian for landscape or countryside rather than the province Campagna in southern Italy.

26 *Valancourt*: Emily's lover, with whom she had been forced to part by her uncle and aunt when they took her from France.

27 *cataract*: a waterfall of considerable size in which the water falls directly over a precipice; originally the word referred to the 'flood-gates of heaven'.

Wild and romantic as were these scenes, their character had far less of the sublime, than had those of the Alps, which guard the entrance of Italy. Emily was often elevated, but seldom felt those emotions of indescribable awe which she had so continually experienced, in her passage over the Alps.

Towards the close of day, the road wound into a deep valley. Mountains, whose shaggy steeps appeared to be inaccessible, almost surrounded it. To the east, a vista opened, that exhibited the Apennine in their darkest horrors; and the long perspective of retiring summits, rising over each other, their ridges clothed with pines, exhibited a stronger image of grandeur, than any that Emily had yet seen. The sun had just sunk below the top of the mountains she was descending, whose long shadow stretched athwart the valley, but his sloping rays, shooting through an opening of the cliffs, touched with a yellow gleam the summits of the forest, that hung upon the opposite steeps, and streamed in full splendour upon the towers and battlements of a castle, that spread its extensive ramparts along the brow of a precipice above. The splendour of these illumined objects was heightened by the contrasted shade, which involved the valley below.

'There,' said Montoni, speaking for the first time in several hours, 'is Udolpho'.

Emily gazed with melancholy awe upon the castle, which she understood to be Montoni's; for, though it was now lighted up by the setting sun, the gothic greatness of its features, and its mouldering walls of dark grey stone, rendered it a gloomy and sublime object. As she gazed, the light died away on its walls, leaving a melancholy purple tint, which spread deeper and deeper, as the thin vapour crept up the mountain, while the battlements above were still tipped with splendour. From those, too, the rays soon faded, and the whole edifice was invested with the solemn duskiness of evening. Silent, lonely, and sublime, it seemed to stand the sovereign of the scene, and to frown defiance on all, who dared to invade its solitary reign. As the twilight deepened, its features became more awful in obscurity, and Emily continued to gaze, till its clustering towers were alone seen, rising over the tops of the woods, beneath whose thick shade the carriages soon after began to ascend. The extent and darkness of these tall woods awakened terrific images in her mind, and she almost expected to see banditti start up from under the trees. At length, the carriages emerged upon a heathy rock, and, soon after, reached the castle gates, where the deep tone of the portal bell, which was struck upon to give notice of their arrival, increased the fearful emotions, that had assailed Emily. While they waited till the servant within should come to open the gates, she anxiously surveyed the edifice: but the gloom, that overspread it, allowed her to distinguish little more than a part of its outline, with the massy walls of the ramparts, and to know, that it was vast, ancient and dreary. From the parts she saw, she judged of the heavy strength and extent of the whole. The gateway before her, leading into the courts, was of gigantic size, and was defended by two round towers, crowned by overhanging turrets, embattled, where, instead of banners, now waved long grass and wild plants, that had taken root among the mouldering stones, and which seemed to sigh, as the breeze rolled past, over the desolation around them. The towers were united by a curtain, pierced and embattled also, below which appeared the pointed arch of a huge portcullis, surmounting the gates: from these, the walls of the ramparts extended to other towers, overlooking the precipice, whose shattered outline, appearing on a gleam, that lingered in the west, told of the ravages of war. – Beyond these all was lost in the obscurity of evening.

While Emily gazed with awe upon the scene, footsteps were heard within the gates, and the undrawing of bolts; after which an ancient servant of the castle appeared, forcing back the huge folds of the portal, to admit his lord. As the carriage-wheels rolled heavily under the portcullis, Emily's heart sunk, and she seemed, as if she was going into her prison; the gloomy court, into which she passed, served to confirm the idea, and her imagination, ever awake to circumstance, suggested even more terrors, than her reason could justify.

Another gate delivered them into the second court, grass-grown, and more wild than the first, where, as she surveyed through the twilight its desolation – its lofty walls, overtopped with bryony, moss and nightshade, and the embattled towers that rose above, – long-suffering and murder came to her thoughts. One of those instantaneous and unaccountable convictions, which sometimes conquer even strong minds, impressed her with its horror. The sentiment was not diminished, when she entered an extensive gothic hall, obscured by the gloom of evening, which a light, glimmering at a distance through a long perspective of arches, only rendered more striking. As a servant brought the lamp nearer, partial gleams fell upon the pillars and the pointed arches, forming a strong contrast with their shadows, that stretched along the pavement and the walls.

5

Crowds

In his important analysis of crowds, Elias Canetti links the experience of being part of a crowd to the sublime: 'in the crowd,' he writes, 'the individual feels that he is transcending the limits of his own person'.[1] Eighteenth-century and romantic-period writing about the crowd reveals that being part of a mass of people can involve the loss of individuated identity, in a two-way process which parallels cotemporary models of the encounter with the sublime, and with the natural sublime in particular. This loss is both belittling for the individual, because of the mass of activity of people and minds all around, and also self-aggrandising, because the individual feels that they have become part of a greater whole. Observing or contemplating a crowd of which one is not a part can similarly be both frightening and exciting, awe-inspiring and exhilarating, as great numbers of humans become one mass, to threaten or inspire the onlooker, as befits the moment. Such experience can also elude representation, because its power and complexity transcends the normal experience of the individual.

Speaking very generally, two types of crowd are dealt with in this section: the political crowd, that has met for a particular reason and with some particular cause in mind, and the more general crowd, whose members are going about their business or leisure, with little unity of purpose, and perhaps even unaware that they *are* a crowd. This distinction is unstable, and has been a vexed question for social historians,[2] but it provides a useful means of distinguishing between the very different experiences treated in this section: on the one hand, riots and protests, and on the other, descriptions of urban living, particularly in London. The eighteenth century inherited a tradition of popular protest, so that the anonymous author of *The Case of the Unfortunate Bosavern Penlez* could claim that the ransacking and burning of a brothel by rioters was a legitimate form of political action; out of the sublime chaos of a tumultuous and drunken riot comes a rational form of justice that transcends the criminal justice system. It is perhaps

---

1 Elias Canetti, *Crowds and Power* (1962), transl. Carol Stewart (London: Phoenix, 2000), p. 20.
2 See for example, George Rudé, *The Crowd in History* (New York: Wiley, 1964), pp. 3–35; and E.P.Thompson, 'The Moral Economy of the Crowd in the Eighteenth Century', in *Customs in Common* (London: Merlin 1991). Elias Canetti provides a detailed taxonomy of crowds in *Crowds and Power*.

with the Gordon Riots (1780) that the potentially unstoppable, revolutionary power of crowds, and the possibility that they could bring down the establishment, became clear to observers, and this was of course confirmed by the French Revolution (1789–95). The sublime power of the crowd can be viewed in either positive or negative terms; a vast mass of people and minds working in unity to transcend what was hitherto thought, or an awful assemblage of people caught up in an ecstatic enthusiasm, losing the will to think.

Those extracts that deal with more general crowds, mostly in London, describe a set of experiences – living in a large urban environment – to which people were still trying to accustom themselves during the period covered by this anthology. It is the shock of the new, of the magnitude, pace and variety of the metropolis, that is registered most often by new visitors to London. The nature of interpersonal relationships in a crowded city is also different from the country, being characterised by promiscuity, surprising intimacies, and competitive comparisons, which are at times self-belittling, at times exhilarating and sparkling with possibilities. In registering such ambiguity, eighteenth-century and romantic-period accounts of the crowd look forward to a modernist experience of the city as both enabling and alienating. Finally, the chaotic and bewildering crowds of London paradoxically go to make a city that is sublime in so far as it transcends any precedent from antiquity or the modern world.

5.1   Anon., *The Case of the Unfortunate Bosavern Penlez, by a Gentleman not concern'd,* 2nd edition (London, 1750), pp. 17–22, 37–47, 53–5.

Bosavern Penlez was a young wig-maker of Cornish origin who was hanged following a riot on 1–3 July 1749, in which a brothel on the Strand in London had been destroyed. The incident became something of a legal test case, and matter of popular debate, in which the competing claims to legitimacy of popular justice and the criminal justice system were played off against each other. Notably, Henry Fielding, then the Chief Magistrate of Bow Street, intervened in the matter by arguing, in A True State of the Case of Bosavern Penlez (1749), that the conviction and execution of Penlez were necessary for the maintenance of public order and defeat of 'mob-rule' in London. The following extracts are from an anonymous reply to Fielding's pamphlet, which not only argues in a limited sense for Penlez's innocence, but also for the legitimacy of the 'mob' in exacting justice not assured by the Law. It is claimed that, out of the passion, confusion and disorder of a riot occasioned by an unreflective desire for vengeance comes reason and a true sense of justice. The mob is not represented in this pamphlet as possessing the same power, and hence relationship to the sublime, it would have later in the century following the Gordon Riots and the French Revolution. However, this account still invests the grotesque crowd with a sublime potential, capable even, as it implies at one point, of justly putting the House of Hanover on the throne. In burning the brothel, the unified crowd creates a kind of public spectacle – like a scene of the burning of Troy at Bartholomew Fair – which enacts a performative and immediate justice upon wrongdoers.

To the point then. A sailor, who had, it seems, reason to complain of ill usage, in a house of ill fame in the *Strand*, where he alleged his having been robbed of a considerable sum of money; and, before he proceeded further, he applied to the keeper of the house for satisfaction of his loss; which was not only denied him, but accompanied with foul language and blows. A man would be enraged at less than such provocation; and, according to the honest tar[3] denounced vengeance to his house, and repaired immediately to his shipmates and brother sailors, whom he made acquainted with his grievances, and by this means became original author and ringleader of the ensuing disturbance: for this gentry, partaking of the roughness of the element they live on,[4] and more used to go to shorthand work with their enemy, than to proceed by way of copy of a writ, or Bill and Answer,[5] immediately espoused his resentment, and resolved to revenge the cause of their injured brother. Here was the plain and true cause of the beginning of this tumult, and no other; not that it was strictly justifiable, but it serves to acquit a parcel of brave unthinking fellows, of any premeditated design to offer an insult to his Majesty's Government, which their body had been the greatest support of, and which some of them had ventured their lives for.

Flushed then with a Sense of the Wrong done, as they imagined, to one of their Body, they got a Party together, and on the evening of the First of *July* last, came to the house pointed out to them for that in which the robbery or injury had been committed; this they presently forced their way into, and acting like true brave fellows, suffered no injury to be done to the poor brave damsels, who got off safe and unhurt; but levelled all their rage against the house and goods of the caitiff,[6] whom they looked on as the author of the villainy exercised on their brother Tar. Accordingly they went to work as if they were breaking up a ship, and in a trice unrigged the house from top to bottom. The movables were thrown out of the windows or doors, to their comrades in the street, where, a bonfire being made, but with so much decency and order, so little confusion, that notwithstanding the crowd gathered together on this occasion, a child of five years old might have crossed the street in the thickest of them, without the least danger.

The neighbours too, though their houses were not absolutely free from danger of fire, by the sparks flying from the bonfire, were so little alarmed at this most bloody outrageous riot, this terrible breach of the public peace, that they stood

---

3 *tar*: sailor.

4 *the element*: the sea.

5 *Bill and Answer*: In Law, charge and defence.

6 *caitiff*: 'contemptible wretch'; the author has previously described brothel keepers as those who prey on women as well as customers.

at their doors, and looked out of their windows, with as little concern, and perhaps more glee and mirth, than if they had been at a droll in Bartholomew Fair,[7] seeing the painted scene of the renowned *Troy* town in flames [...]

[*The following evening*]

A regular bonfire then having been made as before, all the goods of the house were triumphantly conveyed into it; and if the finding of Bundles and effects on any of the actors would have aggravated their guilt, numbers might have been seized with the goods upon them, between the house and the bonfire, where they were all carefully destroyed, to avoid any slur or suspicion of pillage for private use. This was carried to such an exactness, that a little boy, who perhaps thought no great harm to save a gilt cage out of the fire, for his bird at home, was discovered carrying it off; when the leaders of the mob took it from him, and threw it into the fire, and his age alone protected him from severer punishment. Nothing in short was embezzled or diverted, except an old Gown or Petticoat, thrown at a Hackney Coachman's Head, as a Reward for a dutiful Huzza as he drove by [...] When a bundle[8] was objected to [Penlez], it appears that he was perfectly ignorant, as well he might be in such a hurly burly and confusion, himself too disordered with liquor, how such a thing came into his hands [...]

Then as to the shedding the blood of this young man for the example-sake, without regard to the degree of his guilt, there is no room to think, that his death will be no more for the good, than it was to the satisfaction of the public; and that for a plain and obvious reason; because such a severity being too much for the nature of the guilt being actually chargeable on him, will serve to confound and destroy all ideas of right and wrong in the minds of people, who will be too apt to mix the remembrance of the general pity and compassion for his fate, with the crime he suffered for, a remembrance very fit to weaken their apprehension of an act, as a crime, is weakened or taken off, the fear of the punishment is but an inferior restraint, and may only produce more guarded, sullen, fierce and dangerous proceedings in those tumults, which the same levity of the populace that gives rise to them, would probably otherwise of itself put a stop to; and which, it is often more true wisdom than weakness in a government to wink at, especially where there is no reason to treat them as breaches of respect to itself: And indeed, as hot-headed, wild, and impetuous, as an *English* mob, when it is up, appears to be, there is, generally speaking, such a bottom of natural good sense diffused through the common people of *England,* that the least exertion of legal authority will serve to check their fury, or, of itself, set bounds to it, as it mixes with their management a spirit of equity, moderation and even good nature, unknown to the like popular insurrections in other countries, and is

---

7 *Bartholomew Fair*: notorious summer fair in Smithfields, London.
8 *bundle*: the prosecution had alleged at the trial that Penlez was arrested with a bundle of things stolen from the brothel.

perhaps of the best proofs of the peculiar power of liberty, to inspire gentle and governable good sentiments.

But was even this example to strike the intended Terror into the hearts of the people, is it quite clear that this extinction of their fire is a point so desirable? It is but too sensible a complaint, that the spirit of the *English* is already much broke, sunk and declined from its ancient manliness; so that such a further subdual of it might lower and deaden it, so as to leave inanimate the body of the People, and bury it in universal indolence, stupidity and carelessness; than which there cannot subsist a stronger symptom of the approaching dissolution of a free state, thus previously disarmed of no contemptible part of its vigour and defence.

Besides, the Mob is generally seen on the side of Liberty and Property; and everybody knows, that it is on those principles, and more glorious ones there cannot be, that the present family is established on the Throne. And should even those sacred words be ever so far abused, as to raise or revolt the people against its government, their natural common sense would soon open their eyes on the deception, and bring them back to order and submission.

That all mobs too should not be put on a footing, nor involved in one indiscriminate condemnation of riot, let those stand up and attest, who made their first public entry into power at the head of one.[9] [...]

And here the occasion presents itself as justly as it does rarely, of taking notice of such an instance of the old *British* spirit, as shows that still the sacred flame is kept alive in a few breasts, amidst a general conspiracy to its extinction, and that in the right sense and correct conduct of Mr. Sheriff, on this melancholy demand of the law, for the execution of his office; which however offered him so fair an opportunity to convince the world, by the demonstration of fact, that nothing could be falser than the imputation of a riotous seditious humour being prevalent among the people, and which had been the handle made use of to urge the necessity of this bloody example.[10] Nor did Mr. Sheriff miss it: And accordingly, in maintenance of the right and sufficiency of the magistracy to protect itself in the execution of its office, he politely thanked the officer, at the head of a military command, in ready waiting, for his proffer of service, in aid of civil power: And himself, in proof that his majesty's reign was that of the laws, and not of the sword, with no other guards than his own officers, and the ensigns of his office, attended the execution on horseback, when the poor unhappy young man was put to death with all the forms of solemnity of justice, and without the least appearance or shadow of any disturbance: Nor did he submit to it but with a resignation and composure worthy of a less deplorable end. Here then let

---

9 *Those* [...] *one*: presumably a reference to the accession of George I in 1714, or more generally to the widespread use of mobs at election times.
10 *Made* [...] *example*: Fielding argued in *A True State of the Case of Bosavern Penlez* (1749) that the conviction and execution of Penlez was necessary for the maintenance of public order in London.

us leave him, with his only wish, that he may meet with that mercy in the next world which was so *wisely* denied him in this.

5.2 Tobias Smollett, *The Expedition of Humphry Clinker* (1771), I, pp. 192–4.

Smollett's last work of fiction is an epistolary novel that follows a number of upper-middle-class characters and their servants on their journeys around Britain. Much of the interest and humour comes from the various characters' competing descriptions of what they see. The following letter, from the romantic heroine Lydia Melford as she visits London for the first time, is preceded by an account of the same subject by her uncle, Matthew Bramble, who notes in a similar way to his niece the size and voracious growth of the metropolis, and says of the London crowd, 'All is tumult and hurry; one would imagine they were impelled by some disorder of the brain, that will not suffer them to be at rest' (p. 186). But the result is grotesque: 'the capital is become an overgrown monster [with] a dropsical head', and he resolves to, 'explore the depths of this chaos; this misshapen and monstrous capital, without head or tail, members or proportion' (pp. 183, 190). In Lydia's interpretation, this grotesque is converted to the sublime, in a clear demonstration of the proximity and instability of these aesthetic categories; the city's size is invigorating in its unimaginable extent, the rush of the crowd is dizzying, and the splendour and wealth on display are sublimated finally into exotic fantasy.

About five days ago we arrived in London, after an easy journey from Bath; during which, however, we were overturned, and met with some other little incidents, which, had like to have occasioned a misunderstanding betwixt my uncle and aunt; but now, thank God, they are happily reconciled: we live in harmony together, and every day make parties to see the wonders of this vast metropolis, which, however, I cannot pretend to describe; for I have not as yet seen one hundredth part of its curiosities, and I am quite in a maze of admiration.

The cities of London and Westminster are spread out into an incredible extent. The streets, squares, rows, lanes, and alleys, are innumerable. Palaces, public buildings, and churches rise in every quarter; and, among these last, St Paul's appears with the most astonishing pre-eminence. They say it is not so large as St Peter's at Rome; but, for my own part, I can have no idea of any earthly temple more grand and magnificent.

But even these superb objects are not so striking as the crowds of people that swarm in the streets. I at first imagined that some great assembly was just dismissed, and wanted to stand aside till the multitude should pass; but this human tide continues to flow, without interruption or abatement, from morn till night. Then there is such an infinity of gay equipages, coaches, chariots, chaises, and other carriages, continually rolling and shifting before your eyes, that one's head grows giddy looking at them; and the imagination is quite confounded with splendour and variety. Nor is the prospect by water less grand and astonishing than that by land: you see three stupendous bridges, joining the opposite banks of a broad, deep, and rapid river; so vast, so stately, so elegant, that they seem to be the work of the giants; betwixt them, the whole surface of the Thames is covered with small vessels, barges, boats, and ferries, passing to and fro; and below the three bridges, such a prodigious forest of masts, for miles together, that you would think all the ships in the universe were here assembled. All that you read of wealth and grandeur in the Arabian Nights' Entertainment, and the Persian Tales,[11] concerning Bagdad, Diarbekir, Damascus, Ispahan, and Samarkand, is here realized.

Ranelagh[12] looks like the enchanted palace of a genie, adorned with the most exquisite performances of painting, carving, and gilding, enlightened with a thousand golden lamps, that emulate the noon-day sun; crowded with the great, the rich, the gay, the happy, and the fair; glittering with cloth of gold and silver, lace, embroidery, and precious stones. While these exulting sons and daughters of felicity tread this round of pleasure, or regale in different parties, and separate lodges, with fine imperial tea and other delicious refreshments, their ears are entertained with the most ravishing delights of music, both instrumental and vocal. There I heard the famous Tenducci,[13] a thing from Italy – It looks for all the world like a man, though they say it is not. The voice, to be sure, is neither man's nor woman's; but it is more melodious than either; and it warbled so divinely, that, while I listened, I really thought myself in paradise.

5.3 Thomas Holcroft, *A Plain and Succinct Narrative of the Late Riots and Disturbances in the Cities of London and Westminster*, 3rd edition (London, 1780), pp. 24–33.

The Gordon Riots of 2–8 June 1780 were the most serious manifestation of popular disorder in eighteenth-century London. The catalyst for them was the passing of the Papists Act of 1778, which gave to Catholics very moderate relief from the limitations in civil participation imposed a century previously, but the riots fed on popular fears of Catholic conspiracy, and the rioters targeted a number of symbols of property and authority including courts, the Bank of England, houses of prominent individuals and prisons. Most famously, the recently rebuilt Newgate prison was destroyed, together with the house of the judge Lord Mansfield in Bloomsbury,

---

11 *Arabian Nights*[...] *Persian Tales*: two collections of Oriental tales popular throughout the eighteenth century; *The Arabian Nights' Entertainments* (London, 1706), and Montesquieu, *Persian Letters*, trans. Ozell (London, 1722). The names that follow are middle-eastern cities featured in these works.
12 *Ranelagh*: Ranelagh Pleasure Gardens in Chelsea, West London.
13 *Tenducci*: Giusto Ferdinando Tenducci (*c.* 1735–1790), singer and composer.

in riots which became as much drunken revelry and an excuse for looting as they were political protest. For several nights, state authority lost control of the capital, in what was for the polite classes a terrifying demonstration of the power of an urban proletariat. Whereas before the Gordon Riots it had been possible for those of many political persuasions to argue that there was a kind of manly legitimacy in tumult and disorder (see, for example, The Case of Bosavern Penlez*), the crowd's ability to go beyond specific and limited protest was now clear. From 1789, memories of the Gordon Riots became the most important way in which the British public was able to construe the actions of the Parisian crowd in the revolution there, with particular comparisons being made between the destruction of Newgate and of the Bastille.*

What follows is extracted from probably the most comprehensive and influential contemporary account of the riots. Thomas Holcroft – who was later a radical novelist and activist in the London Corresponding Society – notes in his preface that, 'the late riots and popular tumults [...] excited the apprehensions of all ranks of people, to waken curiosity and make a clear and succinct narrative worthy the acceptance of the public' (p. 1). But the magnitude and shocking nature of the events being described confound this stated intention, and Holcroft is forced to use the rhetoric and effects of the sublime. The motor of the narrative, of which a flavour is given here, is that the next event always transcends all previous happenings in depravity and size, with an escalation of violence that is imagined without end. The trope of inability to find words adequate to the situation is used constantly by Holcroft, and the reader is asked to imagine events and affective reactions to these events, which go beyond all previous experience. For the British public, it was perhaps the Gordon Riots that marked the beginning of an era in which the crowd might be able to effect regime change, a fear (or hope) that the French Revolution would only confirm.

[*Holcroft describes the first two days of disturbances, most of which are centred around Westminster and the Houses of Parliament.*]

On Monday the mobs collected again, and became more formidable. They began to put their threats in execution in different quarters of the town. Some paraded with the reliques of havock, which they collected in Moorfield's, as far as Lord George Gordon's house, in Welbeck Street, and afterwards burnt them in adjacent fields. Another party went to Virginia-Lane, Wapping, and a third to Nightingale-Lane, East Smithfield, where they severally destroyed the Catholic Chapels, and committed other outrages. They seemed to have been marshalled out, and different bodies dispatched on these infernal errands [...]

All ranks of people began to be exceedingly terrified at the lawless proceedings of this day, and numbers put blue cockades in their hats (although it might now be said to be the ensign of rebellion), on purpose to avoid personal injury and insult.

We now come to that period of desolation and destruction, when every man began to tremble, not only for the safety of the city, but for the constitution of the kingdom, for property, liberty and life, for everything that is dear to society, or to Englishmen.

About six in the evening one party went to the house of Justice Hyde, near Leicester Fields, which they destroyed in less than an hour; another, shortly after, paraded through Long Acre, down Holborn &c., till they came to Newgate, and publicly declared they would go and release the confined Rioters. When they arrived at the doors of the prison, they demanded of Mr. Akerman the keeper, to have their comrades immediately delivered up to them; and upon his persisting to do his duty, by refusing, they began some to break the windows, some to batter the doors and entrances into the cells, with pick-axes and sledge-hammers, others with ladders to climb the vast walls, while others collected fire-brands, and whatever combustibles they could find, and slung into his dwelling house. What contributed more than anything to the spreading of the flames, was the great quantity of household furniture belonging to Mr, Akerman, which they threw out of the windows, piled up against the doors, and set fire to; the force of which presently communicated to the house, from the house to the chapel, and from thence, by the assistance of the Mob, all through the prison. A party of Constables, nearly to the amount of a hundred, came to the assistance of the keeper; these the Mob made a lane for, and suffered to pass till they were entirely encircled, when they attacked them with great fury, broke their staffs, and conversed them into brands, which they hurled about wherever the fire, which was spreading very fast, had not caught. It is almost incredible to think that it were possible to destroy a building of such amazing strength and extent, with so much swiftness as they accomplished this. As soon as the flames had destroyed Mr. Akerman's house, which was part of Newgate, and were communicated to the wards and cells, all the prisoners, to the amount of three hundred, among whom were four under sentence of death, and ordered for execution on the Thursday following, were released. The activity of the Mob was, in this instance, as well as every other amazing. They dragged out the prisoners, many of them, by the hair of the head, by the legs or arms, or whatever part they could lay hold of: They broke open the doors of the different entrances, as easily as if they had all their lives been acquainted with the intricacies of the place, to let the confined escape. Great numbers were let out at the door that leads to the Session's House; and so well planned were all the manoeuvres of these desperate ruffians, that they had placed sentinels at the avenues, to prevent any of the prisoners from being conveyed to other jails. Thus was the strongest and most durable prison in England, that had been newly erected, and was not yet finished, and in the building of which the nation had expended immense sums demolished, the bare walls excepted, which were too thick and strong to yield to the force of fire, in the space of a few hours.

Even this was but a moiety of the mischief of this terrible night. Not satiated with the destruction of this great building, a party was sent among the Catholics

in Devonshire-Street, Red Lion-Square; another to the house of Justice Cox in
Great Queen-street, which was soon destroyed; a third broke open the doors of
the New Prison, Clerkenwell, and turned out all the confined; a fourth destroyed
the furniture and effects, writings &c. of Sir John Fielding; and a fifth desperate
and infernal gang went to the elegant house of Lord Mansfield, in Bloomsbury-
square, which they, with the most unrelenting fury, set fire to and consumed. The
loss here was immense, both to Lord Mansfield as an individual, and to the public.
A most valuable collection of pictures, some of the scarcest manuscripts said to
be in the possession of any private person in the world, with all his Lordship's
notes on great law cases, and the constitution of England, were all sacrificed by
madmen and villains; and Lord and Lady Mansfield were with difficulty preserved
from their rage, by making their escape through a back door, a few minutes before
these miscreants broke in and took possession of the house [...]

It is impossible to give any adequate description of the events of Wednesday.
Notice was sent round to the public prisons of the King's Bench, &c. by the Mob,
at what time they would come down and burn them down. The same kind of
infernal humanity was exercised towards Mr. Langdale, a distiller in Holborn,
and several other Romish individuals.[14] Three boys went down through the
streets, and in particular down Holborn, in the middle of the day, with iron bars,
got from the railing before Lord Mansfield's house, extorting money at every
shop, huzzaing and shouting, "No Popery!" and though numbers were passing
and repassing, the inhabitants durst not refuse them money; nor durst anyone
secure them, to have them punished [...]

A soon as the day was drawing to a close, one of the most awful and dreadful spectacles this country ever beheld was exhibited. The mob had not only
declared their resolution of firing the prisons, and some private houses, but
had avowed their intention to destroy the Bank, Gray's Inn, Temple, Lincoln's
Inn, the Grand Arsenal at Woolwich, and Royal Palaces. A universal stupor
had seized the minds of men: they looked at one another, and waited with a
resigned consternation for the events which were to follow. Government had
indeed exerted itself to the utmost, as far as their power, under the civil magistrate, would extend. Now, however, it was become necessary to make us of the
royal prerogative, and give discretionary powers to the military. Nothing could
convey a more awful idea of the mischief which was dreaded, than the strong
guard which was placed in the Royal Exchange for the protection of the Bank, as
nothing perhaps could have equalled the national desolation, had the diabolical
purposes of the insurgents upon this place succeeded. Besides this, soldiers were
distributed at Guildhall, in the Inns of Court, in almost every place tenable as a
fortification, and in some private houses; and the cannon was disposed to the
best advantage in the Park.

With minds thus disposed to terror by so many objects of devastation, and
in a city which but a few days before enjoyed the most perfect tranquillity,

14 *Romish individuals*: Catholics.

let those who were not spectators judge what the inhabitants felt when they beheld at the same instant the flames ascending and rolling in vast and voluminous clouds from the King's Bench and Fleet Prisons, from New Bridewell, from the Toll-gates on Blackfriars Bridge, from houses in every quarter of the town, and particularly from the bottom and middle of Holborn, where the conflagration was horrible beyond description. The houses that were first set on fire at this last mentioned place, both belonged to Mr. Langdale, an eminent distiller, and contained immense quantities of spirituous liquors. It is easy to conceive what fury these would add to the flames; but to form an adequate idea of the distress of the neighbouring inhabitants, or indeed of the inhabitants in every part of the city, is not so easy. Men, women and children were running up and down with beds, glasses, bundles, or whatever they wished most to preserve. In streets where there were no fires, numbers were removing their goods and effects at midnight. The tremendous roar of the insatiate and innumerable fiends who were the authors of these horrible scenes, was heard at one instant, and at the next the dreadful report of soldiers' muskets, as if firing in platoons, and at various places; in short, everything which could impress the mind with ideas of universal anarchy, and approaching desolation, seemed to be accumulating. Sleep and rest were things not thought of; the streets were swarming with people, and uproar, confusion and terror reigned in every part.

It is hardly possible to collect, in one point of view, the havock of this night; had half the mischief the Mob had threatened been effected, nothing less than national bankruptcy and destruction could have ensued. [...]

5.4   Edmund Burke, 'Some Thoughts on the Approaching Executions, Humbly Offered to Consideration', 10 July 1780, from *The Works of Edmund Burke* (New York, 1834), II, pp. 386–7.

This text is part of Edmund Burke's contribution to the debate that followed the Gordon Riots about how government should respond; should all perpetrators be severely punished, in a demonstration of the power of the state, or should the state show mercy to the instigators of what was a popular uprising? In a wider sense, Burke's response also concerns a debate about how an urban working class can be controlled psychologically, without the need for military intervention as was the case in June 1780. In effect, Burke suggests the application of some principles of the aesthetics he had earlier laid down in his influential Philosophical Inquiry *(1757). If the intention is to inculcate fear into the minds of the populace, then, so Burke argues, executions must be carried out in such a way as to focus the gaze of the crowd on the solemn objects of the spectacle, so that the occasion produces awe and veneration at the sublime power of the state. The necessity of the state providing sublime spectacle to the public is an idea that Burke would come back to in his* Reflections on the Revolution in France *(1790).*

If I understand the temper of the public at this moment, a very great part of the lower, and some of the middling, people of this city are in a very critical disposition, and such as ought to be managed with firmness and delicacy. In general, they rather approve than blame the principles of the rioters: though the better sort of them are afraid of the consequences of those principles they approve. This keeps their minds in a suspended and anxious state, which may very easily be exasperated by an injudicious severity and desperate resolutions; or by weak measures on the part of government, it may be encouraged to the pursuit of courses, which may be of the most dangerous consequences to the public.

There is no doubt, that the approaching executions will very much determine the future conduct of those people. They ought to be such as will humble, not irritate. Nothing will make government more awful to them than to see, that it does not proceed by chance or under the influence of passion.

It is therefore proposed that no executions should be made, until the number of persons, which government thinks fit to try, is complete. When the whole is at once under the eye, an examination ought to be made into the circumstances of every particular convict; and *six*, at the very utmost, of the fittest examples may then be selected for execution, who ought to be brought out and put to death, on one and the same day, in six different places, and in the most solemn manner that can be devised. Afterwards, great care should be taken, that their bodies may not be delivered to their friends, or to others, who may make them objects of compassion, or even veneration. Some instances of the kind have happened with regard to the bodies of those killed in the riots [...]

This small number of executions, and all at one time, though in different places, is seriously recommended; because it is certain, that great havoc among criminals hardens, rather than subdues, the minds of people inclined to the same crimes; and therefore fails of answering its purpose as an example. Men, who see their lives respected and thought of value by others, come to respect the gift of God themselves. To have compassion for oneself, or to care, more or less, for one's own life, is a lesson to be learned just as every other; and I believe it will be found, that conspiracies have been most common and most desperate, where their punishment has been most extensive and most severe.

Besides, the least excess in this way excites a tenderness in the milder sort of people, which makes them consider government in an harsh and odious light. The sense of justice in men is overloaded and fatigued with a long series of executions, or with such a carnage at once, as rather resembles a massacre, than a sober execution of the laws. The laws thus lose their terror in the minds of the wicked, and their reverence in the minds of the virtuous.

I have ever observed, that the execution of one man fixes the attention and excites awe; the execution of multitudes dissipates and weakens the effect: but men reason themselves into disapprobation and disgust; they compute more as they feel less; and every severe act, which does not appear to be necessary, is sure to be offensive.

5.5   'A Description of the Events in Paris, 12–15 July 1789', in *The Morning Post* (21 July 1789), p. 2.

The interventions of the Parisian crowd during the French Revolution are by some way the most decisive and influential examples of popular protest in eighteenth-century Europe, changing the course of history to a degree that was literally unprecedented. The actions of this crowd were a central subject of the debate on the Revolution that ensued in Britain, as Richard Price in 'Discourse on the Love Our Country' (1789), Edmund Burke in Reflections on the French Revolution in France *(1790) and Thomas Paine in* The Rights of Man *(1791) all tried to impose political form on events that were constantly surprising and often chaotic. Because they are so widely available, none of these texts are included in the current volume, but all these writers are forced in different ways to invoke the tropes of the sublime in order to compensate for lack of historical precedent. We can see this process at work in raw form, however, in the following newspaper reports of the two great interventions by the Parisian crowd in 1789: the taking of the Bastille in July, and the 'October Days', during which the French king was brought to Paris and hence under the control of the revolutionary government.*

In the first of these reports, written by an anonymous French correspondent, it is the controlled and disciplined manner in which the crowd abrogates authority to itself that is astonishing. Surpassing as it does all previous popular protest, the experience of being a part of such a crowd, and the attempt to represent it, have no precedent, and are therefore unrepresentable; the inadequacy of language, and the relative poverty of prior experience, leads to the attempt to grasp the events in terms of the sublime. Further, as events unfold, the power of the crowd becomes ever greater so that by the end it threatens the throne itself. Finally, the Parisian crowd as it is represented here has a kind of mystical unity by which it appears to think with one mind of enormous power. It is this image, in particular, that Thomas Paine picks up on in his description of the days surrounding 14 July in The Rights of Man *(1791).*

An Englishman not filled with esteem and admiration at the *sublime* manner in which one of the most important revolutions the world has ever seen is now effecting, must be dead to every sense of virtue and freedom; not one of my countrymen who has had the *good fortune* to witness the transactions of the last three days, but will testify that my language is not hyperbolical. To give you a detail of one hundredth part of the striking events occurring every moment is impossible – I shall give you a cursory detail of the leading facts and scenes which passed before my eyes, *et quorum pars.*[15]

---

15 *et quorum pars*: 'in which I played a great part'. Taken from *Aeneid* II, 6 where Aeneas is about to relate to Dido the epochal events of the fall of Troy, to which the events in Paris are implicitly compared.

The first acts of revolt naturally took place among the lowest of the populace, who paraded the streets etc., as I have told you, on Sunday night, after the affair with the Hussars at the Place Louis XV, but on Monday the magistrates and principal inhabitants assembled at the Hotel de Ville,[16] and in the different parishes the tocsin, or alarum bell, being rung in all the churches for that purpose; and *before three o'clock* of the same day, registers were opened for the citizens to enrol their names, arms and ammunition were distributed at the Hotel de Ville, and in all the districts, patroles of citizens established, weapons taken out of the hands of populace, and perfect safety established; no man appeared without a cockade, which was at first green, but is now, by order, changed to red and blue.

The French Guards unanimously joined the Citizens, and a set of more noble, orderly men I never saw; in the evening came in many hundreds of the Swiss Guards, bringing with them their cannon, caissons,[17] etc. Dragoons, and other troops from the neighbourhood kept dropping in; detachments were made to all quarters to seize on corn, powder, arms, and ammunition of every sort. The German Hussars, etc., withdrew to the military school, and joined the camp there, consisting of a Swiss regiment or two brought from Arras. Meanwhile all was getting into order. The Prince de Lambeseq, who at the head of his Hussars had killed a French Guardsman and Citizen on Sunday, had a narrow escape, his coach being seized and burnt, and the horses devoted to the public service.

Placards were publicly stuck up by well known persons, setting a price on the heads of the Queen, the Comte D'Artois, the Polignacs, and others. The guard, horse and foot, of Paris, (the horse are a fine body) all joined us in the evening, and at night immense patroles of citizens and soldiers, and string guard-houses, were established everywhere with the most *astonishing* order. All the houses put out lights to prevent surprise, and the Citizens not on duty slept as tranquilly *as in the most profound peace.* – Wonder at what I have seen stops me every instant in giving you the account.

On Tuesday the scene opened out in the same manner, but such *calm activity* never was, I am confident, before displayed, on any similar occasion. Fresh troops kept constantly dropping in. Detachments sent out of town on all sides, were continually returning with corn intended for the hostile troops, cannon, powder, etc. etc. Several wagons were intercepted destined for the King, and brought triumphantly to town, each of them drawn by six royal horses.

Before noon a body of 20,000 Citizens, headed by the French Guard, now joined by many of their officers who had previously taken an oath of fidelity, summoned[18] the Hotel des Invalides in form with cannon; (the Hotel des Invalides is at fifty yards distance from the Military School, where there were now 4000 hostile troops with a park of artillery;) the Governor surrendered, and

---

16 *Hotel de Ville*: Town Hall.
17 *caissons*: chests in which to carry ammunition.
18 *summoned*: called upon to surrender.

immediate possession was taken of 52,000 stand of arms, cannon, ammunition &c. and brought triumphant into town.

On the other side of the town, the Bastille was summoned by Ten or Twelve Thousand citizens, headed by the grenadiers of the French guards, and on the Governor's holding out a white flag, and opening one of the gates, a party of young citizens, with some soldiers, incautiously entered; the Governor instantly drew up the drawbridge, and his troops, consisting of invalids and some traitorous Swiss, fired though loop holes, and killed or wounded the whole party. About thirty were killed. Four times he attempted the same stratagem, but not with the same success; at last the fortress was regularly attacked and cannonaded for three hours, and ditches filled with straw etc. etc. A breach was effected, and first mounted by grenadiers.

The Governor, the Marquis de Delaunay, the Prince de Montbory, the Fort-Major, &c. made prisoners; and all the poor unhappy State Prisoners, many of whom had languished for years in this execrable abode, released.

The great and important scene now followed – The Governor, the Prince de Montbory, the Fort-Major, and Officers, were conveyed to the Hotel de Ville, and after a short trial, (in short form) M. de Delaunay, and the Major were executed by first shooting, and then cutting off their heads.

I was witness to this sad but necessary spectacle, which was conducted with a decency, a firmness, a solemnity worthy of the highest admiration – the officers next underwent the same fate.

But this was not all – M. de Flesselles, the Prevot des Marchands, or first principal officer of Paris, having, in the course of the day, given some reason for suspicion, by refusing arms, powder &c. though President of the Board of Defence, and a courier from the Queen being interrupted with a letter to him, desiring him to hold firm and spin out delays, for that forty thousand men should be here that night (Tuesday), he was seized in the council chamber, examined, similar letters found concealed on him, and shot and beheaded on the Quai de Pelletier. Their bodies were all brought by the stairs to the Town-house, and laid close by my side on the Place de Greve, their heads being conveyed in *calm triumph* to the statue of Henry IV and paraded through all the streets. You see we are in earnest.

All this was performed without the smallest tumult, or even crowding, though the streets were full, nor was there any running, from one place to another, nor a symptom of alarm or terror imprinted on a single countenance. Every man kept his post, every man performed his specific duty.

Thursday, 16.

The first news of yesterday was the retreat of the troops at the Military School, who had stolen off during the night to Versailles, to avoid a siege determined for the morning; immediate possession was taken out of it, and vast magazine of flour etc. Things were now got into complete order – batteries established – the streets in the suburbs unpaved – *chevaux de frize*[19] erected, etc. and barricades prepared for the first alarm of the approach of cavalry. Joy and courage was painted on every face [...]

The news of the taking of the The Bastille, and the beheading of the governor, and the Prevot des Marchands, reached Versailles late on Tuesday evening – The effect was easily to be foreseen. This act of firmness made many an exalted neck creek. The King, *poor soul!* was taken ill; all was alarm at the Court, and we have at least the consolation to know that they slept no better than ourselves.

The Assembly, early in the morning, adopted vigorous measures; the matter now was come to a point. Had the King not given way, the Assembly would not have joined us at Paris, and he must probably have lost the throne (I do not exaggerate).

In the evening a numerous deputation arrived, bringing us his resolution to send off the troops, and his intention to throw himself into the arms of the people this morning, *by continuing here to* the Hotel de Ville. His answer to the commons, however, is still worded in indecent and arbitrary language, and exhibits a mixture of *despotism* and *cowardice*, worthier of a Stuart[20] than a Bourbon.[21] None of his ministers were present with him, but what was as bad, his two unworthy brothers.

The Deputies were received with a discharge of cannon and musquetry at every post and barricade, and by a *feux de joie* from all the Patroles of Citizens, and by applauses that must have touched the most unfeeling heart.

A joint Committee of Electors and Deputies of the National Assembly sat on the evening, to concert measures to be taken with the King this morning. Everything is to be hoped from their firmness and enlightened understandings. Be assured, that the rights of men are well understood here, as is the value of this precious moment. Even the lowest people stopped the Deputies last night; as they passed through the streets, telling them to be firm, not to trust the King – to demand heads, and give them their honest and virtuous minister, Mr. Neckar.

This is a great day; the King will see his people armed; he will discover his own littleness without them. Dreadful accounts are hourly expected from the Provinces.

5.6   An account of the 'October Days' in *The London Chronicle* (10–13 October 1789), LXVI, pp. 353–9.

Just as the preceding extract appears to have informed Thomas Paine's account of the Parisian crowd, so the following extracts, some of which originated in

---

19 *chevaux de frize*: 'Frisian horses', a primitive defensive obstacle made of a single beam with spikes on it.

20 *Stuart*: family name of the British royal household from James I to Queen Anne, and associated for many in Britain with despotism.

21 *Bourbon*: the family name of the ruling French dynasty

The London Gazette, *and many parts of which were reprinted in a number of other newspapers, appear to have conditioned Edmund Burke's notorious description of the alleged attack on the French royal family in* Reflections on the Revolution in France *(1790). The first part, presumably from a correspondent in Paris, contains the basic story of how an entertainment at Versailles, at which demonstrations of loyalty to the King were made, was heard of in Paris, in response to which a large crowd proceeded to Versailles to demand the removal of the King and Queen to Paris, where they could better be brought under the control of the revolutionary government. There follows, under the title 'Postscript', a series of commentaries on the significance of these events, interspersed with information from other sources. At first it seems like a contrast is being made between the sublime proceedings at court, in which an affective response of loyalty to the King and Queen is generated, and the grotesque crowd, which threatens the safety of the protagonists at court. Yet as the account goes on, the power of the crowd increases, producing an unimaginable awe which is itself sublime. The final comments, on the safety of the Queen and the implications given her relations with other European dynasties, present an open-ended question about the previously unimaginable situation that Europe was now in.*

Paris, October 7

It being customary for the Gardes du Corps at Versailles to give an entertainment to any new regiment that arrives there, the Regiment de Flandres was on Thursday last sumptuously entertained by that corps in the palace. After dinner their Most Christian Majesties judged proper to honour the company with their presence, and condescended to show their satisfaction at the general joy which prevailed among the guests. On their appearance the music instantly played the favourite song of '*O Richard, O mon Roi*',[22] and the company, joining in chorus, seemed to unite all ideas in one unanimous sentiment of loyalty and love for the King, and nothing was heard for some time but repeated shouts of *Vive le Roi*, within and without the palace. In the height of their zeal they proceeded to tear the national cockades from their hats, and trampled them under their feet. The Gardes du Corps supplied themselves with black cockades, in the room of those they had treated with such disdain. The news of these proceedings soon reached Paris, where a general humour visibly gained ground.

On Saturday there were great disturbances in the Palais Royal, and it became unsafe for anyone to appear with black cockades, as several foreigners experienced, from whose hats they were torn with much violence and abusive language.

---

22 *O Richard, O mon Roi*: 'O Richard, O my King', an aria from the André Gretry opera *Richard Coeur-de-Lion* (1784), whose subject is loyalty to the King in the face of general abandonment.

On Sunday the confusion increased, and a vast concourse of people tumultu-ously assembled at the Town-house, under the pretence of demanding bread, and enquiring into the real causes of the extreme scarcity of it at this season of the year.

On Monday morning a number of women, to the amount of upwards of 5000, armed with different weapons, marched in regular order to Versailles, followed by the numerous inhabitants of the Fauxbourgs St. Antoine and St. Marceau, with several detachments of the city militia; and in the evening the Marquis de le Fayette, at the head of 20,000 of that corps marched to Versailles.

On Tuesday morning an account was received of some blood having been spilt. The Gardes du Corps fired on the Parisians, and five or six persons, chiefly women, were killed. The Regiment de Flandres was also drawn out to oppose this torrent; but the word to fire was no sooner given, than they all to a man clubbed their arms, and with a shout of *Vive la Nation*, went over to the Parisians. Some troops of dragoons that are quartered at Versailles also laid down their arms, and the Swiss detachments remained motionless, having received no orders from their officers to fire. The Gardes du Corps being thus abandoned, and overpow-ered by numbers, fled precipitately into the gardens and woods, where they were pursued, many of them killed and taken prisoners. Some of the heads of those who were killed were carried to Paris, and paraded through the streets on spikes. The same morning a report came, that the King, the Queen, and Royal Family, were on their way to Paris. Upon this the people began to assemble from all parts of the town, and above 50,000 of the militia proceeded to line the streets and road to Versailles. Their Majesties and the Royal Family accordingly arrived between seven and eight o'clock in the evening, after having been six hours on the road. The carriages all proceeded to the Town-house. The concourse of people that attended is not to be described, and the shouts of *Vive la Nation* filled the air. From the Town-house they were conducted to the palace of the Tuilleries, though totally unprepared for their reception, where they passed the night.

Postscript

Paris, October 7

Further particulars of the present Tumults *in* France

The King's government may now be supposed to be at an end. His situation is truly deplorable. When he was at Versailles he did not think his life secure, though he was surrounded by the corps of Life Guards, the 100 Swiss, and the regiment of dragoons called *Les Trois Eveches*, from the three bishoprics of Toul, Metz and Verdun, in Lorraine, where it was raised. It was resolved therefore, by the Council, in consequence of his Majesty's wish, that another regiment should be ordered to Versailles, to do duty about the King [...]

The military etiquette of France has established a custom through the service, that when a regiment marches into a town where there are troops in garrison, it is always entertained at the expense of those troops. In consequence of this etiquette, and by no means through design, the officers of the Flanders regiment were invited to dinner by the Life Guards. The dinner was served up on the stage of the Opera House in the Palace, as the most capacious place. When the glass had circulated rather freely, some toasts were given by the Life Guards, strongly expressive of loyalty to the King. The officers of the Flanders regiment shouted approbation when they heard them, and drank them in the English style with loud huzzas. This convinced the Life Guards that their guests and they were all of one mind.

The appearance of the King and Queen, with the Dauphin, who entered the place merely to do honour to the guests, increased the flow of loyalty: but when the music struck up the air of, 'O Richard – O my King,' the allusion to his Majesty's situation, which those who ordered the band to play this tune would have thought to be like Richard Coeur de Lion, the situation of a Monarch deprived of his liberty, the officers felt themselves wound up to the highest pitch, and, as if animated by one soul, began to sing the words of the song. The King himself was affected; he immediately walked out, unable to speak, and with his handkerchief up to his eyes. The officers then solemnly pledged themselves to one another, that they would stand by their King, release him from the bondage in which he was kept, or perish in the attempt.

These gentlemen, however, were comparatively few in number; and therefore, although they were approved of their gallantry, they know that if they were not backed by their soldiers, they could do nothing. Such of the non-commissioned officers and privates as were known to have most influence on their fellow soldiers were called in and sounded. They declared their readiness to fight for their king, and second their officers in what they called a glorious cause [...]

The disturbances in Paris, on hearing of these proceedings, became so general on Monday last, that all the districts of the capital were summoned, and the Marquis de la Fayette was ordered to proceed immediately to Versailles, at the head of a large body of troops, and bring the King under his guard to Paris [...] This soon got wind abroad, and the mob, ever ready to catch at anything which could bear an unfavourable construction, insisted that, the Marquis de la Fayette, and the Mayor, whom they likewise suspected, were gained over to betray them. While this suspicion was circulating, another party erected two gallows in the Place de Greve, and threatened to hang them if the orders were not instantly carried out.

At two o'clock on Tuesday morning a considerable number of the persons who were habited in women's dresses, but, as it since appears, were many of them guards, having gained the outward entrances of the castle, forced their way into the palace, and up the staircase leading to the Queen's apartment, with an intent (as it is generally supposed) to seize and murder her; fortunately, a greater number than usual of the King's body guard were ordered to be posted in the ante-chambers leading to it, and be particularly vigilant against any alarm [...]

Nothing can equal the consternation of all ranks of the French now in this kingdom, for their friends and relations whom they have left behind – At the

French Ambassador's all is mystery and silence; and not a post arrives but what is met with countenances of horror.

There was never a moment which excited the anxiety and attention of all ranks of people so much as the present Revolution in France. It is not merely the disputes of the National Assembly, and the new modelling of the French constitution, which claims the attention of our countrymen, in common with all Europe; but the very lives of the Royal Family of France, and the race of a whole monarchy at stake.

At this moment the fate of Europe depends on the actions of a barbarous and unrestrained mob; a mob, which has shown itself so licentious, that the country which claims it, blushes at its cruelties. The murder of the Queen has been attempted in the dead of night, while she was in slumber, and unprepared to appear before the tribunal of her maker, at a time of all others the most awful and barbarous, because the most sacred and inoffensive. Had the attempt succeeded, What must have been the consequence? Or indeed, what may not now be the consequence? For her life is still in danger; a Queen, who is the sister of the Emperor and the Grand Duke of Tuscany, and allied to the Houses of Spain, Sardinia and Naples, and almost all the Princes of Italy!

5.7   Account of the Proceedings at a General Meeting of the London Corresponding Society [...] in an enclosed field, behind the Long Room, Borough Road, St. George's Fields, on Monday, the 29th of June, 1795 (London: 1795), pp. 3–7, 13–14; and from Account of the Proceedings of a Meeting of the London Corresponding Society, held in a field near Copenhagen House, Monday Oct. 26, 1795 (London: Citizen Lee, nd), pp. 3–9.

The following extracts are from pamphlets produced by the London Corresponding Society in 1795, to report on two big meetings held in London in order to press the Society's claims for a reform of Parliament and an end to the war against France. One of the key points made is that a very large meeting is in fact happening – these are highly performative occasions – and that, contrary to the claims of their political opponents who cited the Gordon Riots and events in France, large numbers of people could meet in political assembly and behave in an orderly fashion. Rather like in earlier favourable accounts of the French Revolution (see above pp. 163–66), it is the discipline of such assemblies that is emphasised. But there is more than this; as the Chair John Gale Jones says, 'it seems as if the whole British nation had convened itself on this occasion'. The effect of this, were it actually to happen, would be an assembly that represented the People, being itself the People, perfectly and totally. So the crowd here is sublime, in this case because it bypasses all partial representation, all deputisation, and is the thing itself in all its fullness, acting as one indivisible self. There is also a certain threat in the proceedings; the assembly is an 'awful spectacle', humbling to those opposed to it, inducing the sublime emotions of fear and reverence.

But in a final turn, 'the moment of danger is the moment of inquiry'; the situation of the country is as if on a precipice, and the acknowledgement of danger becomes a cue to rational enquiry and reform.

[*From the address of the Chairman, Citizen [John Gale] Jones, 3 o'clock pm*]

CITIZENS!

It is with infinite satisfaction that I behold here assembled, on this day, so numerous and so respectable a meeting: it presents indeed to my view a spectacle at once sublime and awful, since it seems as if the whole British Nation had convened itself upon this extraordinary occasion to witness the propriety of our conduct, and testify for the legality of our proceedings. They will not, I believe, be disappointed. We meet for no other purpose than our original purpose, a Parliamentary Reform, and disclaim all intention of tumult or violence. I hope, by our firm, yet moderate conduct, we shall gain the good will and concurrence of all who are here present, and convince them that we are, as we ever have been, the sincere advocates and steady promoters of universal peace and tranquillity.

[*Address to the Nation*]

FRIENDS AND FELLOW CITIZENS!

After the lapse of more than a twelve-month, replete with fearful agitation and alarm, the LONDON CORRESPONDING SOCIETY, still firm in its principles, and faithful to its original purpose, again offers itself to your notice, and solicits your immediate attention. Never at any time, from the rude institutions of uncultivated ignorance, to the more polished periods of modern refinement, has there been submitted to the consideration of man a more awful or a more critical moment! It is, indeed, a moment worthy of serious deliberation. To be guilty of rashness or intemperance would serve only to prejudice and inflame; yet to be wholly silent, would betray a criminal indifference.

While the slow, yet steady progression of human improvement, by exciting curiosity, and awakening inquiry, has produced in all countries an insensible revolution of opinion: mankind, as yet unaccustomed to great and novel changes, has too often been inclined to treat them as visionary and impracticable, and has refused to countenance and approve what it has not yet experienced. Hence may we readily account for the existence and perpetuation of abuses, which, having originated in ignorance, are afterwards continued from habit, and supported by folly; hence may we be easily led to distinguish that servile and accommodating disposition which prefers a partial evil to an uncertain good, and contents itself with pursuing the beaten track of uniformity, while it dreads to venture into the unknown, though alluring, path of innovation.

But, with nations as with individuals, it sometimes happens, that the *Hour of Danger is the Hour of Inquiry*; and what would have been withheld from the calm remonstrances of reason is often yielded to the strong impulse of necessity.

At such a time, and in so critical a situation, the collision of contending interests, and the rude shock of adverse powers, are for a while the only arguments of application, and the only effectual means of redress! All deliberation is suspended, and the mind looks forward with fearful horror to the termination of the dreadful contest! Happy the nation which, by lenient and gentle methods, can supersede the necessity of so dreadful a remedy! – Happy the people who are not *compelled* to this ultimate and awful appeal!

To prevent confusion, and preserve tranquillity, is the indispensable duty of every individual, who would enjoy the comforts of civil society; it is necessary, therefore, that he should at all times, and at all hazards, exert his utmost to warn his Fellow Citizens of their impending danger, and oppose the artful and ambitious designs of those who, under miserable pretexts, would enslave and destroy his country. It is not enough that he should boldly disseminate his opinions and propagate his principles; that he should associate with men of similar sentiments and similar views; but he must also, if occasion require, cheerfully consent to be selected from the aggregate mass, AND DIE IN THEIR DEFENCE!

It is now near four years since we first called your attention to the circumstances of the times, and to the situation of your country; if it were necessary *then* to associate, how much more is that necessity *now* increased! We believed a Parliamentary Reform to be the only means of preserving our country from destruction, and is our persuasion become less firm, or are our opinions altered? Did we not foresee the calamities which must result from the want of a fair and equal representation of the People of Britain in the Commons House of Parliament, and call on the united energies of the country to assert its rights? And is it time to relinquish all further exertions, and desert our principles? Surely not! The public mind is at length roused to a sense of its situation; it sees the dreadful precipice on which it stands; it encourages us to proceed in our useful and virtuous career, and assures us it will second our endeavours. Yes, Britons! you begin to exert the privilege of thinking, and mental energy will soon be succeeded by determined resolution! [...] Away with cold calculations of safety and prudence – with paltry expedients and ill-timed fears! It is necessary for all honest men to speak out, *the Times and the Country demand it!* Are we not Men, and shall we not speak? Are we BRITONS, and is not LIBERTY our BIRTHRIGHT! There is no power on Earth shall silence the Voice of an Injured Nation, or prevent the Progress of Free Inquiry! – Bring forth your Whips and Racks, ye Ministers of Vengeance! – Produce your Scaffolds and your Executioners! – Erect Barracks in every Street, and Bastilles in every Corner! – Persecute and punish every innocent Individual! but you will *not* succeed! The Voice of Reason, like the roaring of the Nemean Lion,[23] shall issue from the Cavern's Mouth! The holy Blood of Patriotism, streaming from the severing Axe, shall carry with it the Infant seeds of Liberty, and Men may perish! – but Truth shall be eternal! [...]

Let us entreat you not to fall into those fatal errors which have so frequently misled our ancestors, nor rest your expectations on that delusive phantom – a Change of Ministers! With *such* an House of Commons, no Ministry *can* perform its Duty to the People! – YOUR CHIEF, PERHAPS YOUR ONLY HOPE, IS IN YOURSELVES! [...]

FRIENDS AND FELLOW-CITIZENS!

I hope the event of this truly great and glorious day will fully prove to the world that a very large body of people can, even in the most critical and perilous times, assemble to deliberate upon public measures, without the smallest violation of order or the slightest breach of decorum [...] We have now, I hope, completed in a satisfactory manner the business for which we have assembled; it remains only for me to return you our sincere and hearty acknowledgements for the patient attention and favourable reception which we have this day experienced, and to hope that you will not forget the important cause for which we are associated; and we trust that you will immediately unite your exertions with ours, and that ere long the London Corresponding Society and the British Nation will be ONE AND INDIVISIBLE!

[*from Account of the Proceedings of a Meeting of the London Corresponding Society, held in a field near Copenhagen House*]

The circumstances attending the whole of this meeting are perhaps such as never before were known in the annals of this country. Much has at various periods been said, of the danger of convening large assemblies of the people; but the proceedings of this day evince, beyond a possibility of doubt, that when the people are called together for the discussion and consideration of their essential and inalienable rights and privileges, they not only *can* but *will*, however immense their numbers, demean themselves in such a peaceable and orderly manner, as shall at once give the lie to their servile and prostitute calumniators; and prove to the satisfaction of every reflecting, impartial and disinterested mind, that it is by the efforts of *reason only*, they can ever hope to defend and preserve that inestimable jewel Liberty; and that tumult and disorder are the detestable engines to which their base and bitter enemies alone can wish them to resort.

At nine in the morning, yesterday, the fields about White Conduit House – and the different paths leading from Gray's-inn-land, and other outlets from various

---

23 *Nemean Lion*: in Greek mythology, a monster, offspring of Titans, who is eventually killed by Hercules. Often used as a symbol of terrible invincibility, as in *Hamlet* I, iv, 83.

parts of the town, began to be crowded with Citizens, both male and female, all eagerly and anxiously bending their step towards Copenhagen House, the place mentioned in the advertisement at which the meeting was to be held. – from that time till the hour of taking the Chair, which was twelve o'clock, so grand and extraordinary a *coup d'oeil*[24] was perhaps never seen, as was the continual progress of the people pouring in from every quarter like a torrent – the various streams of which all directed their course to the same central point. At the appointed hour for commencing the business of the day, there could not be less than one hundred thousand persons present [...]

[*Address to the Nation*]

'Once more, dear friends and fellow-citizens, in defiance of threats and insults – of base and unmanly fears – are we met in the open face of day, and call the heavens and earth to witness the purity of our proceedings. Amidst the dreadful storms and hurricanes which at present assail the political hemisphere of our country, with firm and unabated vigour we pursue our avowed purpose, – the grand and glorious cause of Parliamentary Reform! – The rude gales of opposition, and the howling blasts of persecution have served only to assist our career; and where we might have lingered, from choice or indolence, we now steadily advance from the heavy pressure of inevitable necessity.

'With anxious minds and agitated hearts, we are again compelled to address you – and to solicit your patient attention. There was a time, when we might, perhaps, have been startled at the idea of rendering ourselves so conspicuous, and have sought for refuge under the veil of obscurity. When the timid apprehensions of our friends – the loss of our most valuable interests and connexions – the threats of guilty ministers – and the hostile preparations of armed associations, might have forcibly urged us to remain in mournful silence, and to retreat from the eye of observation; – but alas! it is now too late! – When the welfare of society is endangered, what individual is safe? When the public happiness is at stake, what private consideration ought to avail? – When we have been severely persecuted, it is true, but is our cause become less dear? – We have been cruelly and unjustly treated – but has the Majesty of *Truth* suffered in the shameful contest? – No! Away then with lifeless apathy and pale-faced fear! Let every true and sincere friend of Liberty boldly deliver his real sentiments; and, while he professes the bold principles of a *patriot*, assert his independence like *a man*!

'Four months ago we peaceably assembled to deliberate upon the best and most probable mode of recovering our rights, and redressing our numerous grievances: we *addressed* You, and we *petitioned* the King. We believe, if we may judge from the rapid increase of our numbers since our last public meeting, that our sentiments and conduct experience almost general approbation [...]

---

24 *coup d'oeil*: spectacle (French).

'To delineate a faithful portrait of the awful situation of our poor distracted country, would only be to exhibit a scene of misery and desolation; a frightful picture of horror that would sicken the imagination, and appal the stoutest heart [...] The manufacturer has been seduced from his loom – the militia-man swindled from his domestic employment – and the humble cottager kidnapped from the plough. The bread that should support the industrious poor has been exported, either to be abandoned on a foreign shore, or consigned to the bottom of a fathomless ocean – while the helpless widow and wretched orphan, are consoled for their irreparable loss, by the scanty allowance of insolent donation, or a charitable bribe!

'The comfortable and pleasing prospects resulting from an abundant harvest have turned out to be vain and fallacious – and were probably held up only to lull the public into a delusive and fatal security! The approach of famine seems to be inevitable, and we have almost the melancholy and indubitable assurance of being soon in want of bread.

'What is the cruel and insatiate monster that thus piecemeal tears and devours us? – Wherefore in the midst of apparent plenty are we thus compelled to starve? – Why, when we incessantly toil and labour, must we pine in misery and want? What is this subtle and insinuating poison which thus irritates our domestic comforts, and destroys our public prosperity? – It is *Parliamentary Corruption*, which like a foaming whirlpool swallows the fruit of all our labours, and leaves us only the dregs of bitterness and sorrow.

'Those whose duty it is to watch over the interests of the nation, have either proved themselves indifferent to its welfare, or unable to remove the pressure of these intolerable grievances. Let them look to the fatal consequences – we are sincere friends of Peace – we want only a Reform, because we are firmly and fully convinced, that a thorough Reform would effectually remedy those formidable evils; but we cannot answer for the strong and all-powerful impulse of necessity, nor always restrain the aggravated feelings of insulted human nature! – If ever the British Nation should loudly demand strong and decisive measures, we boldly answer – "We have lives! and are ready to devote them, either separately or collectively, for the salvation of our country."'

The reading of this address was, from time to time, interrupted by such loud applauses as are but seldom heard, even in public places – and being ended amidst the warmest and most unanimous acclamations of approbation, the Chairman next proceeded to read the Remonstrance to the King.

5.8 Richard Phillips, *Modern London; Being the History of the Present State of the British Metropolis* (London, 1804), pp. 105–8.

Richard Phillips – writer, publisher, former radical and future sheriff of London – moved to London when he was twenty-nine, and like the accounts of so many visitors to the metropolis, his descriptions of it throughout his life always had the surprise of the new and exotic. 'We roam widely into unhealthy climates', he wrote in 1817, 'and encounter difficulties and dangers, in search of curiosities and knowledge, although if our industry were equally exerted at home, we might find, within our daily reach, inexhaustible sources of inquiry and contemplation'.[25] *The history and guide to London from which the following is extracted presents the reader with a city that is both familiar and exotic, rational and chaotic. London is first compared to great civilisations of antiquity, but surpasses all of these, so that a description can never be adequate to its extent or complexity, which can only be imagined. At street level, only highly complex irregularity can be discerned, but given at a distance, it can be seen that roads, canals and other channels of power and commerce radiate out from it endlessly. From a height, or, in a striking parallel with Wordsworth's famous sonnet, 'from an open space such as Westminster Bridge', the full majesty of the city can be surveyed. In a significant metaphor, a 'forest of spires, steeples, and turrets' can be seen; the man-made environment of buildings, crowds and business, can, in the end, only be (still inadequately) represented in terms of the natural sublime.*

The history of cities is scarcely inferior to the history of empires: the great cities, that have flourished, have not only been the seat of empire, but the general emporium of all that was grand in the productions of human intellect and the accumulated powers of nations. Nineveh, famed for her walls and towers, vast in circumference, height and breadth, Babylon, with her hanging gardens and all her wonders, the self-fortified and proud Persepolis, the magnificent Palmyra buried in the desert, and her sister Balbec, Egyptian Thebes, with her ponderous remains, which in the times of the first Greek historian were, what they still are, ruins beyond the memory of record: each of these, and many more that might be named, excite astonishment, regret, obscure conjectures that are endless, and inferences that may be systematic, but that are hypothetical.

Could a just enumeration be given of that mass of objects which London now contains, and could the grand estimate be read by those ancients who inhabited cities once so great, and still so renowned, London to them might appear still more miraculous. Men are seldom surprised at, nay, they do but rarely even admire or comprehend, the excellence of that which they are in the daily habit of seeing, however admirable it may really be. Any description of London, which words can give, can only be a sketch to suggest that amplitude and grandeur which must be filled by the imagination: it is only thus that objects in detail can be so associated as to form a whole, and portray the diversity, number and magnitude, which actually exist.

Though widely different in its essential qualities, London possesses those grand features which characterised ancient Rome: it is the seat of liberty, the mart of intellect, and the envy of nations. It is a magazine so vast that the whole world is supplied from its stores: it is the centre from which diverge roads, canals, and

---

25 Richard Phillips, *A Morning's Walk from London to Kew* (London: 1817), p. 1.

all those outlets of internal and foreign commerce the activity of which never slumbers. Hence that circulation in the national body, which renders every part healthful; equal in vigour and prosperity; a circulation that benefits alike the heart and the most distant members. In wealth, and even in splendour, the merchant vies with the nobleman: not to the latter, but to the former, the Government applies for loans that appear to be inexhaustible; and not only the wholesale warehouses but the magazines and shops of retail astonish, by their varied, elegant and noble display.

Having taken this brief general view, it is necessary to speak more particularly.

As in the present work the advantages which are enjoyed by London will most of them be recapitulated, it is but just, in these introductory remarks, to notice its most striking defects. Among these, the principal is its irregularity. The plan of London, in its present state, will to the least competent judge appear highly inconvenient, when considered as a grand commercial city, built on the banks of so noble a river as the Thames. The wharfs and quays on each of its shores are many of them extremely mean, confined and inconvenient: what they ought to be may perhaps be best conjectured by contemplating the new docks, with all their warehouses and appurtenances, that are now erecting, and which are likely soon to exhibit a spectacle of commercial grandeur, such as the world must envy, but cannot equal.

The streets that lead to these quays and wharfs are many of them built on declivities, up which it is barely possible to drag heavy loads, and killing to the draught horses. Others are so narrow as to ensure every difficulty which obstruction can offer, and which nothing but the most consummate dexterity can escape. Every day, when business is transacted at the Custom-house, Lower Thames-street presents a scene of hurry, crowd and confusion, such as probably no other city or place on earth can equal: foot passengers, confined to a narrow pavement most carefully guarded by thick and immovable posts, make their way to the Custom-house with the utmost difficulty. The carts, of which the street is absolutely full, though wedged in so that egress and regress are apparently blocked up, yet, when ready to move, make room, and pass each other with an expert facility and order that excite amazement. That these absurd inconveniences, with all their attendant dangers and frequent accidents, should subsist through a lapse of time, is perhaps a subject of greater astonishment.

The modern part of London excepted, there is a winding irregularity and want of uniform appearance, in many of the streets of London, by which it is greatly disfigured and all grandeur of aspect lost. Seen from a height, or even such open places as Westminster-bridge, London presents a forest of spires, steeples, and turrets, appertaining to churches and other public buildings: yet these churches are so built in and locked among alleys, courts and streets, that, with a few exceptions, strangers may traverse the whole metropolis without the least knowledge that such large buildings have any existence.

The roads that lead to London are most of them spacious, in excellent repair, and so well lighted by lamps, to a considerable distance, that foreigners arriving by night have imagined that there was a general illumination; yet, at the edge of London, the entering streets are many of them mean, and calculated to inspire foreigners with very erroneous ideas concerning the real magnificence of this metropolis.

6

The Exotic

Novelty is an important concept in a range of eighteenth-century discourses, including the ongoing enquiries into the causes of progress in the arts and sciences, and into the role of consumerism in promoting economic growth. Adam Smith's essay on 'The History of Astronomy', for example, links the encounter with the new or uncommon to the curiosity that prompts scientific enquiry, while Hume's essay 'Of Commerce' (see p. 50) connects national economic growth with a continuous desire for new commodities.[1] In his 1712 'pleasures of the imagination' essays, Joseph Addison had suggested that the encounter with the new or uncommon also plays a significant role in generating the emotional response associated with the sublime. As the eighteenth century progresses, the relationship between the uncommon and the discourse on the sublime becomes increasingly nuanced and specialised, developing, for example, into the romantic-period valorisation of *originality* in the creative arts (see Mind). A further key locus of interaction between the uncommon and the discourse on the sublime occurs in the increasing public fascination with the *exotic*.

Alongside the growth in popularity of descriptions of European travel following the reopening of the European mainland to British tourists at the end of the Seven Years' War (1756–63), the latter half of the eighteenth century also witnessed the emergence of a new kind of travel writing: the expedition narrative. Published accounts of celebrated journeys into the unknown – to island paradises in the South Pacific, to the Arctic ice, to the jungles of South America, to the Nile and the Niger, to Indonesia and China, to the clouds in hot air balloons – heralded a thrilling new age of discovery and imperial expansion, and introduced the reading public to a range of exotic scenes and cultures. This kind of travel was different from the European Grand Tour: it was conducted not for individual leisure or improvement but for scientific discovery and national commercial interests, often uneasy bedfellows, then as now. And from the published records and reports of these journeys a new persona emerged to captivate the public imagination: supplanting the polite gentleman tourist, figures like Joseph Banks (1743–1820), Alexander Von Humboldt (1769–1859)

---

1 Smith's 'History of Astronomy' was composed in the 1750s, but remained unpublished during his lifetime. It first appeared in the posthumous *Essays on Philosophical Subjects* (1795).

and Mungo Park (1771–1806) come forward as scientific adventurers, troubled geniuses who anticipate and counterpoint the figure of the romantic artist.

Expedition narratives are rich in examples of the exotic sublime: awe-inspiring, terrifying and sometimes baffling encounters with *foreignness* of all kinds. These encounters can be affirming, on both an individual and a national level, expressing wonder at the spectacular phenomena described (e.g. Barrow on the coral reefs), while registering an underlying sense of confidence and pride in the achievements of European science (e.g. Ross and Parry in the Arctic, or Baldwin amongst the clouds). But they can also be terrifying: horrific visions of human brutality and degradation (e.g. Equiano's account of a slave-ship), or of a seemingly godless natural world with no concern for human wellbeing (as in the myth of the deadly Upas tree). At the heart of the encounter with the exotic sublime, then, lie potentially troubling questions about the European. As noted, the encounter with the exotic sublime can support a positive view of European cultural values. But it also has the ability radically to question those values, to destabilise the relationship between the European and the non-European, to undermine and even to collapse the apparent distinction between them. Von Troil's descriptions of disease, De Quincey's 'Asiatic' nightmares, Hazlitt's attitude to the Indian jugglers – each register a fear that the unknown exotic might literally overwhelm the known European.

A similar dynamic of affirmation and threat informs the use of the exotic sublime in the so-called Oriental tale, an increasingly popular literary genre which develops out of the expedition narrative in the last decades of the eighteenth century, dovetailing elements of the Gothic, exotic and erotic into an often-lurid vision of the Middle East (as in Byron's best-selling 'Turkish Tales'). Hence the exotic sublime plays a key role in the development of what would come to be known, following the work of Edward Said, as 'romantic orientalism': the conceptual geography by which romantic-period Britain defined itself and its values in opposition to the those of an *imagined* east, a geography in which the discourse on the sublime is instrumental in bringing the exotic into the fold of European representation.[2]

6.1   John Hawkesworth, *An Account of the Voyages Undertaken by the Order of His Present Majesty for Making Discoveries in the Southern Hemisphere*, 3 vols (London, 1773), III, pp. 140–8.

In 1773, Hawkesworth (1715–73), author and literary editor of the Gentleman's Magazine, *was commissioned by the British Admiralty to compile an official account of the celebrated Admiralty-sponsored expeditions to the South Pacific in 1764–71, based on the records kept by the now-famous explorer James Cook (1728–79) and his fellow officers and naturalists, including Joseph Banks. This extract is taken from Hawkesworth's rendering of Cook's journal entries from 10–11 June 1770, when his*

---

2 Edward Said, *Orientalism* (London: Routledge, 1978).

ship, The Endeavour, *ran aground on the Great Barrier Reef near Cape Tribulation, off the coast of northern Queensland. It encapsulates well the physical, psychological and sociological terrors of shipwreck in exotic waters.*

Hitherto we had safely navigated this dangerous coast, where the sea in all parts conceals shoals that suddenly project from the shore, and rocks that rise abruptly like a pyramid from the bottom, for an extent of two and twenty degrees of latitude, more than one thousand three hundred miles; and therefore hitherto none of the names which distinguish the several parts of the country that we saw, are memorials of distress; but here we became acquainted with misfortune, and we therefore called the point which we had just seen farthest to the northward, Cape Tribulation [...]

We had the advantage of a fine breeze, and a clear moonlight night, and in standing off from six till near nine o'clock, we deepened our water from fourteen to twenty-one fathom, but while we were at supper it suddenly shoaled, and we fell into twelve, ten, and eight fathom, within the space of a few minutes; I immediately ordered everybody to their station, and all was ready to put about and come to an anchor, but meeting at the next cast of the lead with deep water again, we concluded that we had gone over the tail of the shoals which we had seen at sunset, and that all danger was past: before ten, we had twenty and one and twenty fathom, and this depth continuing, the gentlemen left the deck in great tranquillity, and went to bed; but a few minutes before eleven, the water shallowed at once from twenty to seventeen fathom, and before the lead could be cast again, the ship struck, and remained immoveable, except by the heaving of the surge, that beat her against the crags of the rocks upon which she lay. In a few moments everybody was upon the deck, with countenances which sufficiently expressed the horrors of our situation. We had stood off the shore three hours and a half, with a pleasant breeze, and therefore knew that we could not be very near it, and we had too much reason to conclude that we were upon a rock of coral, which is more fatal than any other, because the points of it are sharp, and every part of the surface so rough as to grind away whatever is rubbed against it, even with the gentlest motion.

In this situation all the sails were immediately taken in, and the boats hoisted out to examine the depth of water round the ship: we soon discovered that our fears had not aggravated our misfortune, and that the vessel had been lifted over a ledge of the rock, and lay in a hollow within it [...] during all this time she continued to beat with great violence against the rock, so that it was with the utmost difficulty that we kept upon our legs; and to complete the scene of distress, we saw by the light of the moon the sheathing boards from the bottom of the vessel floating away all round her, and at last, her false keel, so that every moment was making way for the sea to rush in which was to swallow us up [...]

We had indeed some hope from the next tide, but it was doubtful whether she would hold together so long, especially as the rock kept grating her bottom under the starboard bow with such force as to be heard in the fore store-room [...] the men were so far impressed with a sense of their situation, that not an oath was heard among them, the habit of profaneness, however strong, being instantly subdued, by the dread of incurring guilt when death seemed to be so near [...]

About five o'clock in the afternoon, we observed the tide begin to rise, but we observed at the same time that the leak increased to a most alarming degree, so that two more pumps were manned, but unhappily only one of them would work; three of the pumps however were kept going, and at nine o'clock the ship righted, but the leak had gained upon us so considerably, that it was imagined she must go to the bottom as soon as she ceased to be supported by the rock: this was a dreadful circumstance, so that we anticipated the floating of the ship not as an earnest of deliverance, but as an event that would probably precipitate our destruction. We well knew that our boats were not capable of carrying us all on shore, and that when the dreadful crisis should arrive, as all command and subordination would be at an end, a contest for preference would probably ensue, that would increase the horrors even of shipwreck, and terminate in the destruction of us all by the hands of each other; yet we knew that if any should be left on board to perish in the waves, they would probably suffer less upon the whole than those who should get on shore, without any lasting or effectual defence against the natives, in a country, where even nets and firearms would scarcely furnish them with food; and where, if they should find the means of subsistence, they must be condemned to languish out the remainder of life in a desolate wilderness, without the possession, or even hope, of any domestic comfort, and cut off from all commerce with mankind, except the naked savages who prowled the desert, and who perhaps were some of the most rude and uncivilised upon the earth.

To those only who have waited in a state of such suspense, death has approached in all his terrors; and as the dreadful moment that was to determine our fate came on, everyone saw his own sensations pictured in the countenances of his companions [...] I must observe, in justice and gratitude to the ship's company, and the Gentlemen on board, that although in the midst of our distress everyone seemed to have a just sense of his danger, yet no passionate exclamations, or frantic gestures, were to be heard or seen; everyone appeared to have the perfect possession of his mind, and everyone exerted himself to the uttermost, with a quiet and patient perseverance, equally distant from the tumultuous violence of terror, and the gloomy inactivity of despair.

6.2   Uno Von Troil, *Letters on Iceland, Containing Observations* [...] *Made During a Voyage Undertaken in the Year 1772*, 2nd edition (London, 1780), Letter XXIV, pp. 319–22, 331.

Von Troil (1746–1803), later Archbishop of Uppsala, accompanied the famous naturalist Joseph Banks (1743–1820) on his 1772 expedition to Iceland; other notable members of the team included James Lind (1736–1812), who would later tutor the poet Percy Shelley at Eton College. Von Troil's Letters *provide a systematic record of the expedition's cultural, geographical and scientific observations in the geologically spectacular island. The extract given here comes from a letter included by Von Troil concerning Icelandic elephantiasis, a disease triggered by parasitic worms which produces extreme swelling of the infected body parts and numerous other degenerative symptoms. In the* Letters, *this grotesque disease counterbalances Von Troil's response to Iceland's sublime geological and cultural heritage, and instances the frequent collocation, in cotemporary writing, of exotic lands and terrifying disease.*

What Mr. Petersen calls the Icelandic scurvy, is the true elephantiasis, which is nearly related to leprosy[3] [...] it is more terrible than any other disease, producing frequently a dreadful end: it gives a disgusting appearance to the patient, as the body by its colour, roughness, and scaly appearance, resembles the skin of an elephant. Whoever compares your and Mr. Petersen's description of this disease with that of the ancients, will not find it an easy matter to take the Icelandic scurvy for anything else but the elephantiasis [...]

Those of us who have written of the theory of diseases, have with more propriety given the name of scurvy where a gradual increasing languor takes place, together with a bleeding, stinking and putrid breath, and many coloured blackish-blue spots on the body, particularly round the roots of the hair, and which principally proceeds from corrupted salt animal food, and the want of vegetables.[4] The elephantiasis, on the other hand, which is also called *Lepra Arabum*,[5] is rather an hereditary disease; the skin becomes thick, unequal, glossy, and loses its smoothness; the hair falls off, languor and want of feeling take place in the extremities; the face becomes disgusting and full of biles,[6] and the patient gets a hoarse nasal voice. In the real leprosy (impetigo, lepra Græcorum[7]) the skin becomes wrinkled and full of scales, which seem to be strewn with bran,[8] often burst, itch exceedingly, and are filled with a watery moisture [...]

It is very remarkable that this disease has preserved its nature so perfectly in the most northern parts during more than a hundred years, and remained entirely similar to that in the hottest climates [...]

Before this disease breaks out on any person, his breath is disagreeable and stinking for three, and sometimes six years preceding: he has a great appetite to eat sour, half-rotten and unwholesome food; is always thirsty and drinks very much: some are slothful and sleepy, and when asleep are with great difficulty

---

3 *Scurvy* [...] *leprosy*: scurvy is a potentially fatal disease caused by lack of Vitamin C; leprosy, caused by bacterial infection, destroys the skin and extremities.

4 As noted, scurvy is now known to be caused by lack of sufficient Vitamin C.

5 *Lepra Arabum*: literally, 'Arabian leprosy'.

6 *biles*: discoloured swellings.

7 *lepra Græcorum*: psoriasis, a skin disease causing scaly, red patches (literally 'Greek leprosy').

8 *bran*: scales, flakes.

awakened; are short-breathed when the complaint ascends upwards; they spit very much, and complain of weariness in their knees. They shiver violently when they come out of a room into the open air; the eyes and lips become of a brown and blue colour: they have a weak smell; with some the feeling is likewise numbed; others have weak sight; and some lose it entirely when their foreheads begin to swell in the beginning of the disease. They have frequently thin hair, particularly on the eyebrows; the beard likewise grows very thin on both sides of the skin, and the skin becomes glossy, as if it had been rubbed over with grease.

6.3 'Description of the Poison-Tree, in the Island of Java. By N. P. Foersch. Translated from the Original Dutch, by Mr. Heydinger', in *The London Magazine* (December 1783), pp. 511–17.

This spurious article in the natural history section of the London Magazine *describes the sublime spectacle of the* Bohon Upas: *a tree so lethal that nothing can survive within a twelve-mile radius of the spot on which it stands. The* London's *editors admit that 'the account [...] appears so* marvellous, *that even the Credulous might be staggered' (512) but such was the contemporary taste for the 'exotic', and so spectacular did the world being revealed by explorations into previously unknown regions appear, that many took the story at face value. No less a figure that Erasmus Darwin, for example, includes an account of the 'Fell Upas, the Hydra-Tree of death' in his 1791* Botanic Garden *(II, iii, 238), citing the* London Magazine *as his source. Of course, despite the* London's *insistence that 'the existence of the tree, and the noxious powers of its gums and vapours, are certain' (512), the details had been greatly, and perhaps deliberately, exaggerated, as cotemporary travellers to the region were quick to assert: in his 1806* Voyage to Cochinchina, *for example, John Barrow points out that the actual* antiaris toxicaria *was not nearly so lethal as had been suggested. Nevertheless, the original report evidently held a considerable grip on both the romantic and the Victorian imagination: metaphorical uses of the poison tree occur, to give just a few examples, in the work of William Blake, Charlotte Brontë, Lord Byron, Charles Dickens, Thomas Paine, Percy Shelley and Robert Southey, and the Upas was also the subject of a then-celebrated painting by the popular apocalyptic artist Francis Danby, exhibited in London in 1820.*

This destructive tree is called in the Malayan language, *Bohon-Upas*, and has been described by naturalists. But their accounts have been so tinctured with the *marvellous*, that the whole narration has been supposed to be an ingenious fiction by the generality of readers. Nor is this in the least degree surprising, when the circumstances which we shall faithfully consider in this description are considered.

I must acknowledge, that I long doubted the existence of this tree, until a stricter enquiry convinced me of my error. I shall now relate simple, unadorned facts, of which I have been an eye witness. My readers may depend upon the fidelity of this account. In the year 1774, I was stationed at Batavia,[9] as a surgeon of the Dutch East-India Company.[10] During my residence there I received several different accounts of the *Bohon-Upas*, and the violent effects of its poison. They all then seemed incredible to me, but raised my curiosity in so high a degree, that I resolved to investigate this subject thoroughly, and to trust only to *my own observations*. In consequence of this resolution, I applied to the Governor General, Mr. Petrus Albertus van der Parra,[11] for a pass to travel through the country. My request was granted, and having procured every information, I set out on my expedition. I had procured a recommendation from an old Malayan priest to another priest, who lives on the nearest inhabitable spot to the tree, which is about fifteen or sixteen miles distant [from the tree]. The letter proved of great service to me in my undertaking, as that priest is appointed by the Emperor to reside there, in order to prepare for eternity the souls of those who for different crimes are sentenced to approach the tree, and to procure the poison.

The *Bohon-Upas* is situated in the island of *Java*, about twenty-seven leagues from *Batavia*, fourteen from *Soura-Charta*, the seat of the Emperor, and between eighteen and twenty leagues from *Tiukjoe*,[12] the present residence of the Sultan of Java. It is surrounded on all sides by a circle of high hills and mountains, and the country round it, to the distance of ten or twelve miles from the tree, is entirely barren. Not a tree, not a shrub, nor even the least plant or grass is to be seen. I have made the tour all around this dangerous spot, at about eighteen miles distant from the centre, and I found the aspect of the country on all sides equally dreary. The easiest ascent of the hills, is from that part where the old ecclesiastic dwells. From his house the criminals are sent for the poison into which the points of all warlike instruments are dipped. It is of high value, and produces a considerable revenue to the Emperor.

Account of the Manner in which the Poison is Procured.

The poison which is procured from this tree, is a gum that issues out between the bark and the tree itself, like the *camphor*.[13] Malefactors, who for their crimes are sentenced to die, are the only persons who fetch the poison; and this is the only chance they have of saving their lives. After sentence is

---

9 *Batavia*: Jakarta, the capital of Indonesia.

10 *Dutch* [...] *Company*: established by the Dutch government in 1602 to administer its colonies in Indonesia; ostensibly a private trading company but effectively an organ of the state.

11 *Petrus* [...] *Parra*: (1714–75); governor general of the Dutch East Indies from 1761 until his death.

12 *Soura-Charta* [...] *Tiukjoe*: Surakarta and Yogyakarta, both in central Java. This would place the *Upas* in the Mt Dieng area.

13 *camphor*: an aromatic substance, with various medicinal and culinary uses, obtained from a number of laurel species indigenous to Indonesia.

pronounced upon them by the judge, they are asked in court, whether they will die by the hands of the executioner, or whether they will go to the *Upas* tree for a box of poison? They commonly prefer the latter proposal, as there is not only some chance of preserving their lives, but also a certainty, in the case of their safe return, that a provision will be made for them in future, by the Emperor. They are also permitted to ask a favour from the Emperor, which is generally of a trifling nature, and commonly granted. They are then provided with a silver tortoiseshell box, in which they are to put the poisonous gum, and are properly instructed how to proceed while they are upon their danger-ous expedition. Among other particulars, they are always told to attend to the direction of the winds; as they are to go towards the tree before the wind, so that the effluvia from the tree are always blown from them. They are told, like-wise, to travel with the utmost dispatch, as that is the only method of insuring a safe return. They are afterwards sent to the house of the old priest, to which place they are commonly attended by their friends and relations. Here they generally remain for some days, in expectation of a favourable breeze. During that time, the ecclesiastic prepares them for their future fate by prayers and admonitions.

When the hour of their departure arrives, the priest puts on them a long leather cap with two glasses before the eyes, which comes down as far as their breast, and also provides them with a pair of leather gloves. They are then conducted by the priest, and their friends and relations, about two miles on their journey. Here the priest repeats his instructions, and tells them where they are to look for the tree. He shows them a hill, which they are told to ascend; and that on the other side they will find a rivulet, which they are to follow, and which will conduct them directly to the *Upas*. They now take leave of each other, and amidst prayers for their success, the delinquents hasten away.

The worthy old ecclesiastic has assured me, that during his residence there, for upwards of thirty years, he has dismissed above seven hundred criminals in the manner which I have described; and that scarcely two out of twenty have returned. He showed me a catalogue of all the unhappy sufferers, with the date of their departure from his house annexed, and a list of the offences for which they had been condemned. To which was added the names of those who had returned in safety. I afterwards saw another list of these culprits, at the gaol-keeper's at *Soura Charta*, and found that they perfectly corresponded with each other [...]

I was present at some of those melancholy ceremonies, and desired different delinquents to bring with them some pieces of the wood, or a small branch, or some leaves of this wonderful tree. I have also given them silk cords, desiring them to measure its thickness. I never could procure more than two dry leaves, that were picked up by one of them on his return; and all I could learn from him concerning the tree itself, was, that it stood on the border of a rivulet, as described by the old priest, that it was of a middling size, that five or six young trees of the same kind stood close by it; but that no other shrub or plant could be seen near it; and that the ground was of a brownish sand, full of stones, almost impracticable for travelling, and covered with dead bodies [...]

[T]he Malayans consider this tree as an holy instrument of the great prophet to punish the sins of mankind, and, therefore, to die of the poison of the *Upas* is generally considered among them as an honourable death. For that reason I also observed, that the delinquents, who were going to the tree, were generally dressed in their best apparel.

This, however, is certain, though it may appear incredible, that from fifteen to eighteen miles around this tree, not only no human creature can exist; but that, in that space of ground, no living animal of any kind has ever been discovered. I have also been assured by several persons of veracity, that there are no fish in the waters, nor has any rat, mouse, or any other vermin been seen there: and when any birds fly so near this tree, that the effluvia reaches them, they fall a sacrifice to the effects of the poison. This circumstance has been ascertained by different delinquents, who, in their return, have seen the birds drop down, and have picked them up *dead*, and brought them to the old ecclesiastic [...].

6.4 Thomas Baldwin, *Airopaidia: Containing the Narrative of a Balloon Excursion from Chester, the Eighth of September, 1785* (Chester, 1786), pp. 37–43, 171–2.

The first manned balloon flights took place in France in October and November 1783, using the famous Montgolfier brothers' hot air balloon. In the summer of 1784, the Italian balloonist Vincenzo Lunardi (1759–1806) brought a hydrogen balloon to Britain, and, over the next two years, made numerous successful flights over various parts of the country, including one over London witnessed by the Prince of Wales and other dignitaries (on which Lunardi was accompanied by his cat). On 8 September 1785, Lunardi, then at Chester, allowed Thomas Baldwin to make a solo ascent while the balloon was tethered in Chester Castle. Baldwin's normally sober account, delivered in a slightly awkward third-person narrative which was presumably intended to create a sense of scientific objectivity, relies upon the tropes of the discourse on the sublime to describe the wonderful landscapes and cloudscapes visible from the balloon, affirming that they 'overwhelmed' his 'imagination'.

Things taking a favourable turn, he stood up,[14] but with knees a little bent, more easily to conform to accidental motions, as sailors when they walk the deck: and took a full gaze before, and below him.

But what scenes of grandeur and beauty! A tear of pure delight flashed in his Eye! of pure exquisite delight and rapture; to look down on the unexpected

---

14 *he:* that is, Baldwin himself.

change already wrought in the works of art and nature, contracted to a span,[15] by the new perspective, diminished almost beyond the bounds of credibility.

Yet so far were the objects from losing their beauty, that each was brought up in a new manner to the eye, and distinguished by a strength of colouring, a neatness of elegance and boundary, above description charming!

The endless variety of objects, minute, distinct and separate, though apparently on the same plain or level, at once striking the eye without a change of its position, astonished and enchanted. Their beauty was unparalleled. The imagination itself was more than gratified; it was overwhelmed. The gay scene was fairy-land, and Chester Lilliput.[16]

He tried his voice, and shouted for joy. His voice was unknown to himself, shrill and feeble. There was no echo [...].

On looking south by west, the balloon often turning gently to the right and left, and giving the aeronaut an opportunity of enjoying the circular view without a change of attitude; innumerable rays of light darted on the eye as it glanced along the ground: which, though of a gay green colour, appeared like an inverted firmament glittering with stars of the first magnitude.[17] This splendid appearance was owing to the rays of the sun reflected from certain pits or ponds of water [...] The colours of objects shone more brilliant and lively at that amazing height, than if seen on a level with themselves [...] The whole had beautiful and rich look; not like a model, but a coloured map [...] The *greater* the height of the balloon, the more *contracted* was the circle of vapour below it; and the more limited the prospect of the earth's surface below the vapour.

It seemed probable that the sun shone as *bright* on the countries around the observer, as on objects immediately below him: which objects could not have been illuminated by the sun's rays, darting through the apparent and contracted opening under him; as the rays which shone on the balloon, fell beyond the opening, obliquely on clouds which caught the shadow of the balloon.

The extreme rarity or tenuity[18] of the vapours was evident from the progressive course of the balloon, which was always in the centre of a circular opening, limiting the lower prospects; except when the spectator lost all sight of the earth, by dense, watery, intervening clouds.

This *august* central situation, always changing yet still the same, had the most striking effect on the senses and the imagination. Yet, however pleasing the recollection of glorious appearance; however strongly impressed, accurately described, or richly painted; it must fall infinitely short of the original sensation. Unity and sameness were there contrasted with perpetual variety: beauty

---

15 *a span*: that is, the width of a hand.
16 *Lilliput*: in Swift's satirical novel *Gulliver's Travels* (1726), Lilliput is an island-nation inhabited by tiny people.
17 *Firmament* [...] *magnitude*: the firmament is the apparent dome of the night sky; stars are arranged in magnitudes relative to their apparent brightness in the night sky; stars of the first magnitude are the brightest.
18 *tenuity*: tenuousness, that is, in this case, 'lack of thickness'.

of colouring; minuteness; and consummate arrangement; – with magnificence and splendour: actual immensity; – with apparent limitation: – all of which were distinctly conveyed to the mind, at the same instant, through the intervention of the organs of sight: and, to complete the scene, was added the charm of novelty.

6.5 Olaudah Equiano, *The Interesting Narrative of the Life of Olaudah Equiano, or Gustavus Vassa, the African, Written by Himself*, ninth edition (London, 1794), pp. 12–19, pp. 46–52.

Equiano (1745–97), an Igbo native of what is now Nigeria, was captured as a child and sold as a slave to a British naval officer and subsequently to a Quaker merchant, from whom he eventually purchased his freedom, having been permitted to earn money through personal trades. During his captivity, Equiano was taught to read and write, and given a general education. His Interesting Narrative, *first published in 1789, exposed to the general reading public the full horrors of the slave trade, and made a significant contribution to the growth of the Abolitionist movement in Britain. In these two extracts, Equiano presents the reading public with two very different versions of the terrifyingly exotic: in the first, he describes some aspects of his native culture; in the second, he recalls the horrors of the slave ship which transported him from Africa.*

As we live in a country where nature is prodigal of her favours, our wants are few, and easily supplied; of course we have few manufactures. They consist for the most part of calicoes,[19] earthen ware, ornaments, and instruments of war and husbandry. But these make no part of our commerce, the principal articles of which, as I have observed, are provisions. In such a state money is of little use; however we have some small pieces of coin, if I may call them such. They are made something like an anchor; but I do not remember either their value or denomination. We have also markets, at which I have been frequently with my mother. These are sometimes visited by stout, mahogany-coloured men from the south-west of us: we call them *Oye-Eboe*, which term signifies red men living at a distance. They generally bring us firearms, gun-powder, hats, beads, and dried fish. The last we esteemed a great rarity, as our waters were only brooks and springs. These articles they barter with us for odoriferous woods and earth, and our salt of wood-ashes. They always carry slaves through our land, but the strictest account is exacted of their manner of procuring them before they are suffered to pass. Sometimes indeed we sold slaves to them, but they were only prisoners of war, or such among us as had been convicted of kidnapping, or adultery, and some other crimes which we esteemed heinous. This practice of kidnapping induces me to think, that, notwithstanding all our strictness, their

---

19 *calicoes*: cotton textiles.

principal business among us was to trepan our people.[20] I remember too they carried great sacks along with them, which, not long after, I had an opportunity of fatally seeing applied to that infamous purpose.

Our land is uncommonly rich and fruitful, and produces all kinds of vegetables in great abundance. We have plenty of Indian corn, and vast quantities of cotton and tobacco. Our pineapples grow without culture; they are about the size of the largest sugar-loaf, and finely flavoured. We have also spices of different kinds, particularly of pepper; and a variety of delicious fruits which I have never seen in Europe; together with gums of various kinds, and honey in abundance [...]

Our tillage is exercised in a large plain our common, some hours walk from our dwellings, and all the neighbours resort thither in a body. They use no beasts of husbandry; and their only instruments are hoes, axes, shovels, and beaks, or pointed iron, to dig with. Sometimes we are visited by locusts, which come in large clouds, so as to darken the air and destroy our harvest. This however happens rarely, but when it does a famine is produced by it. I remember an instance or two wherein this happened. This common is oftimes the theatre of war; and therefore when our people go out to till their land, they not only go in a body, but generally take their arms with them, for fear of a surprise; and when they apprehend an invasion, they guard the avenues to their dwellings by driving sticks into the ground, which are so sharp at one end as to pierce the foot, and are generally dipped in poison. From what I can recollect of these battles, they appear to have been eruptions of one little state or district on the other, to obtain prisoners or booty. Perhaps they were incited to this by those traders who brought the European goods I mentioned amongst us. Such a mode of obtaining slaves in Africa is common; and I believe more are procured this way, and by kidnapping, than any other.[21] When a trader wants slaves, he applies to a chief for them, and tempts him with his wares. It is not extraordinary, if on this occasion he yields to the temptation with as little firmness, and accepts the price of his fellow creature's liberty with as little reluctance, as the enlightened merchant. Accordingly, he falls on his neighbours, and a desperate battle ensues. If he prevails, and takes prisoners, he gratifies his avarice by selling them; but, if his party be vanquished, and he falls into the hands of the enemy, he is put to death: for, as he has been known to foment[22] their quarrels, it is thought dangerous to let him survive; and no ransom can save him, though all other prisoners may be redeemed.

We have fire-arms, bows and arrows, broad two-edged swords and javelins; we have shields also, which cover a man from head to foot. All are taught the use of these weapons. Even our women are warriors, and march boldly out to fight along with the men. Our whole district is a kind of militia: On a certain signal

---

20 *to trepan*: 'to entrap; ensnare; beguile', *OED* v.2.
21 'See Benezett's Account of Africa through' (Equiano's note). The reference is to the abolitionist Anthony Benezet (1713–84), whose *Short Account of that Part of Africa Inhabited by the Negroes* was published in 1762.
22 *foment*: 'incite, cause'.

given, such as the firing of a gun at night, they all rise in arms and rush upon their enemy. It is perhaps something remarkable, that, when our people march to the field, a red flag or banner is borne before them. I was once a witness to a battle in our common. We had been all at work in it one day as usual, when our people were suddenly attacked. I climbed a tree at some distance, from which I beheld the fight. There were many women as well as men on both sides; among others my mother was there, and armed with a broad sword. After fighting for a considerable time with great fury, and many had been killed, our people obtained the victory, and took their enemy's Chief prisoner. He was carried off in great triumph; and, though he offered a large ransom for his life, he was put to death. A virgin of note among our enemies had been slain in the battle, and her arm was exposed in our market place, where our trophies were always exhibited. The spoils were divided according to the merit of the warriors. Those prisoners which were not sold or redeemed we kept as slaves: but, how different was their condition from that of the slaves in the West Indies![23] With us they do no more work than other members of the community, even their master. Their food, clothing, and lodging, were nearly the same as theirs, except that they were not permitted to eat with those who were free born; and there were scarce any other difference between them than a superior degree of importance which the head of a family possesses in our state, and that authority which, as such, he exercises over every part of his household. Some of these slaves have even slaves under them, as their own property, and for their own use.

As to religion, the natives believe that there is one Creator of all things, and that he lives in the sun, and is girded round with a belt, that he may never eat or drink; but according to some, he smokes a pipe, which is our own favourite luxury. They believe he governs events, especially our deaths or captivity; but, as for the doctrine of eternity, I do not remember to have ever heard of it: some however believe in the transmigration of souls in a certain degree, such as their dear friends or relations, they believe always attend them, and guard them from the bad spirits of their foes. For this reason, they always, before eating, as I have observed, put some small portion of the meat, and pour some of their drink, on the ground for them; and they often make oblations of the blood of beasts or fowls at their graves.[24] I was very fond of my mother, and almost constantly with her. When she went to make these oblations at her mother's tomb, which was a kind of small solitary thatched house, I sometimes attended her. There she made her libations, and spent most of the night in cries and lamentation. I have been often extremely terrified on these occasions. The loneliness of the place, the darkness of the night, and the ceremony of libation, naturally awful and gloomy, were heightened by my mother's lamentations; and these concurring with the doleful cries of birds, by which these places were frequented, have an inexpressible terror to the scene.

---

23 *Slaves* [...] *Indies!*: that is, slaves taken by Europeans.
24 *oblations*: offerings.

The first object that assaulted my eyes when I arrived at the coast was the sea, and a slave ship, which was then riding at anchor, and waiting for its cargo. These filled me with astonishment, which was soon converted to terror, which I am yet at a loss to describe, nor then the feelings of my mind [...] such were the horrors of my views and fears at the moment, that, if ten thousand worlds had been my own, I would freely have parted with them all to have exchanged my condition with that of the meanest slave in my own country [...] I was not long suffered to indulge my grief; I was soon put down under the decks, and there I received such a salutation in my nostrils as I had never experienced in my life; so that with the loathsomeness of the stench, and crying together, I became so sick and low that I was not able to eat, nor had I the least desire to taste anything. I now wished for the last friend, Death, to relieve me; but soon, to my grief, two of the white men offered me eatables; and, on my refusing to eat, one of them held me fast by the hands, and laid me across, I think, the windlass,[25] and tied my feet, while the other flogged me severely [...] still I feared I should be put to death, the white people looked and acted, as I thought, in so savage a manner; for I had never seen among any people such instances of brutal cruelty; and this not only shown towards us blacks, but also to some of the whites themselves. One white man in particular I saw, when we were permitted to be on deck, flogged so unmercifully with a rope near the foremast, that he died in consequence of it; and they tossed him over the side as they would have done a brute [...]

At last, when the ship we were in had got in all her cargo [...] we were all put under deck [...] The closeness of the place, and the heat of the climate, added to the number in the ship, which was so crowded that each had scarcely room to turn himself, almost suffocated us. This produced copious perspirations, so that the air soon became unfit for respiration, from a variety of loathsome smells, and brought on a sickness amongst the slaves, of which many died, thus falling victims to the improvident avarice, as I may call it, of their purchasers. This wretched situation was again aggravated by the galling of the chains, now become insupportable; and the filth of the necessary tubs,[26] into which the children often fell, and were almost suffocated. The shrieks of the women, and the groans of the dying, rendered the whole a scene of horror almost inconceivable.

6.6   Mungo Park, *Travels in the Interior Districts of Africa: Performed under the Patronage and Direction of the African Association, in the Years 1795, 1796, and 1797* (London, 1799), pp. 1–2, 153–4, 189–90.

In 1794, the Scottish surgeon Mungo Park (1771–1806) obtained a commission from the London-based Association for Promoting the Discovery of the Interior Parts

25 *the windlass*: winch for raising the ship's anchor.
26 *the necessary tubs*: for urine and excrement.

of Africa. Park's objective was to determine the course of the river Niger which, the Association hoped, might connect to the Nile, thereby opening up a new trade route from the Atlantic to the eastern Mediterranean, as well as potential new sources of revenue in the African interior. Park's two year-expedition was fraught with mishaps, including some four months as a prisoner of a local ruler. He did, however, succeed in establishing that the Niger flowed in an easterly direction, thus lending credence to the theory of a link with the Nile, and is generally credited as the first European to have seen the river. While Park's highly popular Travels, *compiled after his return in 1797, are rather more sentimental than some cotemporary expedition-narratives (e.g. Barrow, Humboldt), they nevertheless exemplify the combination of disinterested curiosity and commercial interest that characterises many romantic-period engagements with 'exotic' countries. In the three extracts given here, Park describes his motivation for the journey, his impressions of the Sahara desert, and his first glimpse of the Niger.*

Soon after my return from the East Indies in 1793, having learnt that the Noblemen and Gentlemen, associated for the purpose of prosecuting Discoveries in the Interior of Africa, were desirous of engaging a person to explore that continent by way of the Gambia River, I took occasion, through means of the President of the Royal Society,[27] to whom I had the honour to be known, of offering myself for that service. I had been informed, that a gentleman of the name of Houghton, a Captain in the army, and formerly Fort-Major at Gorée,[28] had already sailed to the Gambia, under the direction of the Association, and that there was reason to apprehend he had fallen a sacrifice to the climate, or perished in some contest with the natives; but this intelligence, instead of deterring me from my purpose, animated me to persist in the offer of my services with the greater solicitude. I had a passionate desire to examine into the productions of a country so little known; and to become experimentally acquainted with the modes of life, and character of the natives. I knew that I was able to bear fatigue; and I relied on my youth and the strength of my constitution, to preserve me from the effects of the climate. The salary which the Committee allowed was sufficiently large, and I made no stipulation for future reward. If I should perish in my journey, I was willing that my hopes and expectations should perish with me; and if I should succeed in rendering the geography of Africa more familiar to my countrymen, and in opening to their ambition and industry new sources of wealth, and new channels of commerce, I knew that I was in the hands of men of honour, who would not fail to bestow that remuneration which my successful services should appear to them to merit [...]

---

27 *the President* [...] *Society*: the famous naturalist, Sir Joseph Banks.
28 *Gorée*: Gorée Island, off Dakar, in Western Senegal; first occupied by the Portuguese in 1444, the island was controlled by both the British and the French at various points during Revolutionary and Napoleonic wars.

Ludamar[29] has for its northern boundary, the Great Desert of Sahara. From the best enquiries I could make, this vast ocean of sand, which occupies so large a space in Northern Africa, may be pronounced almost destitute of inhabitants: except where the scanty vegetation which appears in certain spots, affords pasturage for the flocks of a few miserable Arabs, who wander from one well to another. In other places, where the supply of water and pasturage is more abundant, small parties of the Moors[30] have taken up their residence. Here they live, in independent poverty, secure from the tyrannical government of Barbary.[31] But the greater part of the Desert, being totally destitute of water, is seldom visited by any human being: unless where the trading caravans trace out their toilsome and dangerous route across it. In some parts of this extensive waste, the ground is covered with low stunted shrubs, which serve as landmarks for the caravans, and furnish the camels with a scanty forage. In other parts the disconsolate wanderer, wherever he turns, sees nothing around him but a vast interminable expanse of sand and sky; a gloomy and barren void, where the eye finds no particular object to rest upon, and the mind is filled with painful apprehensions of perishing with thirst. 'Surrounded by this solitude, the traveller sees the dead bodies of birds, that the violence of the wind has brought from happier regions; and as he ruminates on the fearful length of his remaining passage, listens with horror to the voice of the driving blast; the only sound that interrupts the awful repose of the Desert'[32] [...]

Just before it was dark, we took up our lodgings for the night at a small village, where I procured some victuals for myself and some corn for my horse, at the moderate price of a button; and was told I should see the Niger (which the Negroes call Joliba or *the great water*), early the next day. The lions are here very numerous: the gates are shut a little after sunset, and nobody allowed to go out. The thoughts of seeing the Niger in the morning, and the troublesome buzzing of mosquitoes, prevented me from shutting my eyes during the night; and I had saddled my horse, and was in readiness before daylight; but, on account of the wild beasts, we were obliged to wait until the people were stirring, and the gates opened. This happened to be a market day at Sego,[33] and the roads were everywhere filled with people carrying different articles to sell. We passed four large villages, and at eight o'clock saw the smoke over Sego.

As we approached the town, I was fortunate enough to overtake the fugitive Kaartans, to whose kindness I had been so much indebted in my journey

---

29 *Ludamar*: an administrative region of the former Bambara Empire, in northern Mali.
30 *Moors*: a term referring, in Park's day, to various North African peoples.
31 *tyrannical* [...] *Barbary*: in Park's day, 'Barbary' was the collective name of the four provinces of the Ottoman Empire on the north coast of Africa, effectively equivalent to modern day Morocco, Tunisia, Algeria and Libya; the region was notorious for harbouring pirates and for the trade in Christian slaves.
32 'Proceedings of the African Association, Part I' (Park's note).
33 *Sego*: the city of Ségou, in Mali; then capital of the Bambara Empire.

through Bambarra.[34] They readily agreed to introduce me to the king; and we rode together through some marshy ground, where, as I was anxiously looking around for the river, one of them called out, *geo affilli* (see the water); and looking forwards, I saw with infinite pleasure the great object of my mission; the long sought for majestic Niger, glittering to the morning sun, as broad as the Thames at Westminster, and flowing slowly *to the eastward*.[35] I hastened to the brink, and, having drank of the water, lifted up my fervent thanks in prayer, to the Great Ruler of all things, for having thus far crowned my endeavours with success.

6.7 John Barrow, *A Voyage to Cochinchina in the Years 1792 and 1793* (London, 1806), pp. 162–3, 165–8.

Sir John Barrow (1764–1848) was a member of the 94-man British ambassadorial visit to China in 1792–4, led by George Macartney, which sought but failed to establish a trade agreement between the two countries. The extracts given here are taken from Barrow's description of 'The Straits of Sunda and the Island of Java', in the seventh chapter of his generally rather sober account of the journey from Britain to Cochinchina (now southern Vietnam), via South America. In the first extract, Barrow recalls an 'alarming' encounter with a three-metre shark. In the second, he describes the 'wonderful [...] inconceivable' spectacle of coral reefs. Later in the same chapter, Barrow refutes the 'fabulous stories' (192) told about the lethal Upas *tree, noting that while such a species exists, and is indeed a source of poisonous resin, the lethal influence reported in the December 1783 number of the* Gentleman's *Magazine had been greatly exaggerated.*

In no other part of the world do I recollect to have observed such shoals of sharks as are constantly prowling near the shore at *Anjerie*,[36] attracted no doubt by the offals that float down the river or are thrown upon the beach. When on board the *Hindostan*, at this anchorage, I hooked one of these voracious animals from the stern gallery, in doing which, however, I had a very narrow escape from being dragged by it into the sea. No sooner did the fish feel the hook in its jaw than, plunging towards the bottom, he drew the line to its full stretch, which, being entangled in the railing of the gallery, swept away at once a great part of the balustrade. In the rapidity with which the rope ran out, a coil of it got round my arm, but just as I was forced among the wreck, the shark, by darting

---

34 *the fugivtive* [...] *Bambarra*: Kaarta was a breakaway province of the Bambara Empire, in Western Mali. Park describes the struggle between the two regions in Chapter VIII, and, in Chapter XIII, explains how a Kaartan attack had helped him escape after he had been held prisoner for four months by the governor of Ludamar.

35 The principal direction of the Niger's flow had been a source of controversy amongst European scientists, and Park notes that he had himself been 'in great hesitation on this subject' (I, 190).

36 *Anjerie*: Anyer, in West Java.

back to the surface, slacked the rope sufficiently to enable me to disengage my arm and to get clear. Greatly as I was alarmed at this accident, a poor Javanese appeared to be still more so, who happened at that moment to be astern of the ship, paddling his canoe with a load of fruit and vegetables. His apprehension lest the wounded shark, in rolling and plunging and lashing the water with its fins and tail, should overturn his little skiff, which was not much larger than the animal itself, his exertions to get out of its reach, and the marks of terror that were visible on his countenance, struck our fellow traveller, Alexander, so forcibly that, though of momentary duration, he caught with his pencil a spirited sketch; which, having the merit at least of being a true representation of a Javanese canoe, with its paddle and bamboo outrigger, was considered as not unworthy of being put into the engraver's hands. The shark being killed with a harpoon, was then hoisted upon deck and opened. The contents of its stomach formed a mass of such magnitude and variety as can scarcely be conceived. It consisted, among other articles, of the complete head of a female buffalo, a whole calf, a quantity of entrails and of bones, and large fragments of the upper and under shells of a considerable sized turtle.[37] The length of the shark was ten feet eight inches [...]

The whole group of the *Thousand Islands*,[38] and indeed the greater part of all those whose surfaces are flat in the neighbourhood of the equator, owe their origin to the labours of that order of marine worms which Linnaeus has arranged under the name of Zoophyta.[39] These little animals, in a most surprising manner, construct their calcareous habitations under an infinite variety of forms, yet with that order and regularity, each after its own manner, which, to the minute inquirer, is so discernible in every part of the creation. But although the eye may be convinced of the fact, it is difficult for the human mind to conceive of the possibility of insects so small being endued with the power, much less of being furnished in their own bodies with the materials, of constructing the immense fabrics which, in almost every part of the Eastern and Pacific oceans[40] lying between the tropics, are met with in the shape of detached rocks, or reefs of great extent just even with the surface, or islands already clothed with plants, whose bases are fixed at the bottom of the sea several hundred feet in depth, where light and heat, so very essential to animal life, if not excluded, are sparingly and feebly felt. Thousands of such rocks and reefs and islands are known to exist in the Eastern Ocean, within, and even beyond, the limits of the tropics. The eastern coast of New Holland[41] is almost wholly girt with reefs and islands of coral rock, rising perpendicularly from the

---

37 This, in all fairness to Barrow, seems unlikely.
38 *the Thousand Islands*: an island chain in the Java Sea.
39 *Linnaeus* [...] *Zoophyta*: the Swedish zoologist, Carl Linnaeus (1707–78) pioneered the modern method of classifying plants and animals. Zoophyte was Linnaeus's term for animals which look like plants.
40 *the Eastern* [...] *oceans*: meaning the Indian Ocean, and the South China, Java and Philippine Seas.
41 *New Holland*: Australia.

bottom of the abyss. Captain Kent of the *Buffalo*,[42] speaking of a coral reef of many miles in extent, on the south-west coast of New Caledonia,[43] observes that 'it is level with the water's edge, and, towards the sea, as *steep to* as the wall of a house; that he sounded frequently within twice the ship's length of it with a line of one hundred and fifty fathoms, or nine hundred feet, without being able to reach the bottom'. How wonderful, how inconceivable, that such stupendous fabrics should rise into existence from the silent, but incessant and almost imperceptible labours of such insignificant worms! [...] The number and magnitude of those wonderful fabrics, dispersed over the Eastern ocean, and daily increasing in bulk and extent, furnish no weak support to that theory which supposes all marbles, limestones, and every species of calcareous rock, to have been the production of animated beings; a theory that is rendered still more plausible from the myriads of minute shells found in many of them, and of which some of the most beautiful of the marbles are almost wholly composed.

6.8   George Gordon, Lord Byron, *The Bride of Abydos: a Turkish Tale* (1813), lines 1–19.

The Bride of Abydos *is one of six 'Turkish tales' written by Byron (1788–1824) in response to the contemporary vogue for so-called Eastern tales: stories of love and adventure, set in Turkey, the Middle East or India, which blended the exotic with the erotic. The* Bride, *which sold six thousand copies in its first month, tells the story of a tragic love affair between the Turkish aristocrat Zuleika and her half-brother Selim, which ends in the deaths of both (Abydos is a town on the southern shore of the Dardanelles, the strait linking the Sea of Marmara to the Aegean). In this extract, the first stanza of the poem, Byron describes the exotic splendour of the Turkish landscape and the no less exotic passions of its inhabitants.*

> Know ye the land where the cypress and myrtle
> Are emblems of deeds that are done in their clime?[44]
> Where the rage of the vulture, the love of the turtle,[45]
> Now melt into sorrow, now madden to crime!
> 5   Know ye the land of the cedar and vine,
> Where the flowers ever blossom, the beams ever shine;
> Where the light wings of Zephyr,[46] oppressed with perfume,

---

42 *Captain Kent*: William Kent (1751–1812).

43 *New Caledonia*: the French territories of Grand Terre and the Loyalty Islands, in the southwest Pacific.

44 *cypress and myrtle*: trees native to the Mediterranean, symbols of death and love respectively.

45 *the turtle*: the turtle dove, an emblem of love.

46 *Zephyr*: in classical myth, the west wind; also associated with love.

Wax faint o'er the gardens of Gúl in her bloom;[47]
Where the citron and olive are fairest of fruit,
10   And the voice of the nightingale never is mute:
Where the tints of the earth, and the hues of the sky,
In colour though varied, in beauty may vie,
And the purple of ocean is deepest in dye;
Where the virgins are soft as the roses they twine,
15   And all, save the spirit of man, is divine?
'Tis the clime of the East; 'tis the land of the Sun –
Can he smile on such deeds as his children have done?
Oh! wild as the accents of lovers' farewell
Are the hearts which they bear, and the tales which they tell.

6.9   Alexander Von Humboldt, *Personal Narrative of Travels to the Equinoctial Regions of the New Continent, During the Years 1799–1804*, transl. Helen Maria Williams, 7 vols (London, 1814–29), IV (1819), pp. 344–50, 443–5.

When the German naturalist and explorer Alexander Von Humboldt (1769–1859) arrived in Cumaná, on the coast of Venezuela, on 16 July 1799, he began what is now routinely referred to as the scientific discovery of the Americas. Over the next five years, Humboldt and his companion Aimé Bonpland (1773–1858) travelled extensively throughout central and southern America, making observations and collecting specimens. On his return to Europe, Humboldt began publication of his Personal Narrative *of the expedition, a compelling combination of scientific record and spectacular travelogue which made the wonders of Latin-American natural history accessible to the reading public and largely created the persona of the scientist-adventurer. In the first of the two extracts from the* Narrative *given here, Humboldt describes the 'very striking spectacle' of 'fishing' for electric eels with horses; in the second, he provides the earliest European description of the ferocious piranha.*

I was impatient from the time of my arrival at Cumana, to procure electrical eels. We had been promised them often, but our hopes had always been disappointed. Money loses its value as you withdraw from the coast; and how is the imperturbable phlegm of the vulgar to be vanquished, when they are not excited by the desire of gain?

The Spaniards confound all electrical fishes under the name of *tembladores* (*producers of trembling*, literally *tremblers*). There are some in the Caribbean Sea, on the coast of Cumana. The Guayqueria Indians, who are the most skilful and industrious fishermen in those parts, brought us a fish, which, they said, had benumbed their hands. This fish ascends the little river Mazanares. It is a new

---

47 *Gúl*: 'gül', the rose (Turkish).

species of the ray, the lateral spots of which are scarcely visible, and which much resembles the torpedo of Galvani.[48] The torpedoes, furnished with an electric organ that is externally visible, on account of the transparency of the skin, form a genus or subgenus, different from the rays properly so called. The torpedo of Cumana was very lively, very energetic in its muscular movements, and yet the electrical shocks it gave us were extremely feeble. They became stronger on *galvanising* the animal by the contact of zinc and gold.[49] Other *tembladores*, real gymnoti or electrical eels,[50] inhabit the Rio Colorado, the Guarapiche, and several little streams, that cross the missions of the Chayma Indians. They abound also in the large rivers of America, the Orinoco, the Amazon, and the Meta; but the strength of the current, and the depth of the water, prevent their being caught by the Indians. They see these fish less frequently than they feel electrical shocks from them when swimming or bathing in the river. In the *Llanos*,[51] particularly in the environs of Calabozo, between the farms of Mondial and the missions *de Arriba* and *de Abaxo*, the basins of stagnant water, and the confluents of the Oroonoko (the Rio Guarico and the *Canos*[52] of Rastro, Berito, and Paloma) are filled with electrical eels. We at first wished to make our experiments in the house we inhabited at Calabozo; but the dread of the electrical shocks of the gymnoti is so great, and so exaggerated among the vulgar, that during three days we could not obtain one, though they are easily caught, and we had promised the Indians two piastres[53] for every strong and vigorous fish. This fear of the Indians is the more extraordinary, as they do not attempt to employ means in which they profess to have great confidence. When interrogated on the effect of the *tembladores*, they never fail to tell the Whites, that they may be touched with impunity, while you are chewing tobacco. This fable of the influence of tobacco on animal electricity is as general on the continent of South America, as the belief among mariners of the effect of garlic and tallow on the magnetic needle.[54]

Impatient of waiting, and having obtained very uncertain results from an electrical eel that had been brought to us alive, but much enfeebled, we repaired to the Cano de Bera, to make our experiments in the open air, on the borders of the water itself. We set off on the 19th of March, at a very early hour, for the village of *Rastro de Abaxo*; thence we were conducted by the Indians to a stream, which,

---

48 *torpedo of Galvani*: the marbled electric ray (torpedo marmorata), a type of fish capable of delivering electric shocks; formerly named after the Italian scientist Luigi Galvani (1737–98) who studied them as part of his research into animal electricity. The naval weapon is named after the fish.
49 *Galvanising* [...] *gold*: the exact process is unclear, but Humboldt presumably means causing the animal to transmit its shock through an attached piece of zinc or gold.
50 *Gymnoti* [...] *eels*: the electric eel is a member of the gymnotidae family and actually, despite its appearance, a species of fish; it is capable of delivering a shock powerful enough to kill a human.
51 *Llanos*: an area of tropical grassland encompassing parts of Colombia and Venezuela.
52 *Canos*: canals.
53 *piastres*: Spanish dollars.
54 *Garlic* [...] *needle*: the strong odours of garlic and animal fat ('tallow') were reputed to affect the accuracy of a compass.

in time of drought, forms a basin of muddy water, surrounded by fine trees, the clusia, the amyris, and the mimosa with fragrant flowers. To catch the gymnoti with nets is very difficult, on account of the extreme agility of the fish, which bury themselves in the mud like serpents. We would not employ the *barbasco*, that is to say, the roots of the piscidea erithryna, jacquinia armillaris, and some species of phyllanthus, which, thrown into the pool, intoxicate or benumb these animals. These means would have enfeebled the gymnoti; the Indians therefore told us, that they would 'fish with horses', *embarbascar con cavallos*.[55] We found it difficult to form an idea of this extraordinary manner of fishing; but we soon saw our guides return from the savannah, which they had been scouring for wild horses and mules. They brought about thirty of them, which they forced to enter the pool.

The extraordinary noise caused by the horses' hoofs makes the fish issue from the mud, and excites them to combat. These yellowish and livid eels, resembling large aquatic serpents, swim on the surface of the water, and crowd under the bellies of the horses and mules. A contest between animals of so different an organisation furnishes a very striking spectacle. The Indians, provided with harpoons and long slender reeds, surround the pool closely; and some climb upon the trees, the branches of which extend horizontally over the surface of the water. By their wild cries, and the length of their reeds, they prevent the horses from running away, and reaching the bank of the pool. The eels, stunned by the noise, defend themselves by the repeated discharge of their electric batteries. During a long time they seem to prove victorious. Several horses sink beneath the violence of the invisible strokes, which they receive from all sides in organs the most essential to life; and stunned by the force and frequency of the shocks, disappear under the water. Others, panting, with mane erect, and haggard eyes, expressing anguish, raise themselves, and endeavour to flee from the storm by which they are overtaken. They are driven back by the Indians into the middle of the water; but a small number succeed in eluding the active vigilance of the fishermen. These regain the shore, stumbling at every step, and stretch themselves on the sand, exhausted with fatigue, and their limbs benumbed by the electric shocks of the gymnoti.

In less than five minutes two horses were drowned. The eel, being five feet long, and pressing itself against the belly of the horses, makes a discharge along the whole extent of its electric organ. It attacks at once the heart, the intestines, and the *plexus cœliacus*[56] of the abdominal nerves. It is natural, that the effect felt by the horses should be more powerful, than that produced upon a man by the touch of the same fish at only one of his extremities. The horses are probably not killed, but only stunned. They are drowned from the impossibility of rising amid the prolonged struggle between the other horses and the eels.

---

55 'Properly *to set to sleep*, or *intoxicate* the fish by means of horses' (Humboldt's note).
56 *the plexus cœliacus*: the solar plexus, a network of nerves in the abdomen.

We had little doubt, that the fishing would terminate by killing successively all the animals engaged; but by degrees the impetuosity of this unequal combat diminished, and the wearied gymnoti dispersed. They require a long rest,[57] and abundant nourishment, to repair what they have lost of galvanic force. The mules and horses appear less frightened; their manes are no longer bristled, and their eyes express less dread. The gymnoti approach timidly the edge of the marsh, where they are taken by means of small harpoons fastened to long cords. When the cords are very dry, the Indians feel no shock in raising the fish into the air. In a few minutes we had five large eels, the greater part of which were only very slightly wounded. Some were taken by the same means toward the evening [...]

Since our departure from San Ferdinando, we have not met a single boat on this fine river. Everything denotes the most profound solitude. In the morning our Indians caught with a hook the fish known in the country by the name of *caribe*, or *caribito*, because no other fish has such a thirst for blood.[58] It attacks bathers and swimmers, from whom it often carries away considerable pieces of flesh. When a person is only slightly wounded, it is difficult for him to get out of the water without receiving a severer wound. The Indians dread extremely these caribes; and several of them showed us the scars of deep wounds in the calf of the leg, and in the thigh, made by these little animals, which the Maypures call umati.[59] They live at the bottom of rivers; but if a few drops of blood be shed on the water, they arrive by thousands at the surface. When we reflect on the number of these fish, the most voracious and cruel of which are only four or five inches long; on the triangular form of their sharp and cutting teeth, and on the amplitude of their retractile mouth, we need not be surprised at the fear which the caribe excites in the inhabitants of the banks of the Apure and Oroonoko. In places where the river was very limpid,[60] and where not a fish appeared, we threw into the water little morsels of flesh covered with blood. In a few minutes a cloud of caribes came to dispute the prey [...] As no one dares to bathe where it is found, [the caribito] may be considered as one of the greatest scourges of those climates, in which the stings of the mosquitoes, and the irritation of the skin, render the use of baths so necessary.

6.10   John Ross, *A Voyage of Discovery* [...] *Enquiring Into the Probability of a North-West Passage*, 2 vols (London, 1819), I, pp. 22–3, 52–3.

In 1818, Ross (1777–1835) commanded a two-ship expedition commissioned by the British Admiralty to investigate the possibility of a route from the North Sea to the

---

57 'The Indians assured us, that when the horses are made to run two days successively into the same pool, none are killed the second day' (Humboldt's note).

58 *Caribe* [...] *caribito*: presumably because the Carib Indians, native to the Orinoco area, were reputed to be cannibals.

59 *Maypures*: the Maipure Indians are native to the upper Orinoco region.

60 *limpid*: clear.

*Pacific Ocean through the Arctic Ocean, the so-called Northwest Passage, potentially
a quicker and safer alternative to the normal route around Cape Horn. In these brief
extracts from his account of the journey, Ross describes the expedition's encounter with
the sublime spectacle of icebergs, noting their appeal to the imagination and drawing
particular attention to his crew's highly-politicised re-imagining of one distant berg,
a process which bears comparison with radical-materialist critiques of the religious
response to the natural sublime as nothing more than superstitious anthropomorphism
(see Mountains). Ross's expedition failed to discover a navigable route through the ice
and returned to England the same year.*

At two o'clock on this day [26 May], we had the first sight of an iceberg, covered
with snow, bearing N.N.E., at a distance of eight or nine miles. From a calculation made by means of comparison between two objects, it appeared to be about
forty feet in height, and a thousand feet long.

Imagination presented it in many grotesque forms: at one time it looked something like a white lion and a horse rampant, and served to amuse the sailors,
who naturally enough shaped it into the lion and unicorn of the King's arms,
and were accordingly delighted with the notion of good luck which it seemed
to them to augur.

It is hardly possible to imagine anything more exquisite than the variety of
tints which these icebergs display; by night as well as by day they glitter with
a vividness of colour beyond the power of art to represent. While the white
portions have the brilliancy of silver, their colours are as various and splendid
as those of the rainbow; their ever-changing disposition producing effects as
singular as they were to us new and interesting [...]

On the following day [17 June] we worked with all sail to the northward;
Disco[61] was in sight; and no ice except the bergs was to be seen.

A current was found here, running south (true), a quarter of a mile an hour. In
the afternoon we boarded several Greenlandmen,[62] and learnt that none of their
ships had been able to penetrate further north than 70°30´, and that we should
fall in with ice in two hours, through which we might sail as far as Hare Island,[63]
where it became a solid body. At six we fell in with loose ice, and continued sail-
ing through it. Firm ice was seen to the westward.

We proceeded next day, steering along the edge of the main ice, and a firm
field stretching from north to south; we sailed on between large floes and among
loose ice, the former becoming more numerous as we advanced, and the latter
more closely packed, till at length we had only a narrow and crooked channel
for our passage. At eight we saw a ridge of icebergs, of every variety and shape
that can be imagined; many of them forming objects no less singular than

---

61 *Disco*: Disko Island, in Baffin Bay, off the west coast of Greenland.
62 *Greenlandmen*: ships from Greenland.
63 *Hare Island*: Hareø, a small island north of Disko.

picturesque, and presenting an infinite diversity in their grouping and in the splendour and brilliancy of their colouring.

6.11   William Edward Parry, *Journal of a Voyage for the Discovery of a North-West Passage from the Atlantic to the Pacific: Performed in the Years 1819–1820* (London, 1821), pp. 134–6, 141, 155–6, 162–3.

Parry (1790–1855) had captained one of the two ships on Ross's unsuccessful 1818 attempt to discover a Northwest Passage through the Arctic ice to the Pacific Ocean (see previous extract). In 1819, Parry commanded another two-ship, Admiralty-commissioned expedition with the same goal, although it, too, was unsuccessful. In these extracts from his Journal, *Parry describes various 'magnificent' atmospheric phenomena witnessed by the expedition. The extracts reveal a tension between the sublime effect of these phenomena and the need to provide sober, scientific witness of them, a tension encapsulated in Parry's reliance on the testimony of other members of the expedition as a counterbalance to his own 'inadequate' impressions.*

On the evening of the 15th [of January, 1820], the atmosphere being clear and serene, we were gratified by a sight of the only very brilliant and diversified display of Aurora Borealis,[64] which occurred during the whole winter; I believe it to be almost impossible for words to give an idea of the beauty and variety which this magnificent phenomenon displayed; I am at least certain, that no description of mine can convey an adequate conception of it, and I therefore gladly avail myself of the following account, by Captain Sabine, which was furnished by my request at the time for insertion in my Journal.[65]

'Mr. Edwards,[66] from whom we first heard that the Aurora was visible, described it as forming a complete arch, having its legs nearly north and south of each other, and passing a little to the eastward of the zenith.[67] [...] The distribution of light has been described as irregular and in constant change: the various masses, however, seemed to have a tendency to arrange themselves into two arches, one passing near the zenith, and a second about midway between the zenith and horizon, both having generally a north and south direction, but curving towards each other, so that their legs produced would complete an ellipse;[68] these arches were as quickly dispersed as formed. At one time a part of the arch near the zenith was bent into convolutions, resembling those of a snake in motion, and undulating rapidly; an appearance which we had not before

---

64 *Aurora Borealis*: 'the Northern Lights', an atmospheric phenomenon produced by the collision of solar particles with the earth's magnetic field.

65 *Captain Sabine*: a captain in the British Army, the astronomer and scientist Edward Sabine (1788–1883) had also been with Parry on Ross's 1818 expedition.

66 *Mr Edwards*: John Edwards, chief medical officer on the expedition.

67 *the zenith*: the point of the sky directly overhead.

68 *so that [...] ellipse*: imaginary lines continued from the feet of each arch would form an ellipse.

observed [...] It is difficult to compare the light produced by an Aurora with that of the moon, because the shadows are rendered faint and indistinct by reason of the general diffusion of the Aurora; but I should think the effect of the one now described, scarcely equal to that of the moon when a week old. The usual pale light of the Aurora strongly resembles that produced by the combustion of phosphorus [...]'

This Aurora had the appearance of being very near us, and we listened attentively for the sound which is said sometimes to accompany brilliant displays of this phenomenon, but neither on this nor on any other occasion, could any be distinguished.

[*from Parry's entry for 7 February 1820*]

As we were now, however, approaching the coldest part of the season, it became more essential than ever to use the utmost caution in allowing the men to remain for any length of time in the open air, on account of the injury to their general health, which was likely to result from the inactivity requisite to the cure of some of the most trifling frost-bites. Mr Edwards has favoured me with the following brief account of such cases of this nature as occurred on board the *Hecla*:[69] – 'The majority of the men who came into the sick-list in consequence of frost-injuries during the severity of the winter, suffered mostly in their feet, and especially in their great toes; and, although none of them were so unfortunate as to lose a toe, yet few cures were effected without the loss of the nail and cuticle, in which the vital power was invariably destroyed. The exfoliation of these dead parts was always slow, and often attended with small ulcerations at the extremity of the toe. The comparatively languid action which is always going on in the feet, owing to their dependent situation, and their remoteness from the centre of circulation, is much increased by the rigour of so severe a climate, and also by the state of inactivity in which it is necessary to keep the patient; so that these trifling sores were found to heal with extreme difficulty. Occasional negligence and irregularities in the patients also served at times to protract the cure. It may further be observed, that the ulcerations alluded to seldom took place, even in some of the more severe cases, when circumstances would allow of timely attention being paid to them".

[*from Parry's entry for 8 March 1820*]

From ten till eleven am this day, a halo and three parhelia[70] were seen about the sun [...] About one pm, there being a fresh breeze from the northward, with some snow drift, the parhelia reappeared, being much more bright and prismatic

---

69 *the Hecla*: Parry's two ships were the *Hecla* and the *Griper*.
70 *three parhelia*: a parhelion is an atmospheric phenomenon whereby a bright spot of white light appears in the sky adjacent to the sun; it is caused by the refraction of sunlight through ice crystals or cirrus cloud.

than in the forenoon, and accompanied by the usual halo, which was nearly complete, and whose radius measured 22½°. The parhelia [...] on each side of the sun were at times so bright as to be painful to the eye in looking steadfastly at them. When they were brightest, the light was nearly white, and this generally occurred when the wind was most moderate, and when there was consequently less snow-drift. When, on the other hand, the wind and drift increased, they became of a deeper tint, but the red and a pale yellow were the only distinguishable colours, the former being as usual, next the sun. These parhelia were much better resemblances of the sun than any we had seen before, being smaller, more compact and circular, and better defined about their edges, than usual, approaching, in every respect, near to that appearance of the sun's disk, which has obtained for them the name of mock suns.

[from Parry's entry for 5 April 1820]

At nine am, on the 5th, the weather being very fine, and the thermometer at −18°, we observed a halo round the sun, which was at times nearly complete. There was, as usual, a parhelion on each side of the sun, at the same altitude, and distinctly prismatic. There was also a third parhelion in the part of the circle immediately above the sun, and this had a peculiarity attending it which we had never before observed. Although the weather was remarkably fine and clear, the atmosphere was full of innumerable minute *spiculæ*[71] of snow glittering in the sun, which we had never before seen on a bright sun-shiny day, though we had constant occasion to remark such a deposit, at times when the weather could by no means be called hazy, and when the heavenly bodies were distinctly visible. The parhelion above the sun appeared to be evidently formed by the reflection of the sun's rays to the eye, by an infinite number of these spiculæ, commencing close to the observer, and continuing so as to be easily distinguishable for at least one or two hundred yards from the eye. This parhelion might at times be easily seen to consist of the intersection, or rather the touching, of two circles turning opposite ways, of which the plainest was generally the upper one, or that which had its convex side downwards. At about 22° above the parhelion, being nearly the same distance that the latter was above the sun, a streak of glittering spiculæ was permanently seen in a horizontal direction; but there was so little of it, that it was difficult to say of what regular figure it formed a part. This phenomenon continued above an hour.

6.12 Thomas De Quincey, *Confessions of an English Opium-Eater*, in *The London Magazine*, Number 22, Part 4 (October 1821), pp. 375–6.

De Quincey's pseudo-autobiographical account of his experience as an opium addict, serialised in the London Magazine *in 1821 and published as a book the following*

---

71 *spiculæ*: tiny crystals.

year, was an immediate sensation, offering unprecedented, and occasionally lurid,
insight into the related psychologies of addiction and artistic creativity. In this often-
anthologised extract from the 'Pains of Opium' section of the Confessions, *headed*
'May 1818', De Quincey recounts the opium-fuelled nightmares which, he says, were
triggered by the unexpected arrival of a Malay at his cottage in the English Lake
District. The passage typifies the psychological (as it would now be called) approach of
the Confessions, *with its emphasis on the analysis of dreams as an index of person-*
ality. De Quincey's configuration of 'Asiatic scenes' as the source of an 'awful' excess
of 'images and associations' also typifies that strand of romantic writing in which the
sublime effect of the exotic leads to 'horror' at the apparent instability of personal and
national identity.

The Malay has been a fearful enemy for months. I have been every night,
through his means, transported into Asiatic scenes. I know not whether others
share in my feelings on this point; but I have often thought that if I were
compelled to forgo England, and to live in China, and among Chinese manners
and modes of life and scenery, I should go mad. The causes of my horror lie
deep; and some of them must be common to others. Southern Asia, in general,
is the seat of awful images and associations. As the cradle of the human race,[72]
it would alone have a dim and reverential feeling connected with it. But there
are other reasons. No man can pretend that the wild, barbarous, and capricious
superstitions of Africa, or of savage tribes elsewhere, affect him in the way that
he is affected by the ancient, monumental, cruel, and elaborate religions of
Indostan, etc.[73] The mere antiquity of Asiatic things, of their institutions, histories, modes of faith, etc. is so impressive, that to me the vast age of the race and
name overpowers the sense of youth in the individual. A young Chinese seems
to me an antediluvian man renewed.[74] Even Englishmen, though not bred in
any knowledge of such institutions, cannot but shudder at the mystic sublimity
of *castes* that have flowed apart, and refused to mix, through such immemorial
tracts of time; nor can any man fail to be awed by the names of the Ganges, or
Euphrates.[75] It contributes much to these feelings, that southern Asia is, and has
been for thousands of years, the part of the earth most swarming with human
life; the great *officina gentium*.[76] Man is a weed in those regions. The vast empires
also, into which the enormous population of Asia has always been cast, give a
further sublimity to the feelings associated with all oriental names or images.
In China, over and above what it has in common with the rest of southern
Asia, I am terrified by the modes of life, by the manners, and the barrier of utter
abhorrence, and want of sympathy, placed between us by feelings deeper than

---

72 Early nineteenth-century anthropology suggested that the human race arose in the Kashmir Valley,
    south of the Himalayan mountain range.
73 *Indostan*: one of a number of cognate, nineteenth-century terms for the Indian Peninsula.
74 *Antediluvian*: 'from before the (biblical) flood.'
75 *Ganges* [...] *Euphrates*: major rivers in India and the Middle East.
76 *officina gentium*: 'workshop of peoples', that is, factory where peoples are produced.

I can analyse. I could sooner live with lunatics, or brute animals. All this, and much more than I can say, or have time to say, the reader must enter into before he can comprehend the unimaginable horror which these dreams of oriental imagery, and mythological tortures, impressed upon me. Under the connecting feeling of tropical heat and vertical sun-lights, I brought together all creatures, birds, beasts, reptiles, all trees and plants, usages and appearances, that are found in all tropical regions, and assembled them together in China or Indostan. From kindred feelings, I soon brought Egypt and all her gods under the same law. I was stared at, hooted at, grinned at, chattered at, by monkeys, by paroquets, by cockatoos.[77] I ran into pagodas: and was fixed, for centuries, at the summit, or in secret rooms; and I was the idol; I was the priest; I was worshipped; I was sacrificed. I fled from the wrath of Brama through all the forests of Asia: Vishnu hated me: Seeva laid wait for me.[78] I came suddenly upon Isis and Osiris: I had done a deed, they said, which the ibis and the crocodile trembled at.[79] I was buried, for a thousand years, in stone coffins, with mummies and sphinxes, in narrow chambers at the heart of eternal pyramids. I was kissed, with cancerous kisses, by crocodiles; and laid, confounded with all unutterable slimy things, amongst reeds and Nilotic mud.[80]

6.13   William Hazlitt, 'The Indian Jugglers', in *Table-Talk, or, Original Essays on Men and Manners* (1821), pp. 181–5.

In this extract from the first, 1821 volume of his Table-Talk *collection, the essayist William Hazlitt (1778–1830) describes the sublime skill of the Indian jugglers, who could be seen performing in various locations around London. In the passage extracted here, Hazlitt, rates the 'witchcraft' of the juggler's act far above his own aptitude as an essay writer. Although this comparison could be disingenuous since Hazlitt goes on to rate athletic or physical ability in general above intellectual attainments, the passage nevertheless registers a sense, familiar from much cotemporary writing (e.g. De Quincey), in which the sublime effect of the exotic questions both the supposed security and superiority of British cultural values.*

Coming forward and seating himself on the ground in his white dress and tightened turban, the chief of the Indian Jugglers begins with tossing up two brass balls, which is what any of us could do, and concludes with keeping up four at the same time, which is what none of us could do to save our lives, not if we were to take our whole lives to do it in. Is it then a trifling power we see at work,

---

77 Parakeets and cockatoos are types of parrot.
78 *Brama* [...] *Seeva*: the three principle gods in Hindu mythology: Brahma was the god of creation, Vishnu of preservation, and Shiva of destruction.
79 *Isis and Osiris*: in Egyptian mythology, Isis was the goddess of nature and Osiris the god of the afterlife. The ibis and the crocodile are sacred animals in Egyptian mythology.
80 *Nilotic*: of the river Nile.

or is it not something next to miraculous? It is the utmost stretch of human ingenuity, which nothing but the bending the faculties of body and mind to it from the tenderest infancy with incessant, ever-anxious application up to manhood, can accomplish or make even a slight approach to. Man, thou art a wonderful animal, and thy ways past finding out! Thou canst do strange things, but thou turnest them to little account! – To conceive of this effort of extraordinary dexterity distracts the imagination and makes admiration breathless. Yet it costs nothing to the performer, any more than if it were a mere mechanical deception with which he had nothing to do but to watch and laugh at the astonishment of the spectators. A single error of a hair's-breadth, of the smallest conceivable portion of time, would be fatal: the precision of the movements must be like a mathematical truth, their rapidity is like lightning. To catch four balls in succession in less than a second of time, and deliver them back so as to return with seeming consciousness to the hand again, to make them revolve round him at certain intervals, like the planets in their spheres, to make them chase one another like sparkles of fire, or shoot up like flowers or meteors, to throw them behind his back and twine them round his neck like ribbons or like serpents, to do what appears an impossibility, and to do it with all the ease, the grace, the carelessness imaginable, to laugh at, to play with the glittering mockeries, to follow them with his eye as if he could fascinate them with its lambent fire,[81] or as if he had only to see that they kept time with the music on the stage – there is something in all this which he who does not admire may be quite sure he never really admired anything in the whole course of his life. It is skill surmounting difficulty, and beauty triumphing over skill. It seems as if the difficulty once mastered naturally resolved itself into ease and grace, and as if to be overcome at all, it must be overcome without an effort. The smallest awkwardness or want of pliancy or self-possession would stop the whole process. It is the work of witchcraft, and yet sport for children. Some of the other feats are quite as curious and wonderful, such as the balancing the artificial tree and shooting bird from each branch through a quill; though none of them have the elegance or facility of the keeping up of the brass balls. You are in pain for the result, and glad when the experiment is over; they are not accompanied with the same unmixed, unchecked delight as the former; and I would not give much to be merely astonished without being pleased at the same time. As to the swallowing of the sword, the police ought to interfere to prevent it. When I saw the Indian Juggler do the same things before, his feet were bare, and he had large rings on his toes, which kept turning round all the time of the performance, as if they moved of themselves. – The hearing a speech in Parliament, drawled or stammered out by the Honourable Member or the Noble Lord, the ringing the changes on their common-places,[82] which anyone could repeat after them as well as they, stirs me not a jot, shakes not my good opinion of myself: but

---

81 *lambent*: brightly shining.
82 *Ringing* [...] *common-places*: 'variations of the same arguments'.

seeing the Indian Jugglers does. It makes me ashamed of myself. I ask what there is that I can do as well as this? Nothing. What have I been doing all my life? Have I been idle, or have I nothing to show for all my labour and pains? Or have I passed my time in pouring words like water into empty sieves, rolling a stone up a hill and then down again, trying to prove an argument in the teeth of the facts, and looking for causes in the dark, and not finding them? Is there no one thing in which I can challenge competition, that I can bring as an instance of exact perfection, in which others cannot find a flaw? The utmost I can pretend to do is to write a description of what this fellow can do. I can write a book: so can many others who have not even learned to spell. What abortions are these Essays! What errors, what ill-pieced transitions, what crooked reasons, what lame conclusions! How little is made out, and that little how ill! Yet they are the best I can do. I endeavour to recollect all I have ever observed or thought upon a subject, and to express it as nearly as I can. Instead of writing on four subjects at a time, it is as much as I can manage to keep the thread of one discourse clear and un-entangled.

Suggestions for Further Reading

The Sublime

Albrecth, William, *The Sublime Pleasures of Tragedy: A Study of Critical Theory from Dennis to Keats* (Lawrence: University of Kansas Press, 1975).

Crowther, Paul, *The Kantian Sublime* (Oxford: Clarendon Press, 1989).

De Bolla, Peter, *The Discourse of the Sublime: Readings in History, Aesthetics and the Subject* (Oxford: Basil Blackwell, 1989).

De Bolla, Peter and Ashfield, Andrew (eds), *The Sublime: A Reader in British Eighteenth-Century Aesthetic Theory* (Cambridge: Cambridge University Press, 1996).

Duffy, Cian, *Shelley and the Revolutionary Sublime* (Cambridge: Cambridge University Press, 2005).

Ferguson, Frances, *Solitude and the Sublime: Romanticism and the Aesthetics of Individuation* (London: Routledge, 1992).

Freeman, Barbara, *The Feminine Sublime: Gender and Excess in Women's Fiction* (Berkeley: University of California Press, 1995).

Furniss, Tim, *Edmund Burke's Aesthetic Ideology: Language, Gender and Political Economy in Revolution* (Cambridge: Cambridge University Press, 1993).

Hertz, Neil, *The End of the Line: Essays in Psychoanalysis and the Sublime* (New York: Columbia University Press, 1985).

Holmes, Richard, *The Age of Wonder: How the Romantic Generation Discovered the Beauty and Terror of Science* (London: Harper Press, 2008).

Hipple, Walter, *The Beautiful, the Sublime, and the Picturesque in Eighteenth-Century British Aesthetic Theory* (Carbondale: Southern Illinois University Press, 1957).

Knapp, Stephen, *Personification and the Sublime: Milton to Coleridge* (Cambridge, Mass.: Harvard University Press, 1985).

Maxwell, Catherine, *The Female Sublime from Milton to Swinburne: Bearing Blindness* (Manchester: Manchester University Press, 2001).

Monk, Samuel Holt, *The Sublime: A Study in Critical Theories in Eighteenth-Century England* (New York: MLA, 1960).

Nicolson, Marjorie Hope, *Mountain Gloom and Mountain Glory: The Development of the Aesthetics of the Infinite* (Ithaca: Cornell University Press, 1959).

Weiskel, Thomas, *The Romantic Sublime: Studies in the Structure and Psychology of Transcendence* (Baltimore: Johns Hopkins University Press, 1976).

Wlecke, Albert, *Wordsworth and the Sublime* (Berkeley: University of California Press, 1973).

Wood, Theodore, *The Word 'Sublime' and its Context 1650–1760* (The Hague: Mouton, 1972).

Yaeger, Patricia, 'Toward a Female Sublime', in Linda Kaufmann (ed.), *Gender and Theory: Dialogues on Feminist Criticism* (Oxford: Blackwell, 1989).

Žižek, Slavoj, *The Sublime Object of Ideology* (London: Verso, 1989).

Mountains

Anne Colley, Anne, *Victorians in the Mountains: Sinking the Sublime* (London: Ashgate, 2010).
De Beer, Gavin, *Early Travellers in the Alps*, second edn. (New York: October House, 1967).
Heringman, Noah, *Romantic Rocks, Aesthetic Geology* (Ithaca: Cornell University Press, 2004).
Labbe, Jacqueline, *Romantic Visualities: Landscape, Gender and Romanticism* (Basingstoke: Macmillan, 1998).
Macfarlane, Robert, *Mountains of the Mind: A History of a Fascination* (London: Granta, 2003).
Ring, Jim, *How the English made the Alps* (London: Murray, 2000).

Money

De Bolla, Peter, *The Discourse of the Sublime: History, Aesthetics, and the Subject* (Oxford: Wiley-Blackwell, 1989).
Brewer, John, *The Sinews of Power: War, Money and the English State 1688–1783* (Boston: Harvard, 1990).
Chancellor, Edward *Devil take the Hindmost: A History of Financial Speculations* (London: Macmillan, 1999).
Clark, Gregory 'Debt, Deficits and Crowding Out: England 1727–1840' in *European Review of Economic History* 5 (2001), pp. 403–36.
Copeland, Edward, *Women Writing about Money: Women's Fiction in England 1790–1820* (Cambridge: Cambridge University Press, 1995).
Foucault, Michel, *The Order of Things: An Archaeology of the Human Sciences* (London: Routledge, 2001).
Neal, Larry, *The Rise of Financial Capitalism: International Capital Markets in the Age of Reason* (Cambridge: Cambridge University Press, 1990).
Nicholson, Colin, *Writing and the Rise of Finance: Capital Satires of the Early Eighteenth Century* (Cambridge: Cambridge University Press, 1994).
Pocock, J. G. A., *Virtue, Commerce and History: Essays on Political Thought and History, Chiefly in the Eighteenth Century* (Cambridge: Cambridge University Press, 1985).
Poovey, Mary, *Genres of the Credit Economy: Mediating Value in Eighteenth- and Nineteenth-Century Britain* (Chicago: Chicago University Press, 2008).
Rowlinson, Matthew, *Real Money and Romanticism* (Cambridge: Cambridge University Press, 2010).
Samuels, Warren J., Biddle, Jeff E., and Davis, John B. (eds) *A Companion to the History of Economic Thought* (Oxford: Blackwell-Wiley, 2007).

Mind

Foucault, Michel, *Madness and Civilisation*, transl. Richard Howard (New York: Pantheon, 1965).
Ingram, Allan and Faubert, Michelle, *Cultural Constructions of Madness in Eighteenth-Century Writing: Representing the Insane* (Basingstoke: Palgrave Macmillan, 2005).

Jackson, Noel, *Science and Sensation in Romantic Poetry* (Cambridge: Cambridge University Press, 2008).

Macdayter, Ghislaine (ed.), *Untrodden Regions of the Mind: Romanticism and Psychoanalysis* (London: Associated University Presses, 2001).

Maclane, Maureen, *Romanticism and the Human Sciences* (Cambridge: Cambridge University Press, 2006).

Porter, Roy, *Mind forg'd manacles: A History of Madness in England from the Restoration to the Regency* (London: Athlone, 1987).

Richardson, Alan, *British Romanticism and the Science of Mind* (Cambridge: Cambridge University Press, 2001).

Gothic

Botting, Fred, *Gothic* (London: Routledge, 1995).

Clery, Emma (ed.) *Gothic Documents, a Sourcebook 1700–1820* (Manchester: Manchester University Press, 2000).

Ellis, Markman, *The History of Gothic fiction* (Edinburgh: Edinburgh University Press, 2000).

Gamer, Michael, *Romanticism and the Gothic: Genre, Reception and Canon Formation* (Cambridge: Cambridge University Press, 2006).

Hills, Matt, *The Pleasures of Horror* (London: Continuum, 2005).

Miles, Robert, *Gothic Writing 1750–1820: A Genealogy* (London: Routledge, 1993).

Mishra, Vijay, *The Gothic Sublime* (New York: State University of NY Press, 1994).

Punter, David (ed.) *A Companion to the Gothic* (Oxford: Blackwell, 2000).

Sedgwick, Eve Kosovsky, *The Coherence of Gothic Conventions* (London: Methuen, 1986).

Wallace, Diana and Smith, Andrew (eds), *The Female Gothic: New Directions* (London: Palgrave Macmillan, 2009).

Crowds

Le Bon, Gustave, *The Crowd: A Study of the Popular Mind* (New York: Viking, 1960).

Canetti, Elias *Crowds and Power* trans. Carol Stewart (London: Phoenix Press, 2000).

Foucault, Michel, 'On Popular Justice: A Discussion with Maosists' in Michel Foucault, *Power/Knowledge*, ed. Colin Gordon (Harlow: Longman, 1980), pp. 1–36.

Ogborn, Miles, *Spaces of Modernity: London's Geographies, 1680–1780* (New York: Guilford Press, 1998).

Ozouf, Mona, *Festivals and the French Revolution*, trans. Alan Sheridan (Cambridge, MA and London: Harvard University Press, 1988).

Paulson, Ronald, *Representations of Revolution 1789–1820* (New Haven: Yale University Press, 1987).

Porter, Roy, *London: A Social History* (London: Penguin, 2000).

Rudé, George, *The Crowd in History* (London: Serif, 2005).

Shoemaker, Robert, *The London Mob: Violence and Disorder in Eighteenth-Century England* (New York: Hambeldon Continuum, 2004).

Thompson, E. P., 'The Moral Economy of the Crowd in the Eighteenth Century' in *Customs in Common* (London: Merlin, 1991).

The Exotic

Fulford, Tim, Lee, Debbie and Kitson, Peter (eds), *Literature, Science and Exploration in the Romantic Era: Bodies of Knowledge* (Cambridge: Cambridge University Press, 2004).

Leask, Nigel, *Curiosity and the Aesthetics of Travel Writing, 1770–1840: From an Antique Land* (Oxford: Oxford University Press, 2003).

——, *British Romantic Writers and the East: Anxieties of Empire* (Cambridge: Cambridge University Press, 1992).

Morton, Timothy, *The Poetics of Spice: Romantic Consumerism and the Exotic* (Cambridge: Cambridge University Press, 2000).

Said, Edward, *Orientalism* (London: Routledge, 1978).

Sharafuddin, Mohammed, *Islam and Romantic Orientalism: Literary Encounters with the Orient* (London: Tuaris, 1994).

Turhan, Filiz, *The Other Empire: British Romantic Writings about the Ottoman Empire* (London: Routledge, 2003).

Index